IMAGES
of America

FRANKLIN

On the Cover: With banners and flags waving overhead, the Franklin High School band makes its way down Main Street, past thousands of fans, announcing the opening of the annual rodeo in the Noon Rotary 1957 Rodeo Parade. Throughout its history, downtown Franklin has been known for its festivals and parades, and locals and tourists alike are still drawn to the city's hospitality. (Courtesy of Bob Canaday.)

IMAGES
of America

FRANKLIN

Joe Johnston

ARCADIA
PUBLISHING

ISBN 978-1-4671-1293-2

Published by Arcadia Publishing
Charleston, South Carolina

Printed in the United States of America

Library of Congress Control Number: 2014938791

For all general information, please contact Arcadia Publishing:
Telephone 843-853-2070
Fax 843-853-0044
E-mail sales@arcadiapublishing.com
For customer service and orders:
Toll-Free 1-888-313-2665

Visit us on the Internet at www.arcadiapublishing.com

Dedicated to Eli Evrett Johnston, with love.

CONTENTS

ACKNOWLEDGMENTS

It was my hope in beginning this work that I would contribute a new viewpoint to Franklin's historic record and make some new friends along the way. To all of the welcoming people of Franklin, thank you for your handshakes and smiles.

This book would not have been possible without the enthusiastic help of our longtime family friend Russell Hooper III. A big thank-you to Scott Smith, who loves sharing the history of Franklin and helped us get started on this journey. And thanks to Billy Baskin for friendship, encouragement, and the fun he added to the project.

Special thanks to the generous and caring Joanna Stephens, the curator of Carnton House and the Battle of Franklin Trust. And also to my new friend J.T. Thomson at Lotz House, whose passion for history is contagious.

I'm especially indebted to the generosity of many people and organizations who participated in this project, including Mark Tolley of the Tennessee Ancient Sites Conservancy, the Tennessee State Library and Archives, the Downtown Franklin Association, and Tennessee state archeologist Aaron Deter-Wolf. Also Pam Horne, managing editor of the *Williamson County Herald*; Aimee Saunders, at the Williamson County Archives; Jack Grant, at the Factory; Randall Bedwell; Donna O'Neil; Shari Lacy, at Good Stuff PR; Rick Warwick; Joni Cole; Tosha Robinson Baugh; Alma McLemore; Debbie Smartt; and Scott Ducaj. Cassandra Taylor, great granddaughter of A.N.C. Williams, also went the extra mile to help us tell this story.

I would also like to give a salute to Bob Canaday for caring for the photographic history of Franklin and for his help with this book. And, it is impossible to overstate the importance of the tireless contributions that Thelma Battle and Mary Mills have made to this book and to the community.

Finally, I offer my deep gratitude to my beautiful, encouraging, and patient wife, Becky.

All photographs are from the author's personal collection unless otherwise noted. Many photographs were generously provided for this book, for which the contributors declined credit.

BFTC The Battle of Franklin Trust Collections
RWC Collection of Rick Warwick
TNA Tennessee State Division of Archeology, Department of Environment and Conservation
WCA Williamson County Archives
RHC Russell Hooper III personal collection
LOC Library of Congress
TDA The Tennessee Division of Archaeology and the Center for the First Americans at Texas A&M University
TSL Tennessee State Library

Introduction

Ask folks about Franklin, Tennessee, and some will tell you about what happened there during the Civil War. Some will focus on the public square celebrations that started over 200 years ago and never seem to stop. For others, it will be the new housing development west of town, or the mall north of town that changed everything a few years ago. But everybody will agree that Franklin is a town with one eye on the past and one eye on the future. Shaped by what it has been, and embracing what it will be. Nurturing its legacy, while dancing into the future.

The Franklin area was once home to Native Americans of the Mississippian Culture, who thrived along the meandering banks of the Harpeth River. Those original people thrived here as long as 14,000 years ago, making this one of the oldest inhabited places in North America. Nomadic hunters settled down, planted crops, and built villages, which gradually became large towns with cultural centers. Then, about 500 years ago, these sites were largely abandoned. When the Europeans arrived, there were no Native American tribes living permanently in the area, although for the Cherokee, Choctaw, and others it was still prime hunting ground with important trade routes.

We know all this because archeologists have found the remains of ancient homes, gardens, fires, burial mounds, and stone box graves, even though many sites and artifacts were destroyed by building and mining—some of it done as recently as the 20th century. Since then, more enlightened thinking, and the efforts of citizen organizations, have identified and preserved several ancient historic sites. The Glass Mounds, just five miles from downtown Franklin, were protected by the neighborhood's developer, and have been preserved so that they can educate future generations in the midst of homes and a golf course. That is the spirit of Franklin.

Just like the Native Americans, settlers were drawn to the twisting Harpeth watershed, with its rolling lands, abundant timber, clear creeks, and rich soil. The area would prove to be perfect for agriculture, especially sprawling plantations raising rye, corn, oats, tobacco, potatoes, wheat, peas, barley, horses, and the main cash crop: cotton.

In 1878, Ewen Cameron built the first house in what is now Franklin. His son Duncan was born there, and their descendants live in the area to this day. Within a year, Fort Nashborough, the future Nashville, was established, and some adventurous families pressed south from there. Soon, the Franklin area was dotted with family farms. Around the same time, Revolutionary War veterans were moving to Tennessee to take advantage of land grants for their service. Major Anthony Sharp sold 640 acres of his grant to Abram Maury Jr., who set aside 109 acres to lay out the city of Franklin in 1799, naming it to honor Benjamin Franklin. On October 26 of that year, the Tennessee General Assembly carved off the southern part of Davidson County to create Williamson County, with Franklin serving as county seat.

Franklin Pike became a busy toll road, skirting the Brentwood Hills and connecting with Nashville. Wilson Pike, originally called the Harpeth Turnpike, was a toll road built around 1840, spurring a population boom to the east. In the 1850s, visionary investors built two railroad lines into the county, and Franklin's concrete and brick freight depot was built in 1858. These developments allowed farmers to ship out their produce and livestock, and storeowners to ship in the latest manufactured goods.

Over the next few years, Williamson County became one of the wealthiest counties in the state. Magnificent homes were built, and Franklin's Episcopal, Presbyterian, and Methodist churches were the pride of the city. The courthouse, with its two-story columns made of iron smelted and cast at a local foundry, stood over the town square. The future was bright in Franklin.

Then war stole the smiles from the faces of Franklin's residents. In 1862, unwelcome Union forces occupied the city. They needed food, horses, and mules, as well as places to sleep, store supplies, build fortifications, and stable their animals. Homes were turned into officers' headquarters. Farms were ravaged. Trees were cut down for firewood and breastworks, and, when the trees were gone, the soldiers took the church pews, pillars, and whatever they could find.

Then, on the evening of November 30, 1864, the Confederate army under Gen. John Bell Hood marched across the field south of town, and into the teeth of the Yankee guns. Scared but courageous men walked across the bodies of those who fell before them, reaching the streets and yards of the city and engaging in hand-to-hand combat. Sometime in the night, the battle ended with a Union victory. Among the nearly 10,000 casualties were generals, chaplains, and boys too young to shave. The Union troops moved on to Nashville, leaving behind the dead, dying, and wounded. Floorboards ran red with blood, as many houses and virtually all the public buildings—about four dozen in all—were pressed into service as hospitals and morgues. It fell to a few Confederate soldiers, along with the women, children, and old men of Franklin, to nurse, comfort, and bury all of those men in gray and blue.

Miraculously, the people of Franklin found a place to start recovering from this trauma. By digging one grave at a time, replacing one board, planting one row, or holding one baby, they began to rebuild their city. There were elections to be held, laws to be enforced, and businesses to be started. The trains came back, and the crops grew again. For the townspeople, it was an uncommon time of faith in each other, in the good, nurturing earth, and in the city of Franklin.

Some 12,000 local slaves were freed in the war, and years of social uncertainty followed their emancipation. But these newly freed people had marketable skills. Some saved their money—eventually investing it in real estate or new businesses—and new partnerships were born with the people who had once owned them. Leaders rose up, and African American churches became the heart of their social lives, while families made sure their children got a good start with their education.

There were Civil War monuments and reunions, and the battlefield was graced with the building of the Battle Ground Academy. But, at the same time, building and street construction chipped away at this sacred ground. It became industrialized and cluttered with signs. Eventually, in an odd mix of pride and sadness, of progress and regret, the city and its economy languished for decades.

Then, around 1960, the construction of Interstate 65 made it easier to commute to the state capital and other points. Beginning in the 1980s, several other factors gradually contributed to a rebirth of Franklin as well. As the population and industrial base of Nashville grew, its suburbs stretched toward Franklin. Shopping improved, and manufacturing moved in. But perhaps the most significant factor in Franklin's new vigor is that the city rediscovered its beautiful and inspiring legacy, embracing both its past and its future. Tourism increased, and stories that were once only of the bloody battle began to be about the experiences of civilians before, during, and after the battle. Once a Confederate town, Franklin grew up to be a Civil War town, and a new generation began to understand that there is no gray without the blue, and that the Battle of Franklin is a shared experience with a multitude of meanings. Today, Franklin is a living testament to the idea that history belongs to everyone.

As any city grows, progress takes a toll, and so Franklin's historic homes, roads, cemeteries, streams, springs, and fields have all paid a price. But, before it was too late, some people in Franklin realized what a treasure they had to lose. Unlike some communities, where history has been paved over with a glut of concrete and neon, Franklin has faced progress with an uncommon spirit for preservation, repurposing, and reuse, but changes still bring new questions at every turn. Which houses, roads, and sites will be preserved? How can they best be used? What will their role be in a forward-looking city? With these questions in mind, citizen groups have led governments in the fight to save historic structures and sites, and enterprising merchants have turned abandoned buildings into inviting shops, offices, and restaurants.

The results are astounding. Franklin's beautiful old buildings and homes are unique. Where else can people park downtown for free and walk to so many great restaurants, shops, art exhibits, and historic sites? The town has always been ready to celebrate with a veterans' parade, children's "blue ribbon day," or countywide booster tour, and that tradition has continued and grown. Today, Franklin hosts street festivals, music on porches, art on the sidewalks, and a river of charity benefits. No wonder folks say there's always something going on in Franklin.

In the 1990s, the whole county's population increased by over 50 percent. In 1980, the population of Franklin was about 12,000, and today it is over 60,000. And yet, in the midst of so much that's new and exciting, the public square is still the center of life—the place where everyone passes through, and crowds gather. There are some 35 structures from the 19th century still standing in the city, and an entire 15-block area around the square is listed in the National Register of Historic Places.

What follows is a sampling of Franklin's rich history, and a taste of all that's waiting to be discovered. People and places have been included not just because they are exceptional but also because they exemplify the city and people of Franklin. Each one is representative of countless others with the same spirit, doing the same sort of work with the same care and passion.

Slaves and slave owners—and their descendants—have not lived separate black and white histories, but one grand history full of heartache, joy, and discovery. We are all part of one unending story that began with the first people in North America. Magic Chef ovens were made here. The first man to chart the ocean currents was educated here. Music stars call Franklin home. Some folks who live here are the seventh, eighth, or ninth generations of their family to live in Franklin, and they have a certain view of what the city is and what it should be. Tourists and new neighbors arrive every year by the thousands, and they contribute to that vision as well. More than a city, Franklin is a place of people, homes, offices, and open spaces—all connected through a web of history that we are still weaving. And this alone is enough to make Franklin a great American treasure.

One

The First People

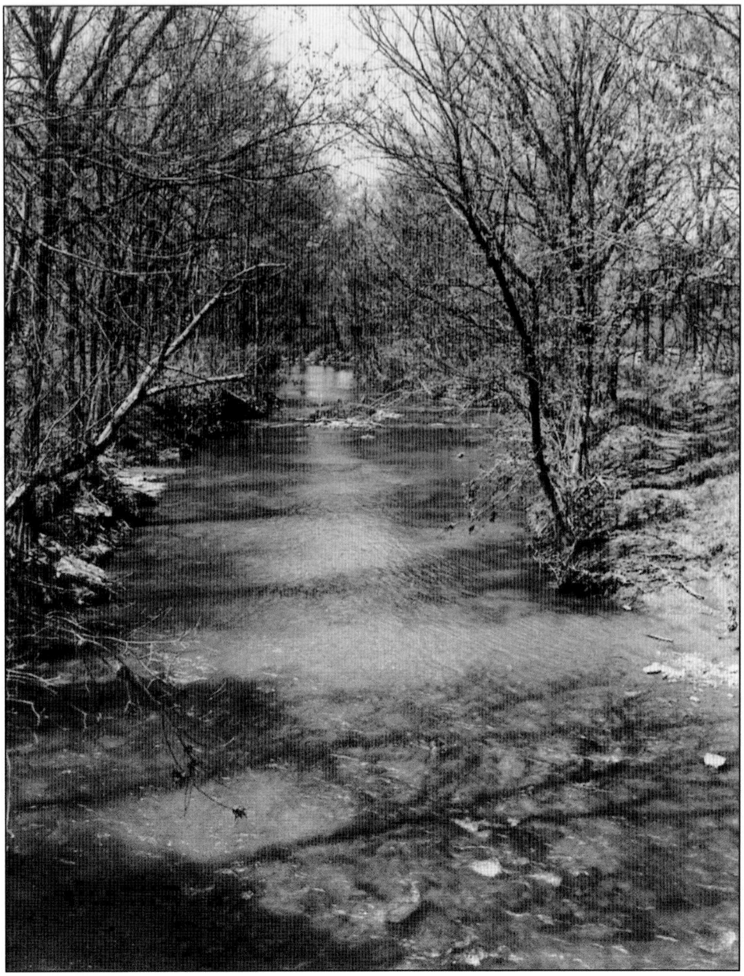

The Harpeth and Little Harpeth Rivers come together at Franklin, and almost anywhere that either of them made a bend was a good place for early people to live. The rivers supplied water for cooking, drinking, and bathing; food in the form of fish and mussels; and even transportation routes for canoes. Later, the same land was best for farm families. (TSL.)

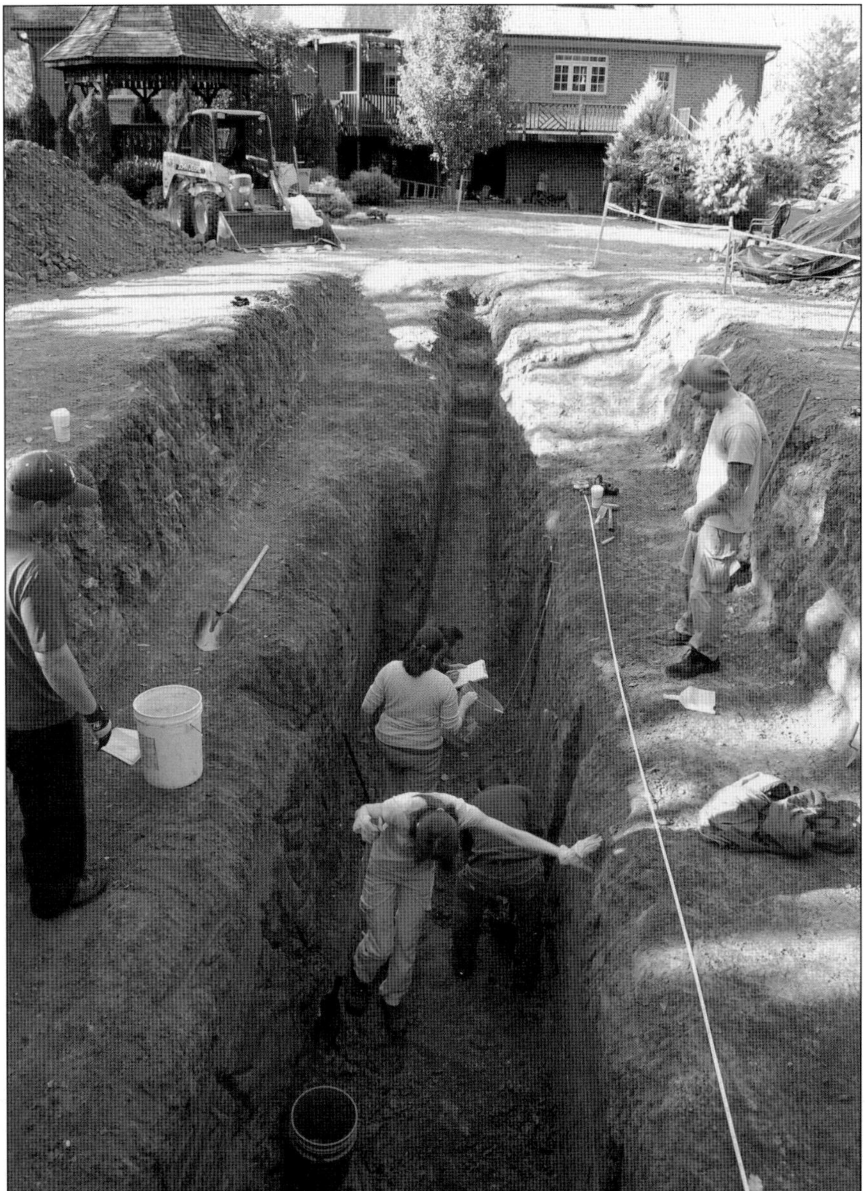

The excavation in this photograph was performed by Middle Tennessee State University students under the supervision of state archeologists in the yard of a home east of I-65 near the CoolSprings Galleria. It went down six feet to reveal evidence of Paleo-Indian habitation and contained the fossil remains of a young mastodon butchered by humans using stone tools. The tools and bones found at the site have been dated to at least 12,000 BCE, making it the oldest archeological find in Tennessee, and Franklin one of the oldest inhabited places in North America. A site in New Mexico was long considered the location of North America's oldest human habitation, and a unique type of stone point for weapons—called a Clovis point—was found there. However, Clovis points have since been found at other sites, including those in the Franklin area. This site on Moores Lane is now listed in the National Register of Historic Places. (TDA.)

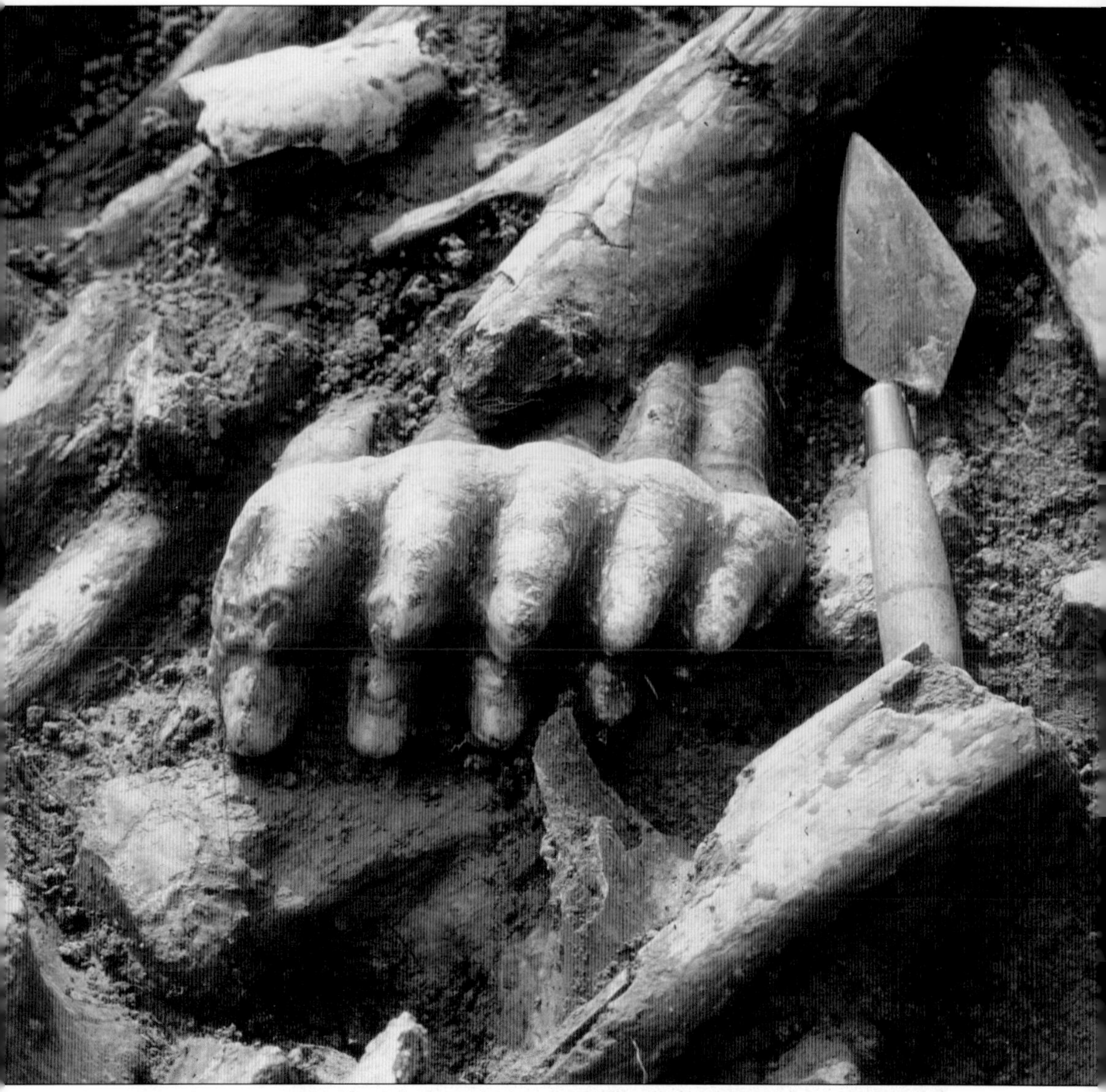

The molar of a young male mastodon can be seen at the center of this photograph, with a trowel to the right for size comparison. The animal was butchered by Paleo-Indians around 14,000 years ago. This molar was unearthed at a site located under a recent housing development, alongside other bones that show marks from butchering by humans using stone knives and axes. (TDA.)

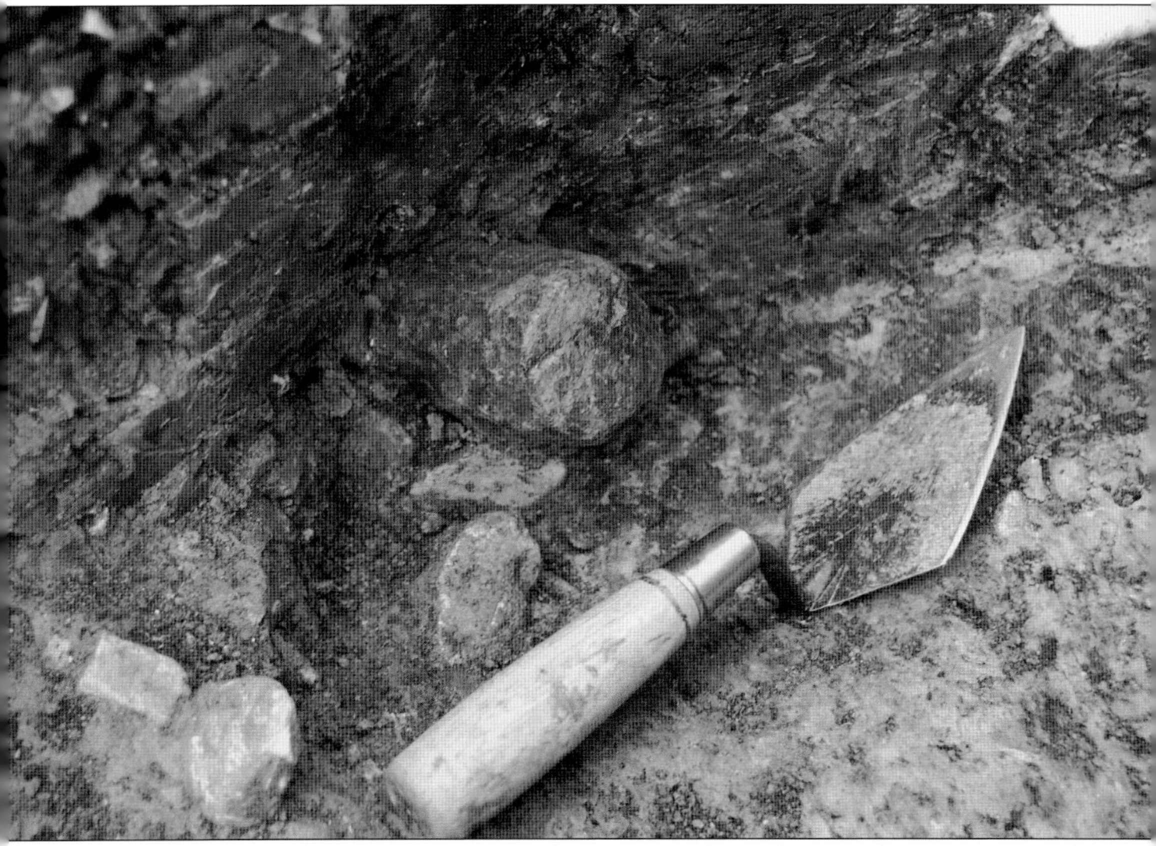

In another photograph from an archeological dig in a Franklin yard, a mastodon's femur protrudes from the soil beside a trowel. The bones were found almost 10 feet below the surface. This dig was conducted by students under the direction of Tennessee state archeologists. (TDA.)

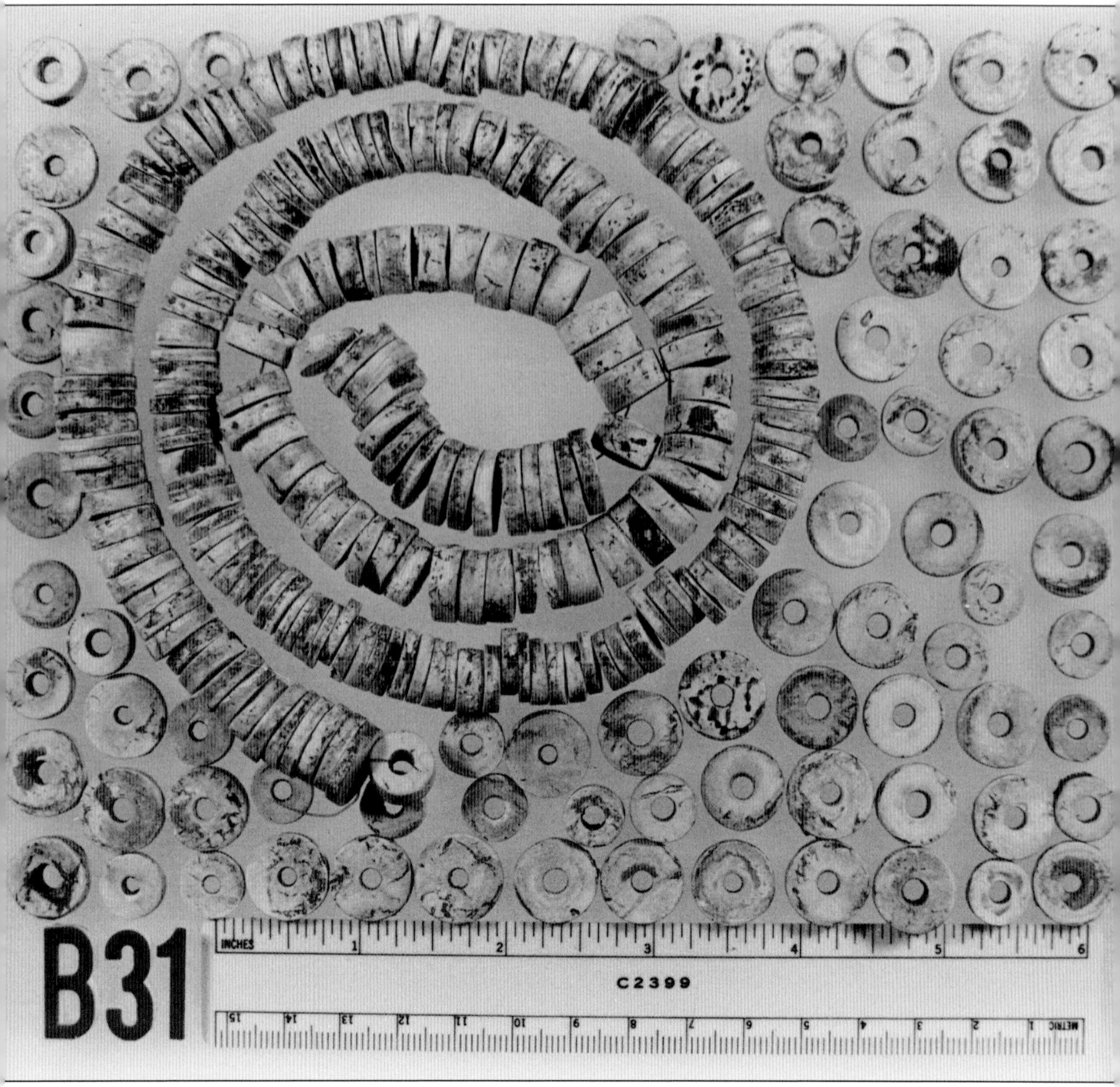

Native Americans of the Mississippian period were living in the Franklin area thousands of years ago, building flat mounds for their council houses. These beads, made of shells from the Gulf of Mexico that were traded until they reached Tennessee, were found along the Harpeth River in Franklin at the site of an ancient village dating to about 7,000 years ago. (John T. Dowd, courtesy TDA.)

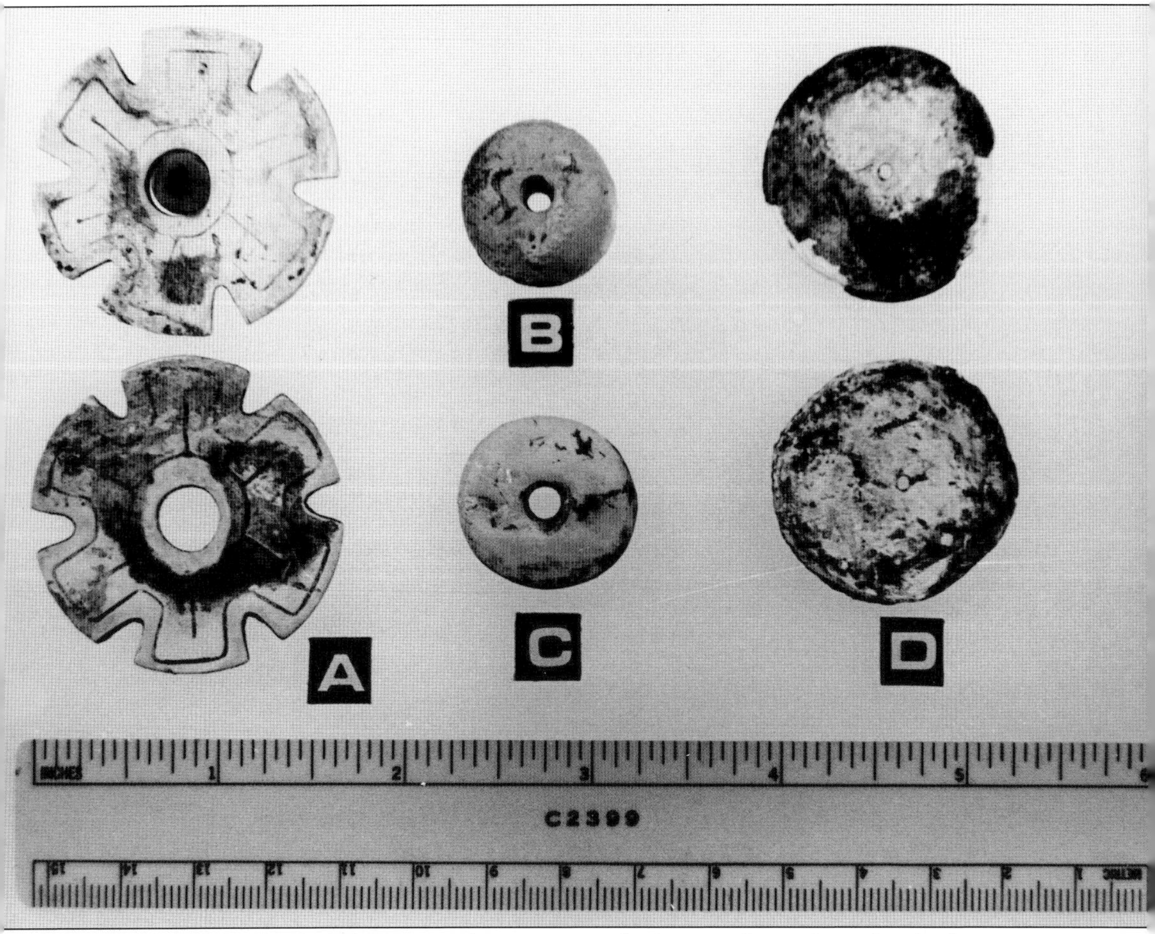

These shell beads, including some that are ornately decorated, are from the Anderson site in Franklin—a village of the Middle Archaic period that was occupied from about 3,500 to 5,000 BCE. The Native Americans living there made fishhooks, ate mussels, carefully buried their dead, and kept dogs as pets. (John T. Dowd, courtesy TDA.)

Triangular arrowheads like this one were used by the Cherokee, Choctaw, Creek, Chickasaw, and other tribes that formed after the Mississippian period. Hunters would pass through the area, but there were no permanent settlements in Middle Tennessee after about 1300 CE. Why people left the area after it was populated for so long is not certain, but a series of social changes in the tribes, combined with weather and environmental changes, likely fractured these communities. (TDA.)

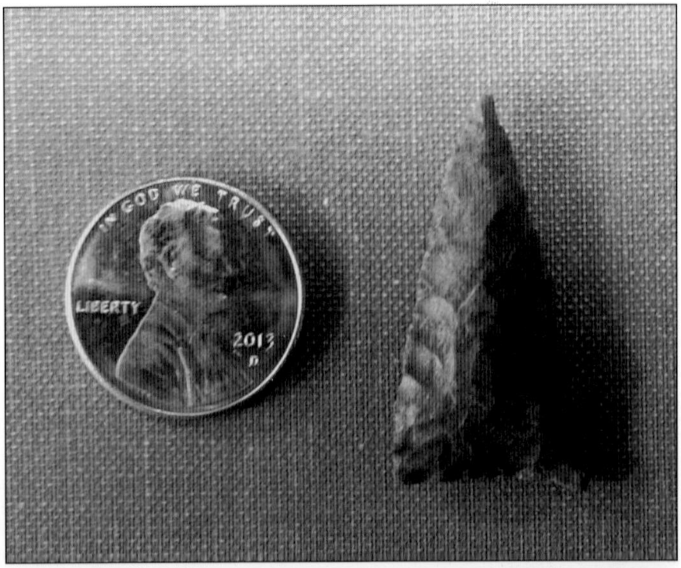

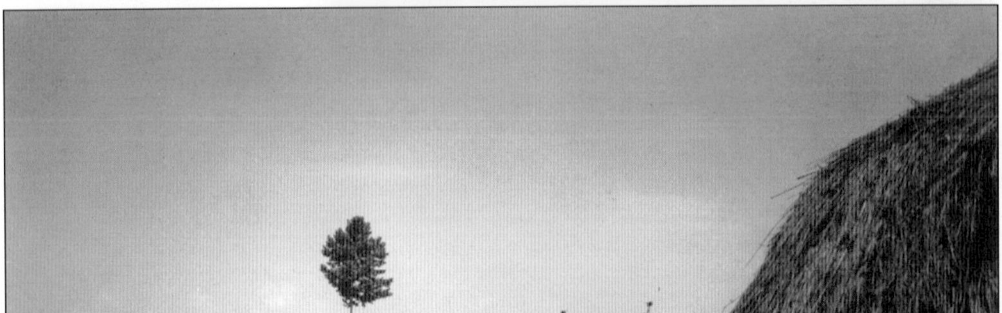

The Chucalissa Indian Village, reconstructed on a bluff overlooking Memphis, is typical of the Mississippian period settlements of Middle Tennessee. By the time European Americans arrived in the Franklin area there were no Native American tribes living in the area, but their mounds are still considered sacred. It is almost certain that the people moved east, and the Southeastern tribes, including the Cherokee, Choctaw, and Chickasaw, are their descendants. (TSL.)

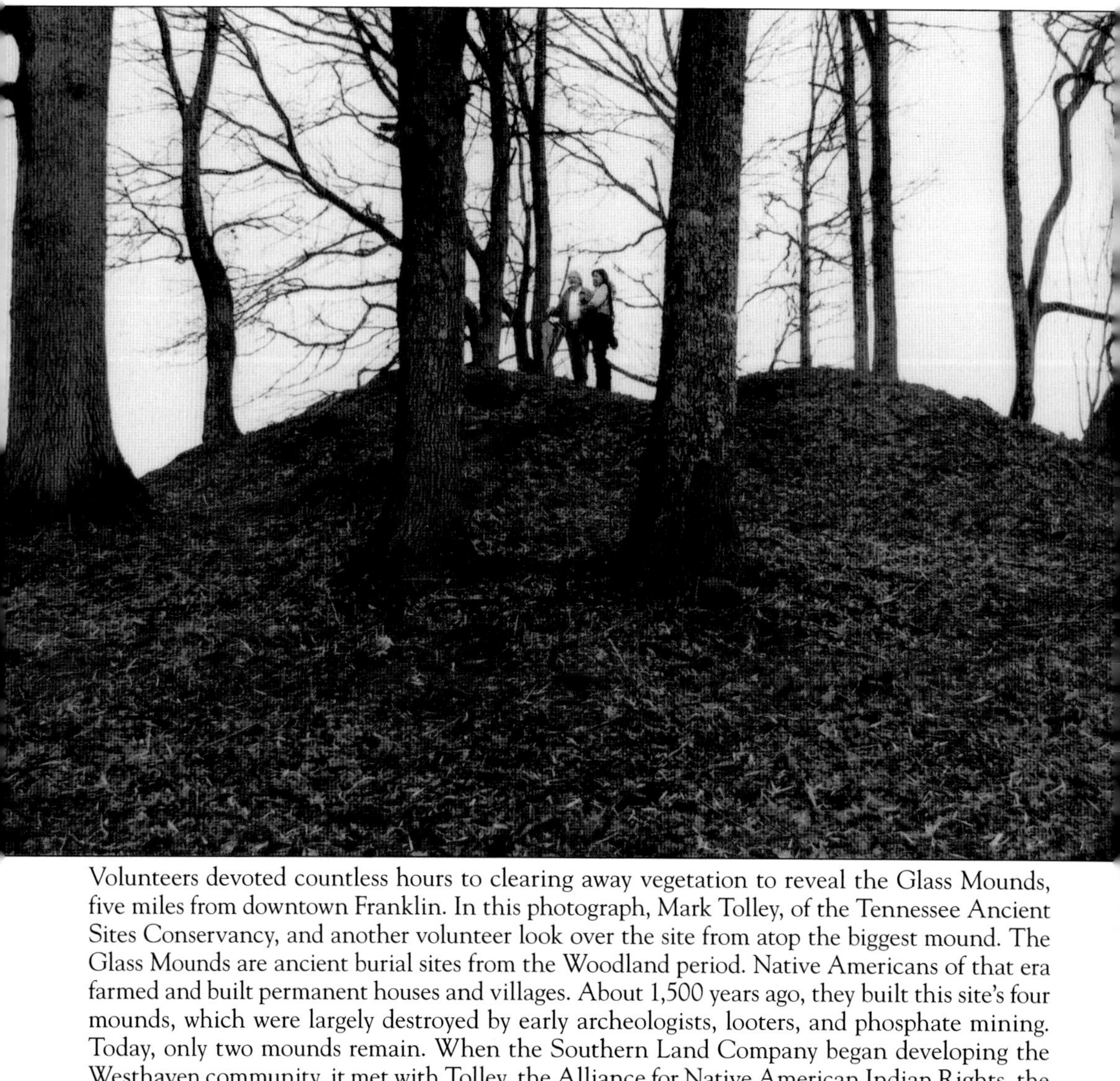

Volunteers devoted countless hours to clearing away vegetation to reveal the Glass Mounds, five miles from downtown Franklin. In this photograph, Mark Tolley, of the Tennessee Ancient Sites Conservancy, and another volunteer look over the site from atop the biggest mound. The Glass Mounds are ancient burial sites from the Woodland period. Native Americans of that era farmed and built permanent houses and villages. About 1,500 years ago, they built this site's four mounds, which were largely destroyed by early archeologists, looters, and phosphate mining. Today, only two mounds remain. When the Southern Land Company began developing the Westhaven community, it met with Tolley, the Alliance for Native American Indian Rights, the Tennessee Commission of Indian Affairs, and the Tennessee Division of Archaeology. After tests by archeology students from MTSU confirmed the archeological value of the mounds, Southern Land and the other groups made a plan for preserving the site as a permanent educational resource and sacred site. (Courtesy Mark Tolley.)

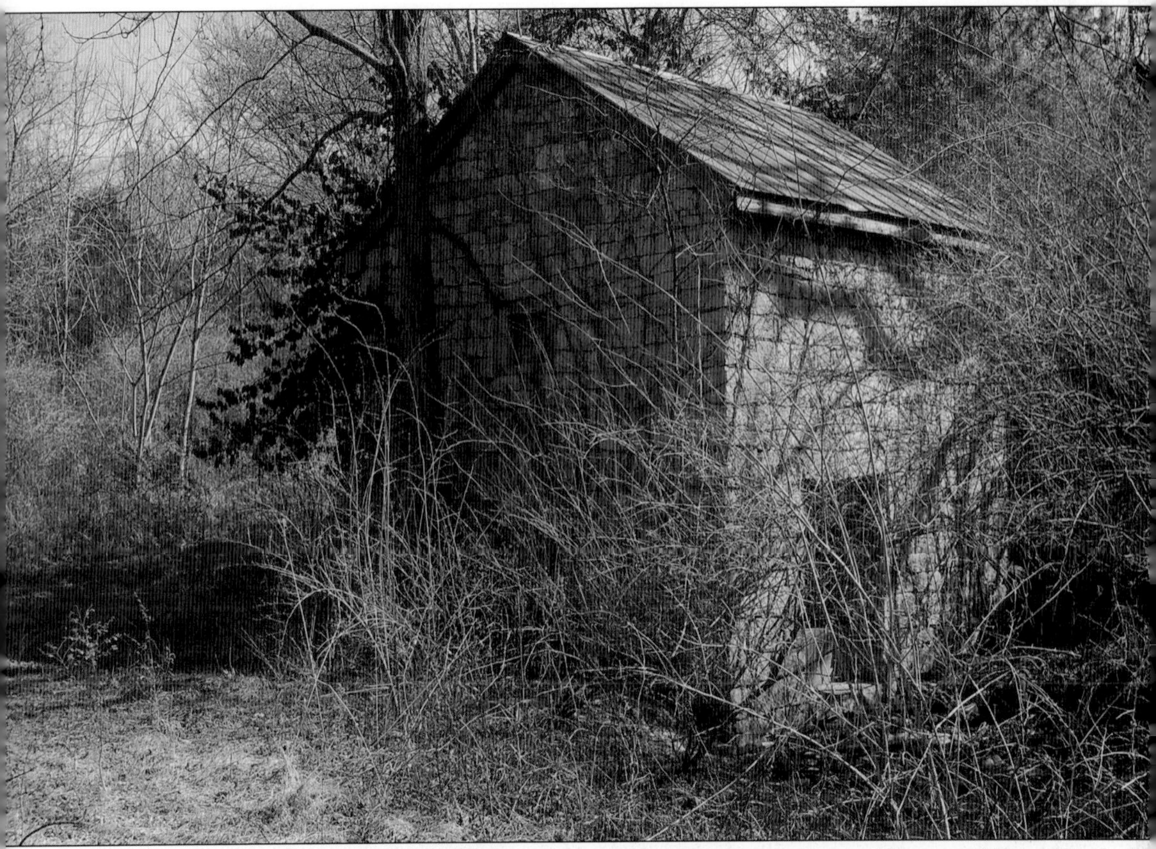

At the heart of the thriving, modern Cool Springs shopping area stands a 200-year-old stone springhouse, and below it flows a spring that is nobody knows how old. Prehistoric people who lived in large villages nearby left stone tools, weapons, and other evidence that they drank from these waters. Then, for hundreds of years, the only visitors were Native American hunters passing through. In 1788, after explorers and trappers had come through the area, the 320 acres around the spring became the land grant of Revolutionary War veteran Thomas Sharp Spencer. John and Sarah Crockett bought 105 acres of this land in 1813 and built the springhouse. Over time, the spring supplied a dairy and four farm families. Additionally, thirsty students of the Mallory School carried buckets of water from the spring until the school closed in 1949.

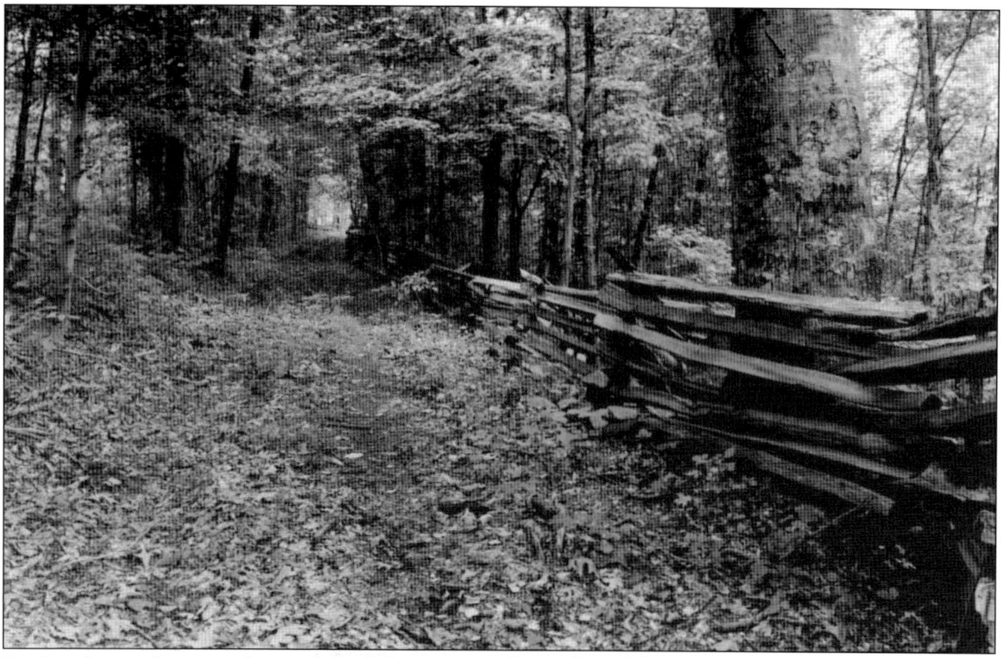

In the above photograph, a split rail fence runs along the Old Natchez Trace, which began as a migratory trail for prehistoric animals. Native Americans, traders, and settlers further defined it, linking the Mississippi River to the Cumberland River and passing west of Franklin. The trace was improved under Pres. Thomas Jefferson, making it important to New Orleans and the Louisiana Purchase. As riverboat traffic increased and more roads were built, the trace fell to disuse, but today it is honored by the 444-mile Natchez Trace Scenic Parkway and the Natchez Trace National Scenic Trail. Offering places where visitors can hike and camp, the route also features a soaring double arch concrete bridge that is one of only two of its type in the world. Stretching almost 1,600 feet across the valley, the bridge is a scenic wonder that spans Highway 96 about 145 feet below. (Above, TSL; below, courtesy of Brent Moore.)

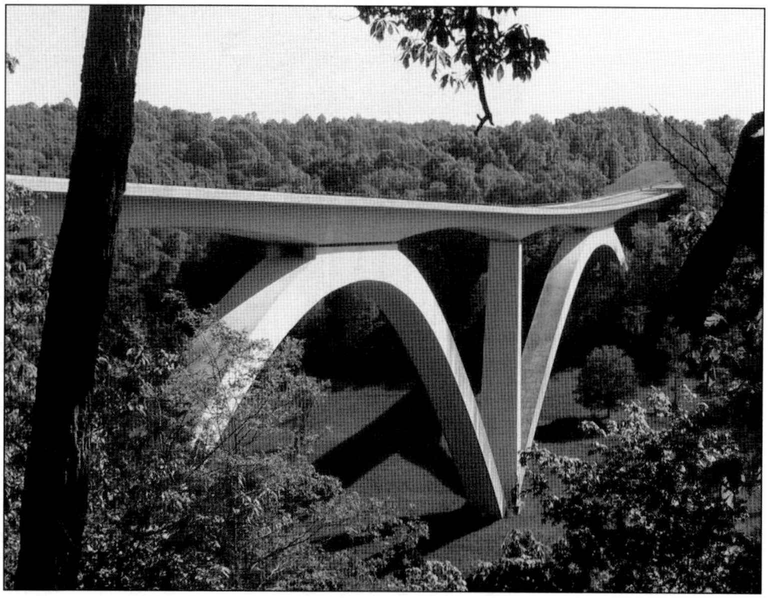

Two

A Few of the Founders

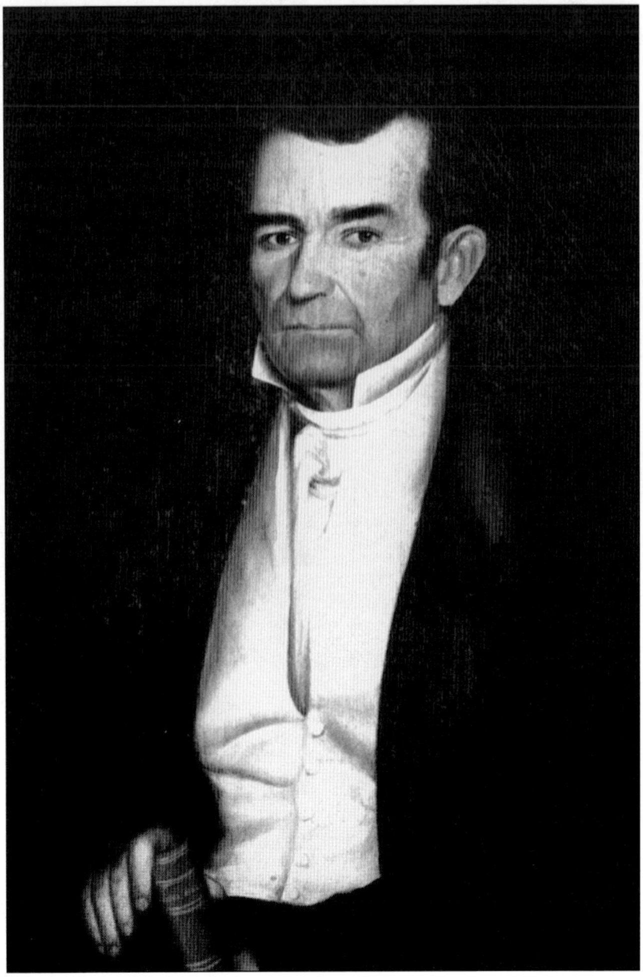

Virginia native Nicholas "Bigbee" Perkins practiced law in Alabama, and helped to write that state's constitution. While in Alabama, Perkins aided in the 1807 capture of former vice president Aaron Burr and escorted him back to Washington to be tried for treason. Moving to Franklin in 1808, Perkins became register of lands and, thanks to the reward for Burr's capture, was at one time the county's largest slaveholder and landowner, with over 12,000 acres. (LOC.)

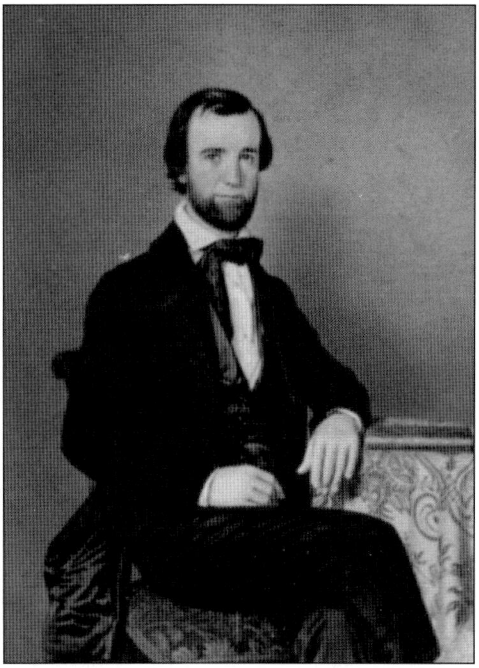

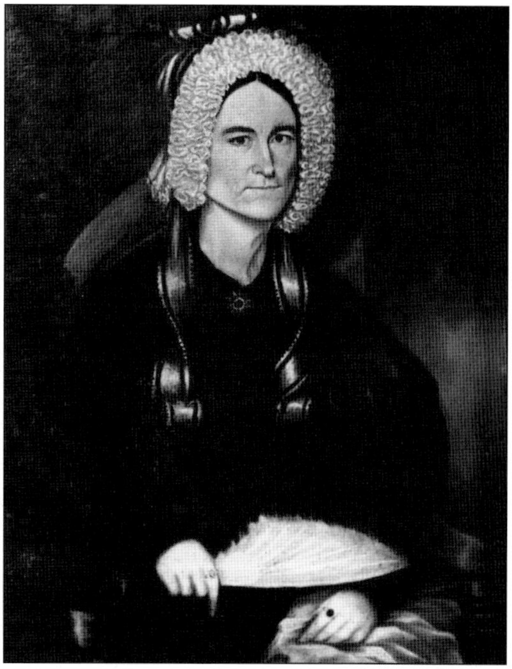

Soon after coming to Franklin in 1808, Nicholas "Bigbee" Perkins married his teenaged cousin, Mary Hardin Perkins. Their son Nicholas Edwin Perkins and his family lived at Meeting of the Waters, which was built at the confluence of the Harpeth and Little Harpeth Rivers by his grandfather, Thomas Hardin Perkins. Nicholas's mother and father also lived at Meeting of the Waters for a time. The home would stay in the Perkins family for several generations. (Both, TSL.)

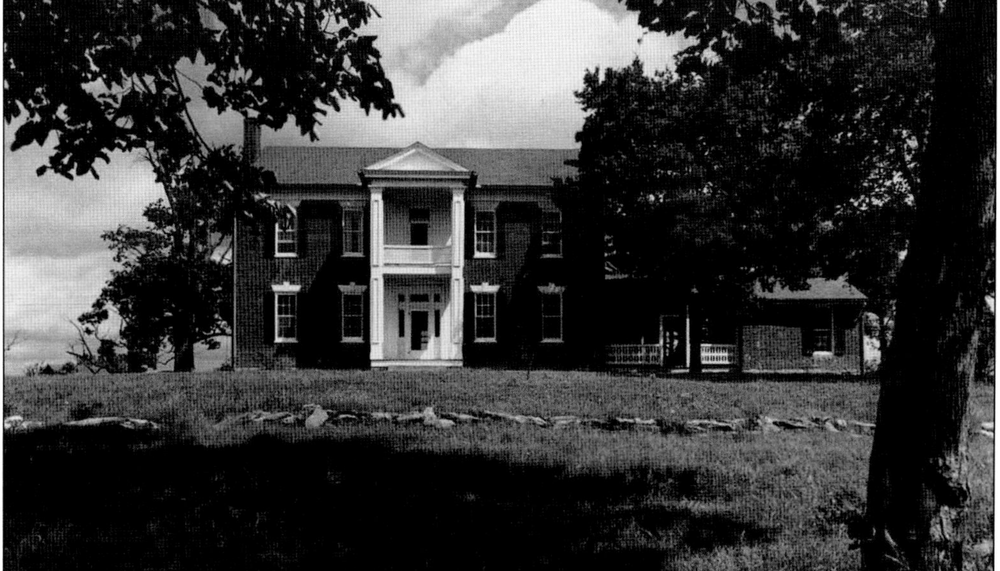

Nicholas and Mary Perkins built this beautiful home, which they named Montpier, in 1821. Mary and Nicholas would have 12 children. In 1835, Perkins built another beautiful home nearby, Walnut Hill, for a daughter and her family. (TSL.)

The only time a president met with Native Americans to negotiate a treaty for their lands was when Andrew Jackson (pictured at right) and leaders of the Chickasaw Nation met in Franklin. Jackson, who the Indians called "Sharp Knife," was joined by his chief negotiator, Gen. John Coffee (pictured below), and Secretary of War John Eaton at the Hiram Masonic Lodge on September 26, 1830. The tribe agreed to trade their land in Mississippi and Alabama for a home in Indian Territory, plus cash and travel expenses. However, the Chickasaw leader, Levi Colbert, insisted on a provision that if they didn't find land they liked in the Territory, they could void the treaty. After a Chickasaw delegation looked in vain for a good place to move the tribe, they cancelled the treaty with a letter and postponed their removal by several years. Neither Coffee nor Colbert would live to see the removal completed. (Both, LOC.)

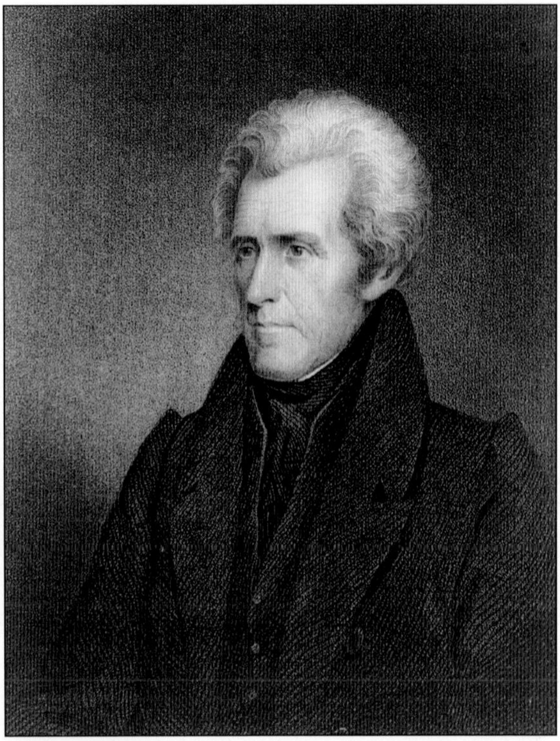

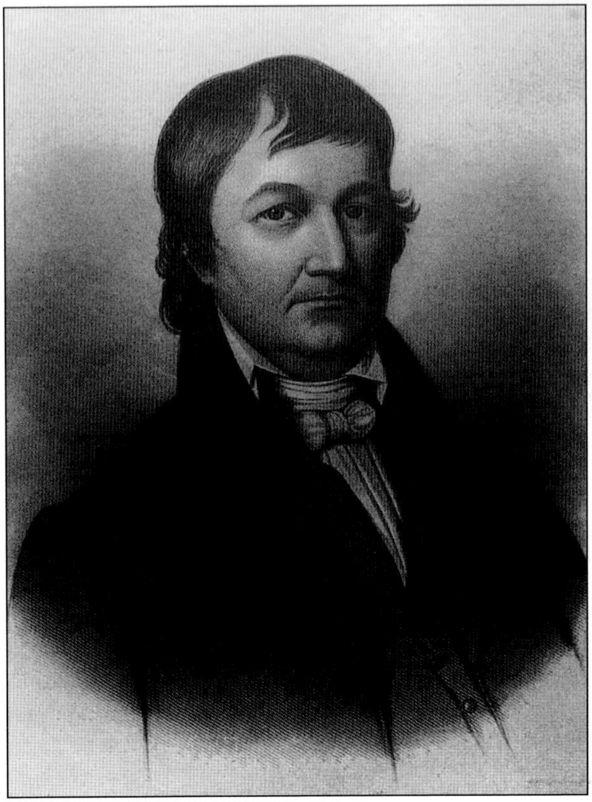

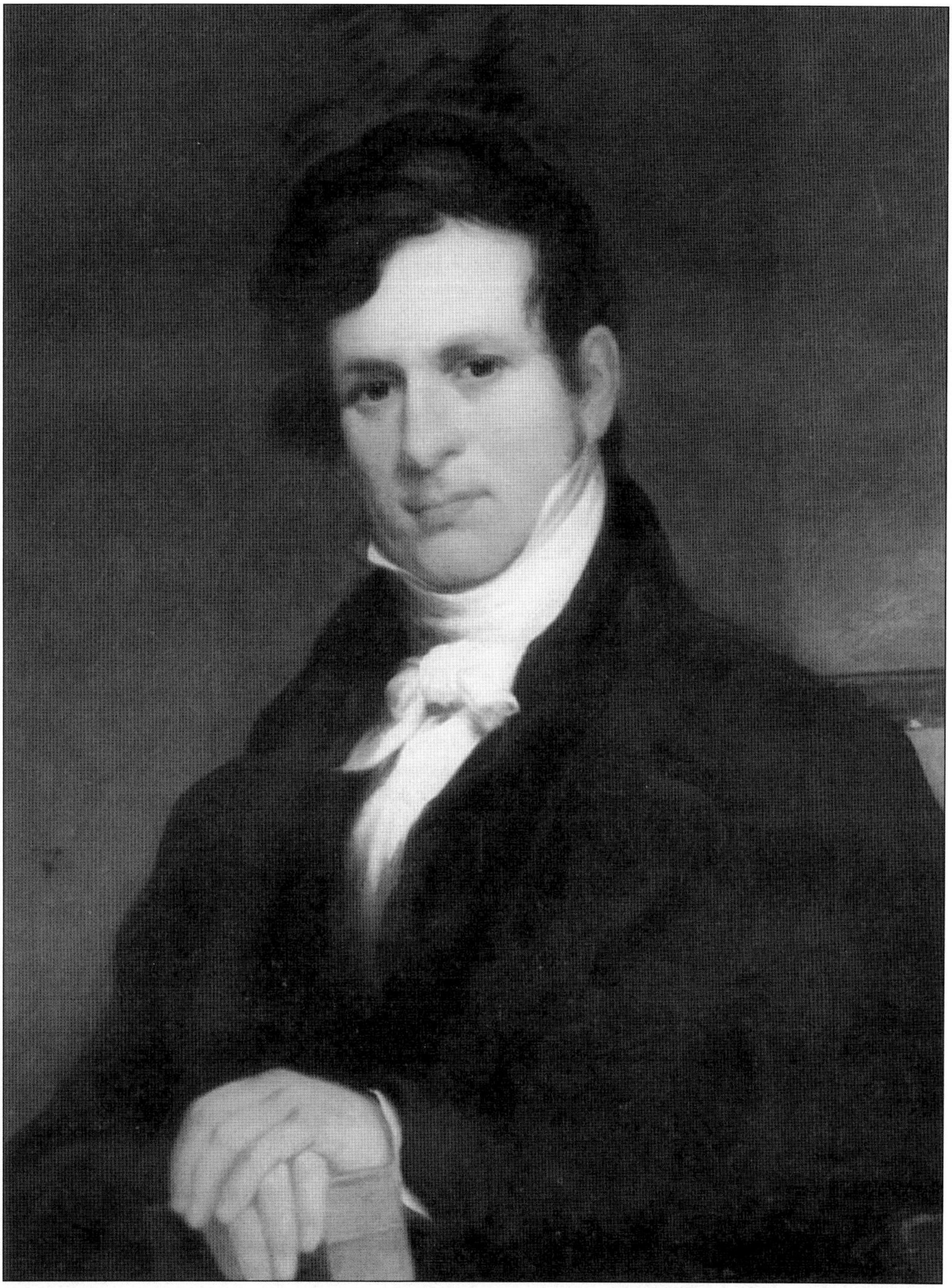

As secretary of war under Andrew Jackson, Franklin's John Henry Eaton participated in the Chickasaw treaty negotiations. He and his brash, opinionated wife, Peggy, were close friends of President Jackson and played a central role in the scandalous collapse of Jackson's first cabinet. John was a senator and diplomat, and the Eatons continued to live in Franklin, mainly during the summers, until his death in 1856. (LOC.)

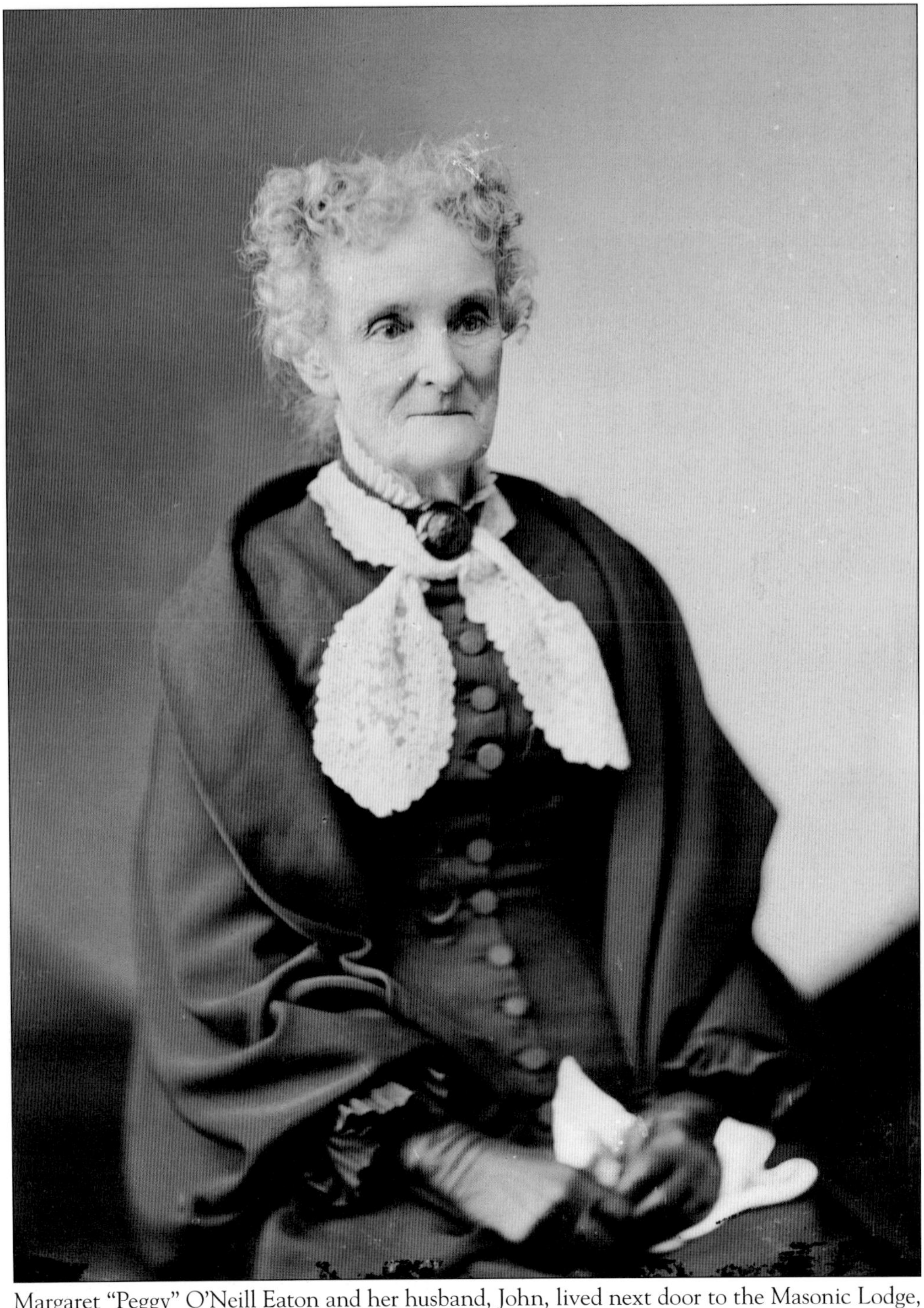

Margaret "Peggy" O'Neill Eaton and her husband, John, lived next door to the Masonic Lodge, where the local Episcopal congregation first met. The lodge had no piano, but the Eatons did, so Peggy had her piano moved to that side of the room and would accompany the hymns through the open windows. Having grown up in a Washington boardinghouse, she was opinionated and loved to talk politics. (LOC.)

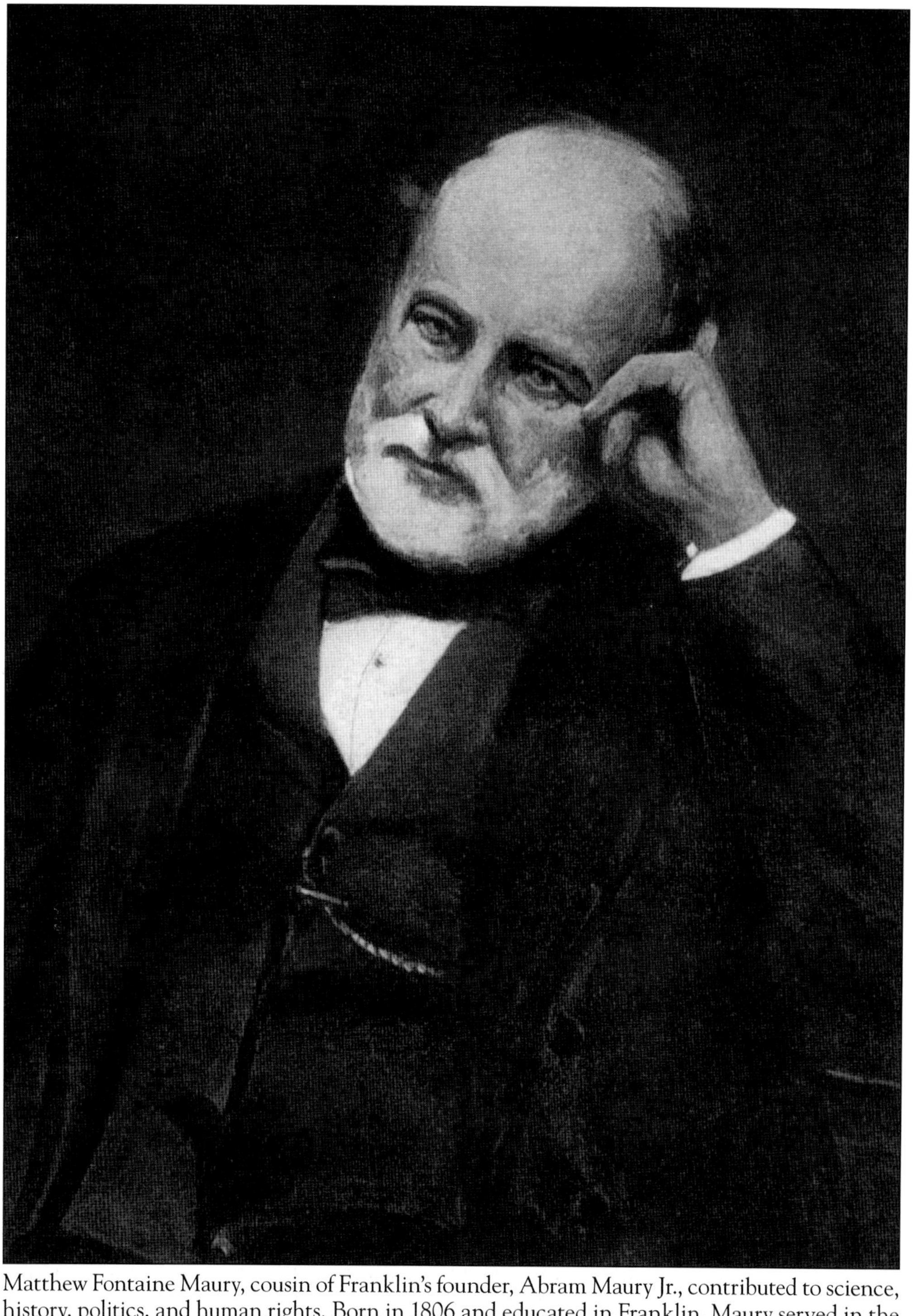

Matthew Fontaine Maury, cousin of Franklin's founder, Abram Maury Jr., contributed to science, history, politics, and human rights. Born in 1806 and educated in Franklin, Maury served in the Navy and then created maps of ocean currents and shipping lanes—revolutionizing worldwide ocean traffic. Maury was the first to chart weather patterns, and the first to map the migration of whales. He is considered by many one of the world's most widely accomplished men. (RHC.)

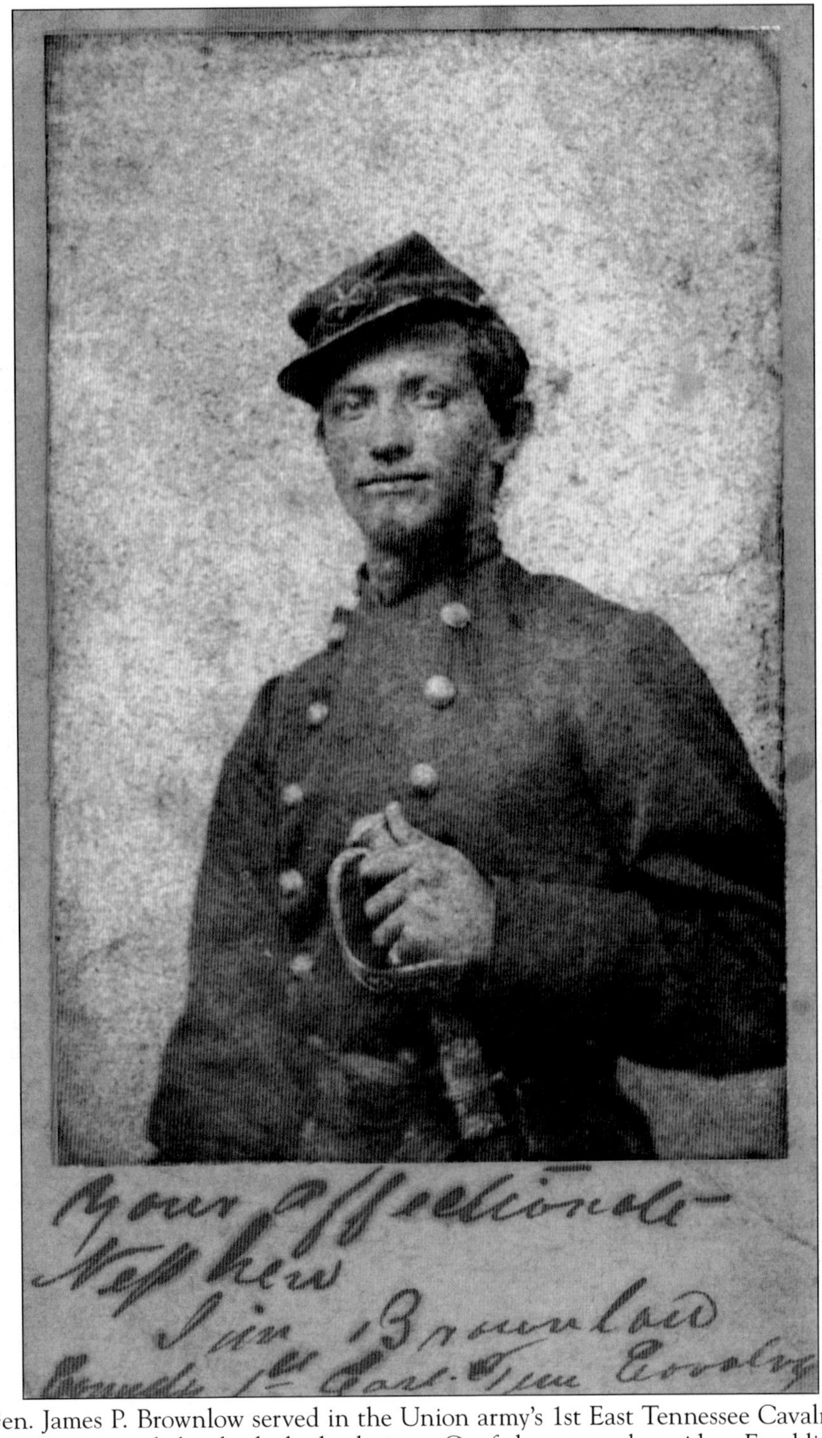

Brig. Gen. James P. Brownlow served in the Union army's 1st East Tennessee Cavalry during the Civil War. Wounded in both thighs during a Confederate cavalry raid on Franklin, he was treated by Dr. Daniel N. Cliffe. Brownlow fell in love with his nurse, Cliffe's daughter Isabella, and they married. When his father was elected governor, he became state adjutant general. He died at the age of 36. (LOC.)

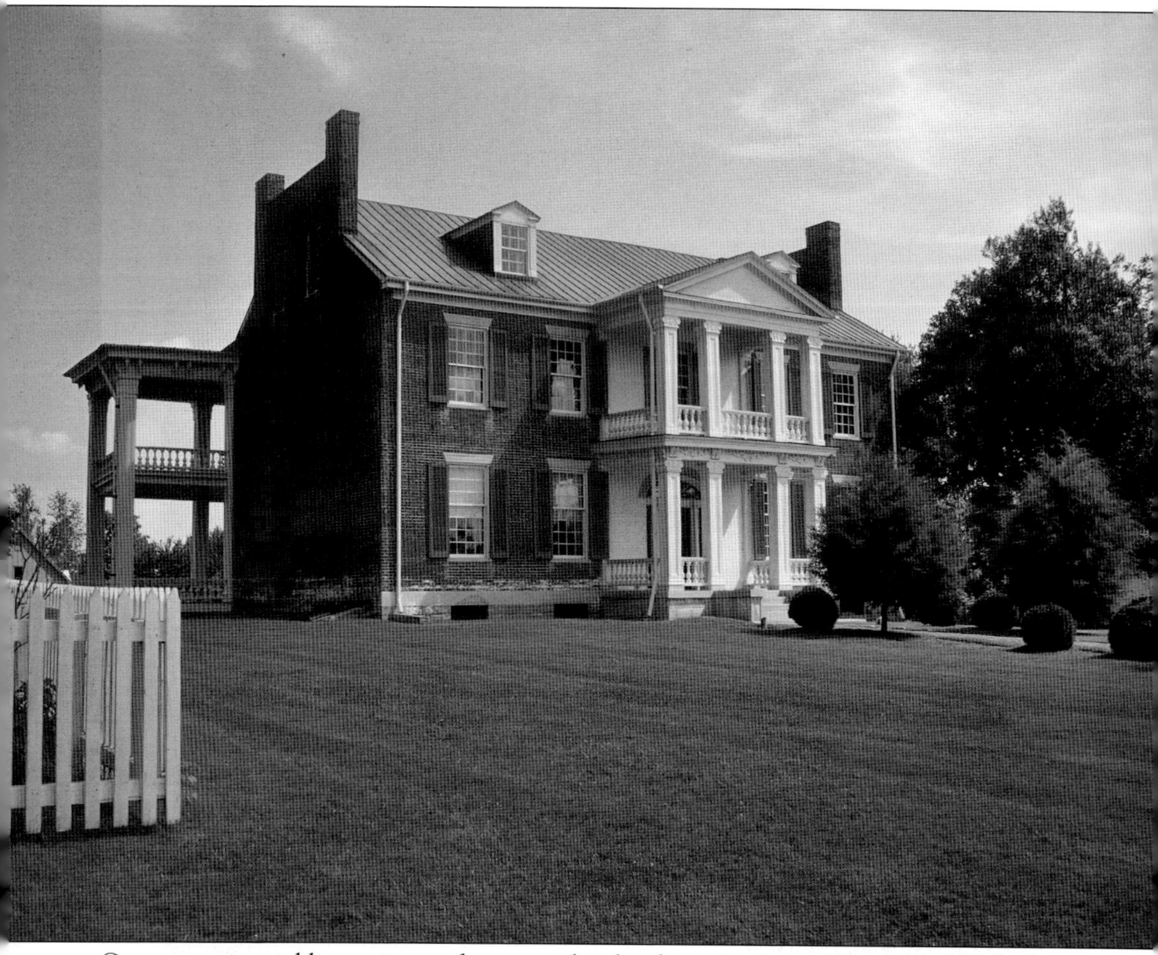

Carnton—pictured here—is a perfect example of a plantation home. It once overlooked 1,400 acres, with white fences, thoroughbred horses, and 500 cultivated acres of wheat, corn, oats, potatoes, and hay. After the house passed from the McGavock family, it fell into decay until being restored by private citizens. Carnton is now a beautiful, fully restored museum that is open to the public. (BFTC.)

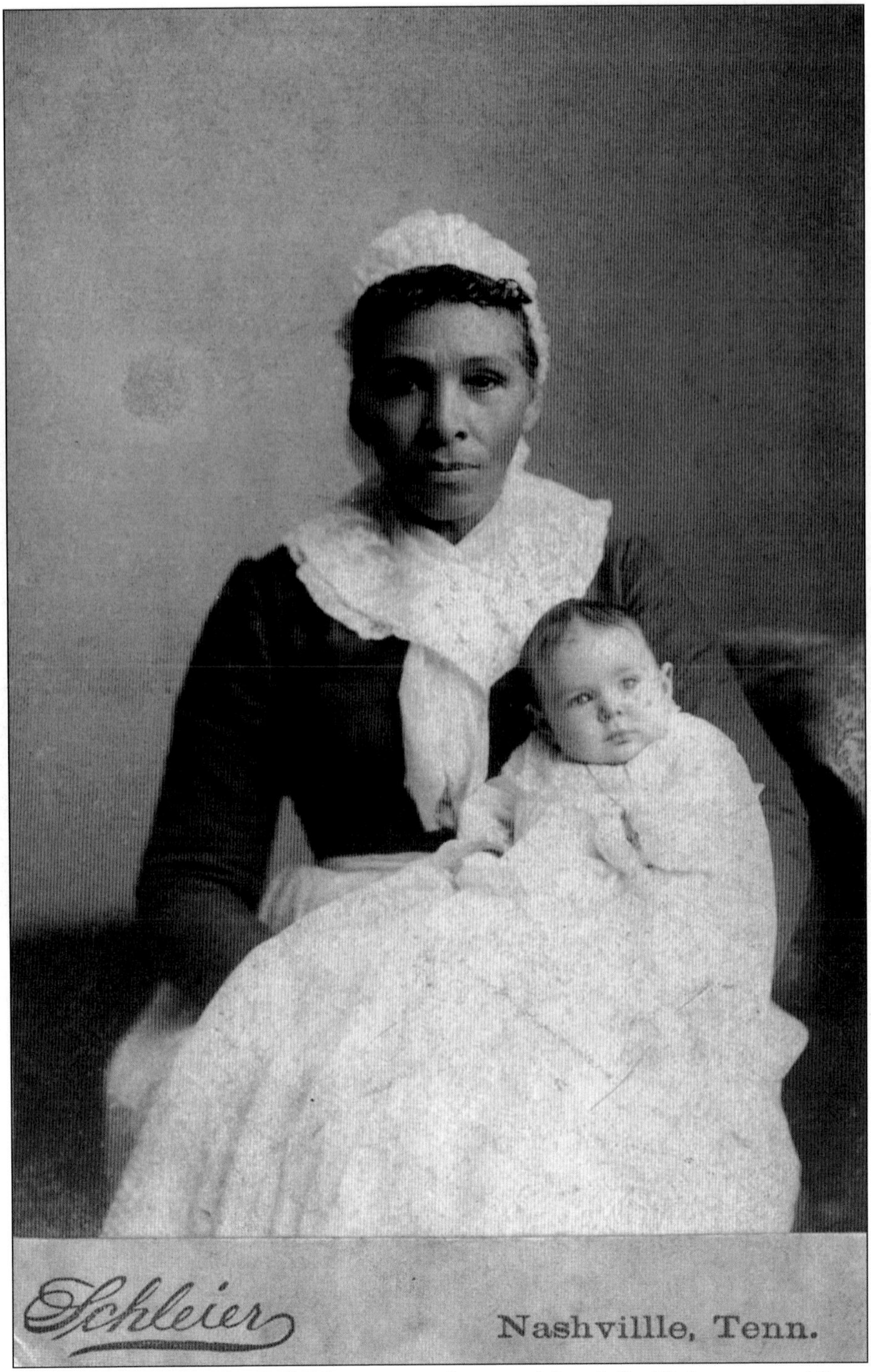

John and Carrie McGavock's faithful servant and nanny, Mariah Reddick, was a wedding gift to Carrie in 1848. She is pictured here holding John and Carrie's granddaughter Carrie. As a slave of the McGavocks, Mariah was head of the household staff and attended the births of generations of McGavock children. After emancipation, Franklin women frequently called upon Mariah as a midwife. (BFTC.)

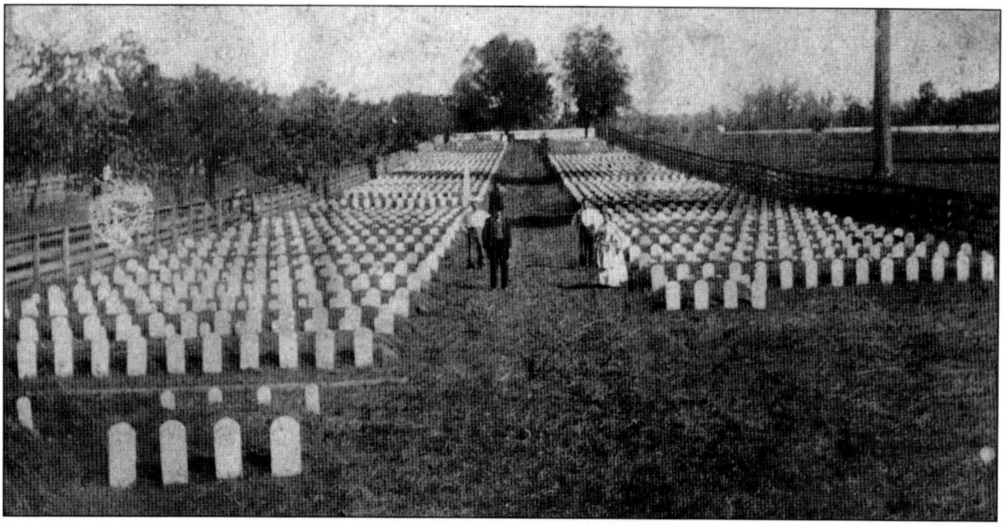

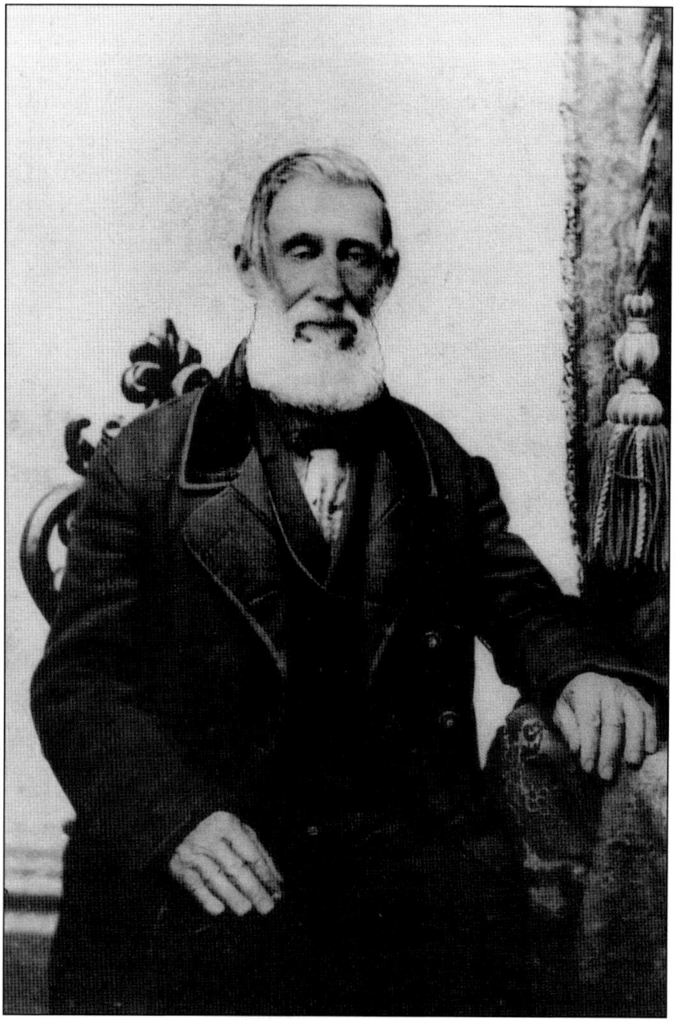

After the Battle of Franklin, some 1,500 Confederate dead were hastily buried in shallow graves with wooden markers. In June 1866, the bodies were reinterred on land donated by the McGavock family at Carnton and marked with stone markers. Carrie McGavock and the United Daughters of the Confederacy devoted themselves to caring for the graves, which the organization still does today. (BFTC.)

Fountain Branch Carter was a local shoemaker and farmer who, in one of the most important commercial accomplishments of the time, built a cotton gin to the east of his home. Carter owned 288 acres and 28 slaves by 1861. His wife, Mary Atkinson Carter, gave birth to 12 children, but she died in 1852, and only three of their sons lived until the time of the Civil War. (BFTC.)

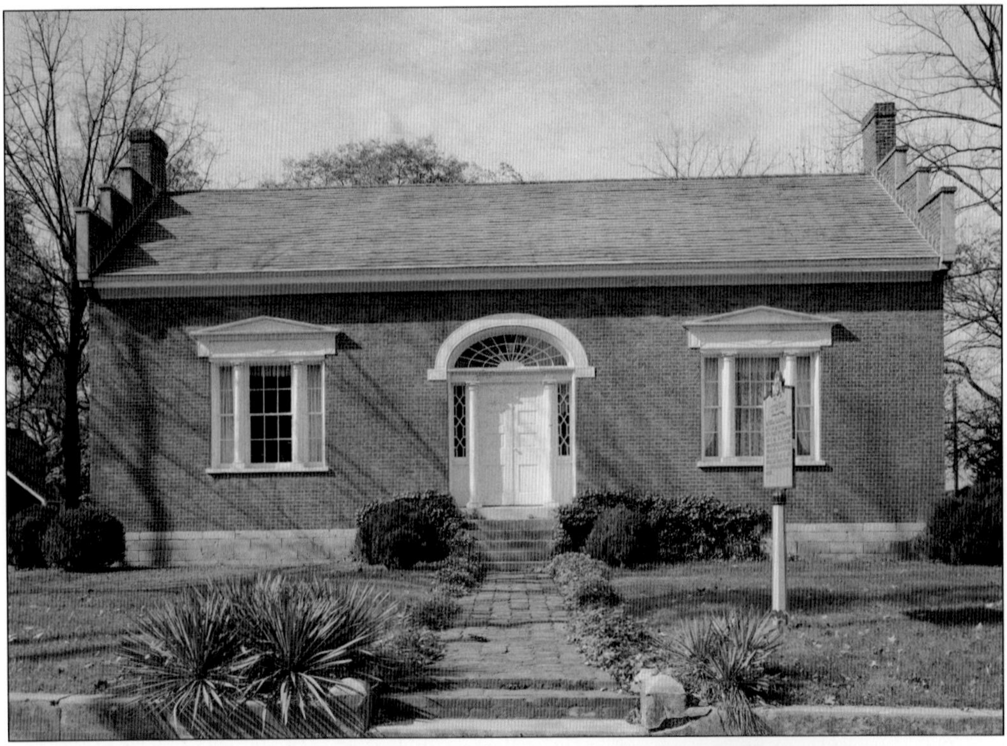

The Federal-style Carter House, home of the Fountain Branch Carter family, was built in 1830. It stood just behind the Union lines during the Battle of Franklin, and the fighting reached its zenith in the house's yard. Over the years the home has been renovated several times, and, thanks to citizen preservation groups, has been restored to its original, pastoral beauty. (LOC.)

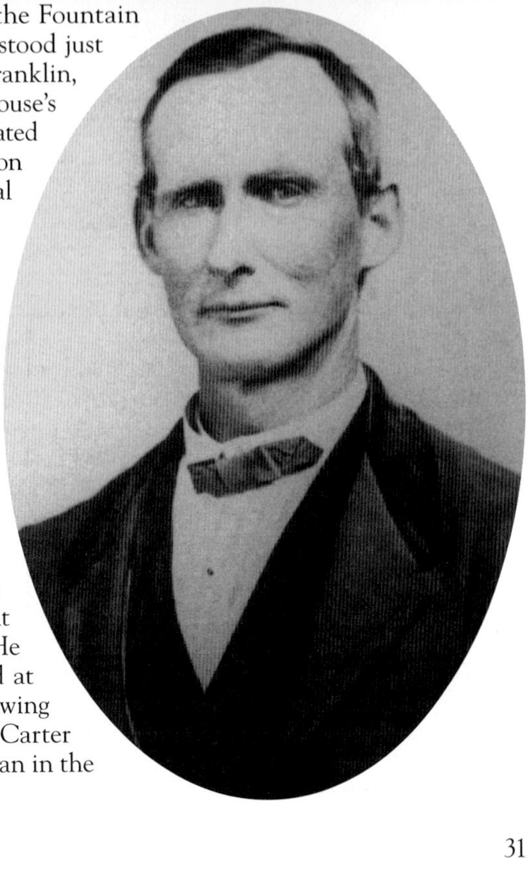

Col. Moscow B. Carter, son of F.B. Carter, served in the Mexican-American War, then returned to farming north of Franklin. When the Civil War broke out, he joined the Confederate army and became a lieutenant colonel in the 20th Tennessee Regiment. He fought in several skirmishes, was captured at Fishing Creek, and later rejoined his unit following a prisoner exchange. When he died at 76, Carter was the oldest Mexican-American War veteran in the county. (BFTC.)

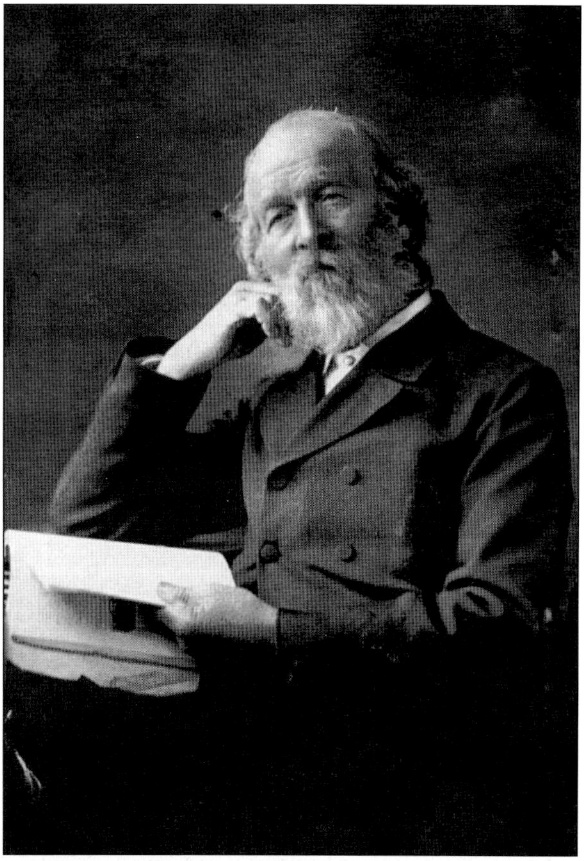

German immigrant Albert Johann Lotz bought five acres from Fountain Branch Carter to build his Columbia Avenue home. Lotz was a master woodcarver, and, with his own hands, fashioned the ornate woodwork in the home. Lotz is pictured here in his 70s, long after the family moved to California, where he continued to excel at woodworking and made guitars, dulcimers, and even pianos. (Lotz House.)

Albert Johann Lotz spent three years building his home. Insisting on building without the assistance of slave labor, Lotz made the house a showcase for his skill as a master carpenter and woodcarver. The exquisite home was all but destroyed during the Battle of Franklin, so Lotz spent another four years rebuilding. Today, the Lotz House Museum showcases some of his finest work, including three carved fireplace mantles. (Lotz House.)

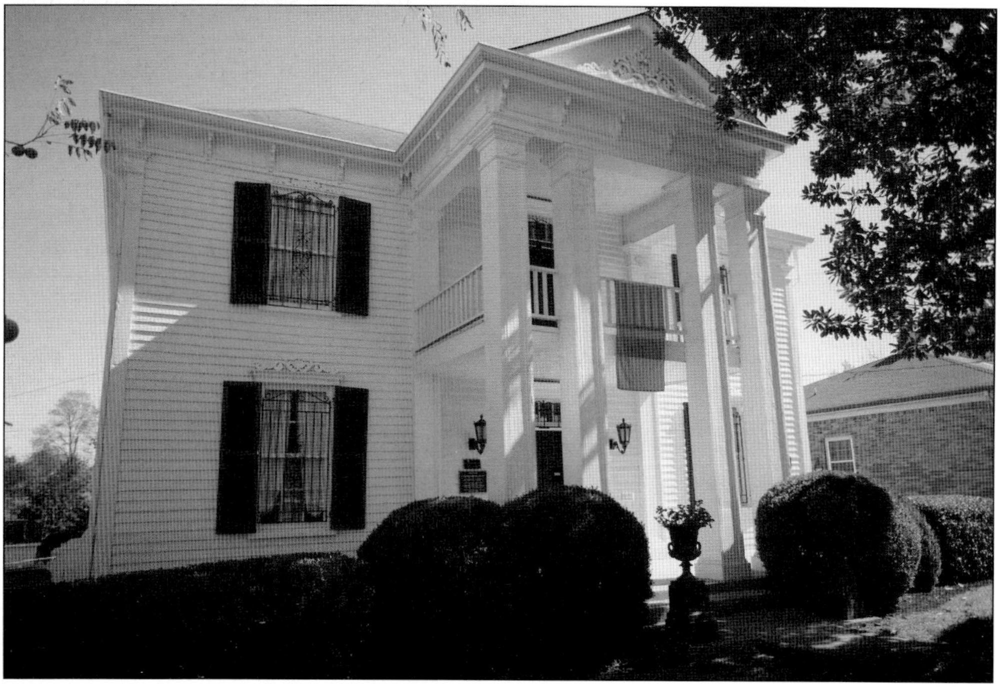

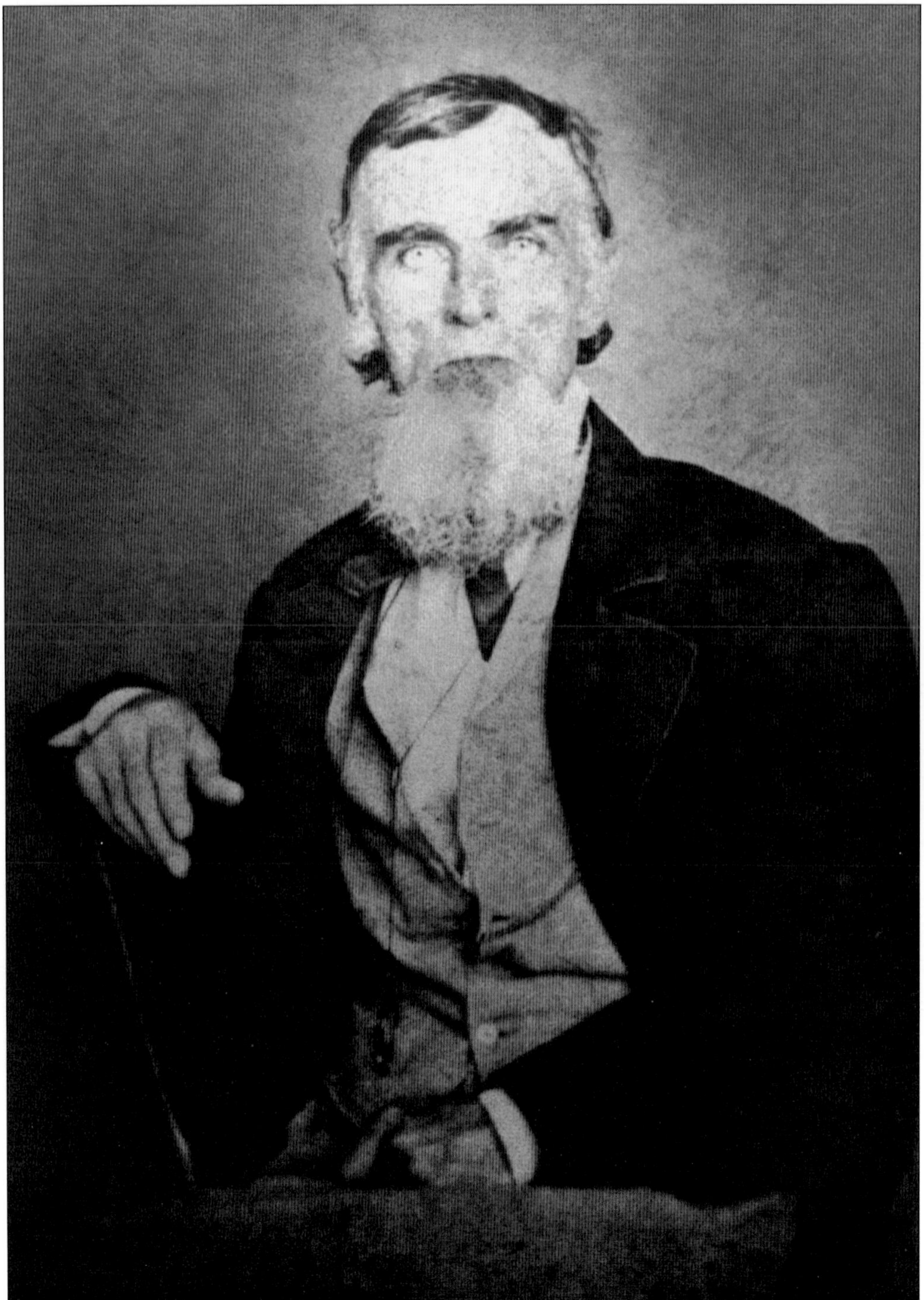

Randal McGavock, who once served as mayor of Nashville, finished Canton plantation in 1826. His son John, pictured here, renovated the house in the Greek Revival style, adding the two-story portico. John and his wife Carrie farmed the place until his death in 1893. They had five children, but only two survived to adulthood. (BFTC.)

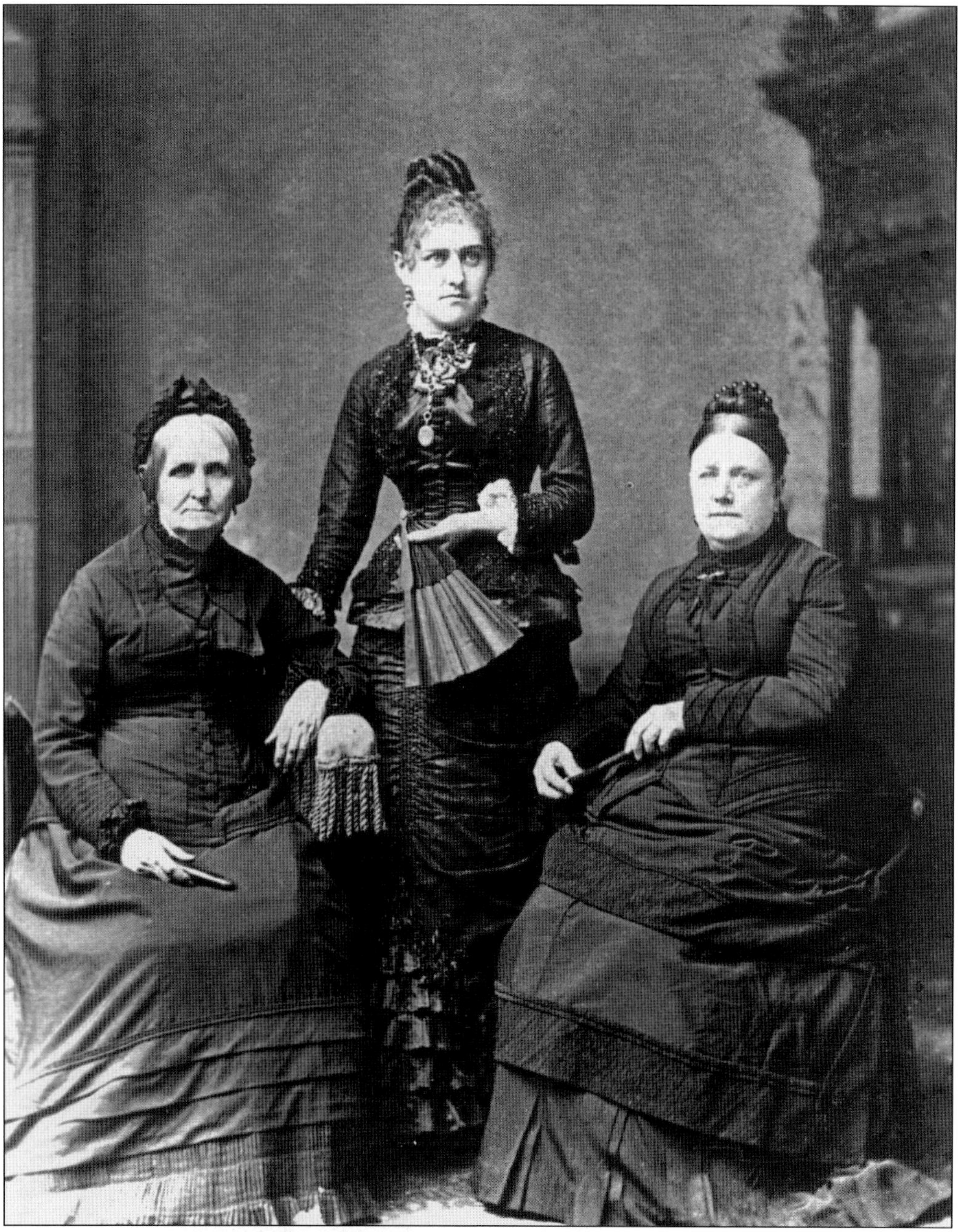

Carrie Winder McGavock (right) is shown with her daughter, Hattie Cowan and her mother, Martha Winder, on a visit to Carnton. After the death of three children, Carrie was overwhelmed with grief. Then, while tending the hundreds of dead, dying, and wounded after the Battle of Franklin, she found a new purpose and devoted her life to ongoing advocacy for Civil War veterans. Carrie lived until 1905. (BFTC.)

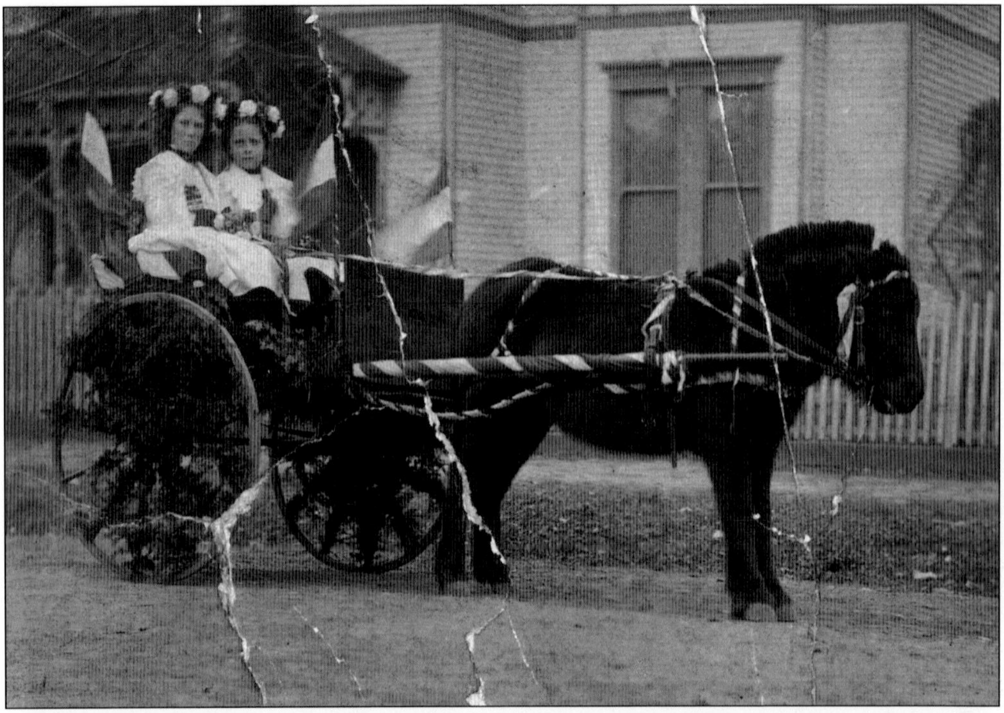

On November 30, 1899, Leah Cowan and Susie Winstead, grandchildren of the McGavocks, drove their pony cart, decorated with flowers, bunting, and fresh greens, to the Franklin square. There, at the dedication of the city's iconic Confederate Monument, they had the honor of pulling the drape to unveil the statue. (BFTC.)

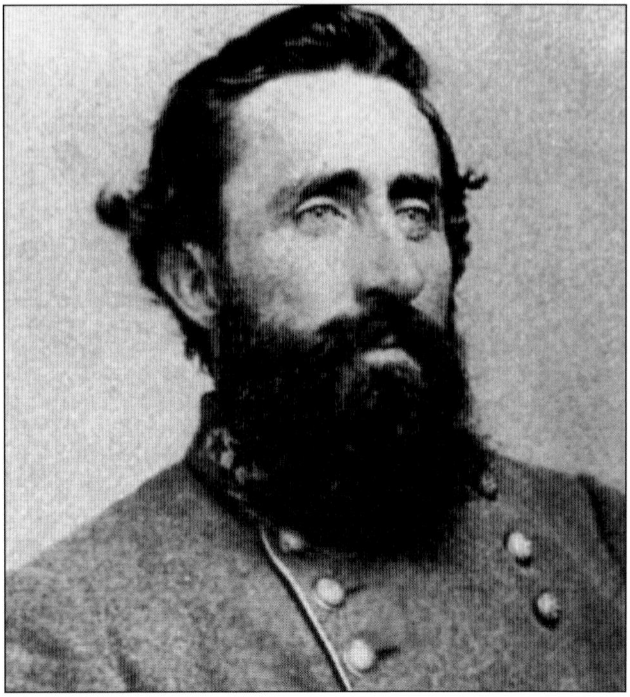

William Brimage Bate served in the US Army before becoming a major general for the Confederacy and seeing action at the Battles of Franklin and Nashville. He was governor of Tennessee from 1883 to 1887, and was elected to four terms as US senator. At the opening of Battle Ground Academy on October 5, 1889, he spoke on the same bloody ground where he had led his command. (LOC.)

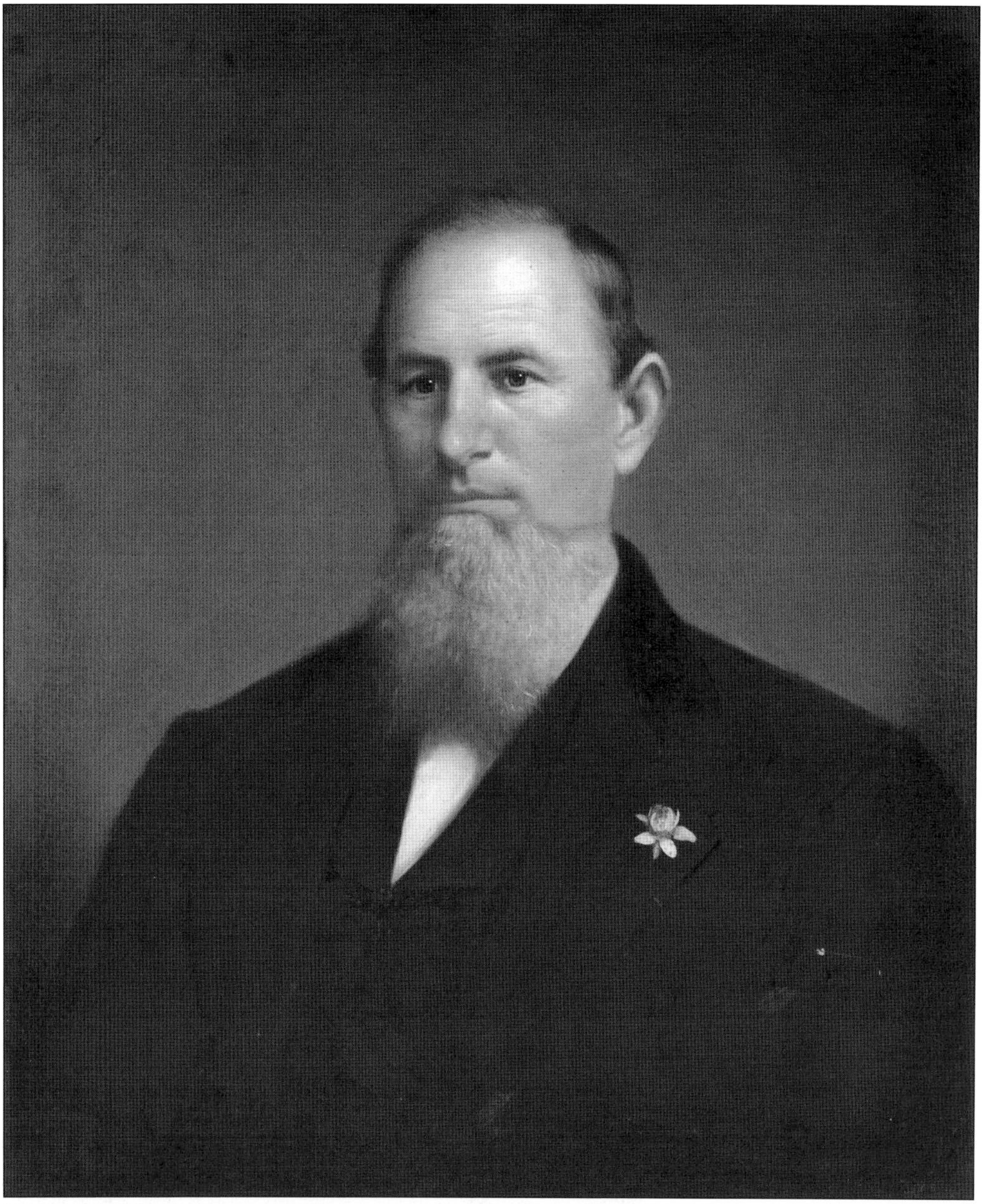

Born in 1820, John Brown McEwen was the grandson of David McEwen, who was one of the first settlers of the area in 1798. He was an innovative farmer who experimented with crops and livestock and wrote about his experiments for agricultural publications. He was also a lawyer and served as Franklin's mayor during the Civil War, and it fell to him to make the difficult decision to surrender the city to the occupying Federal troops. Following the death of their son, McEwen and his wife raised several orphan children. In the 1870s, in his most generous show of public service, McEwen organized Franklin's first public schools on an unpaid, volunteer basis. (BFTC.)

Three

The Civil War

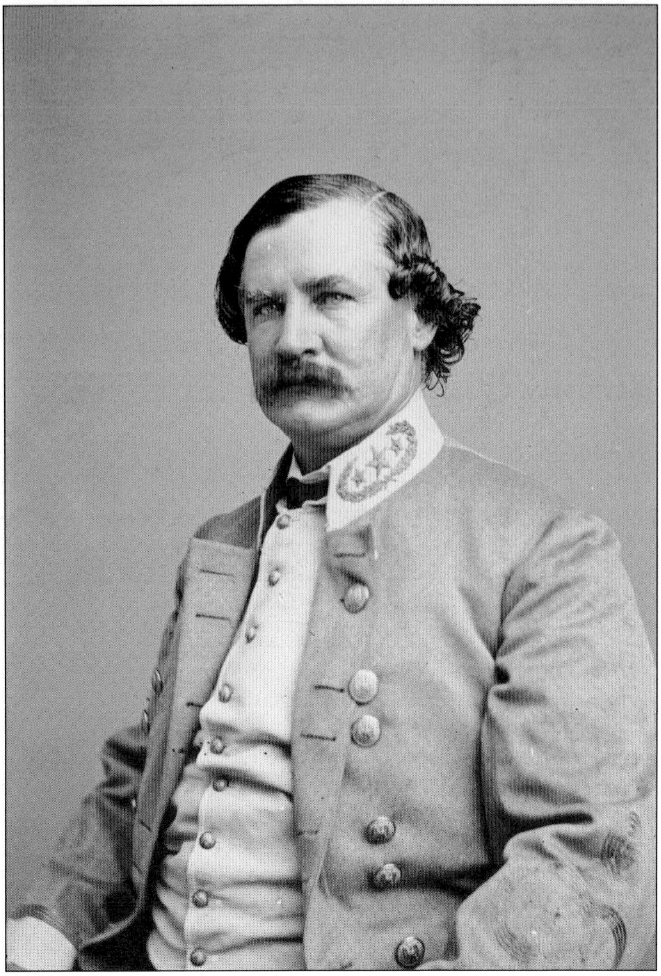

Benjamin Frank Cheatham grew up on a Nashville plantation. At the Battle of Franklin, he was a Confederate brigadier general and an experienced commander. He advised General Hood not to make the frontal assault on Franklin, but his command then bore the brunt of the fighting. Cheatham survived the battles at both Franklin and Nashville, and would be one of the last Confederate generals to surrender with General Johnston in North Carolina. (LOC.)

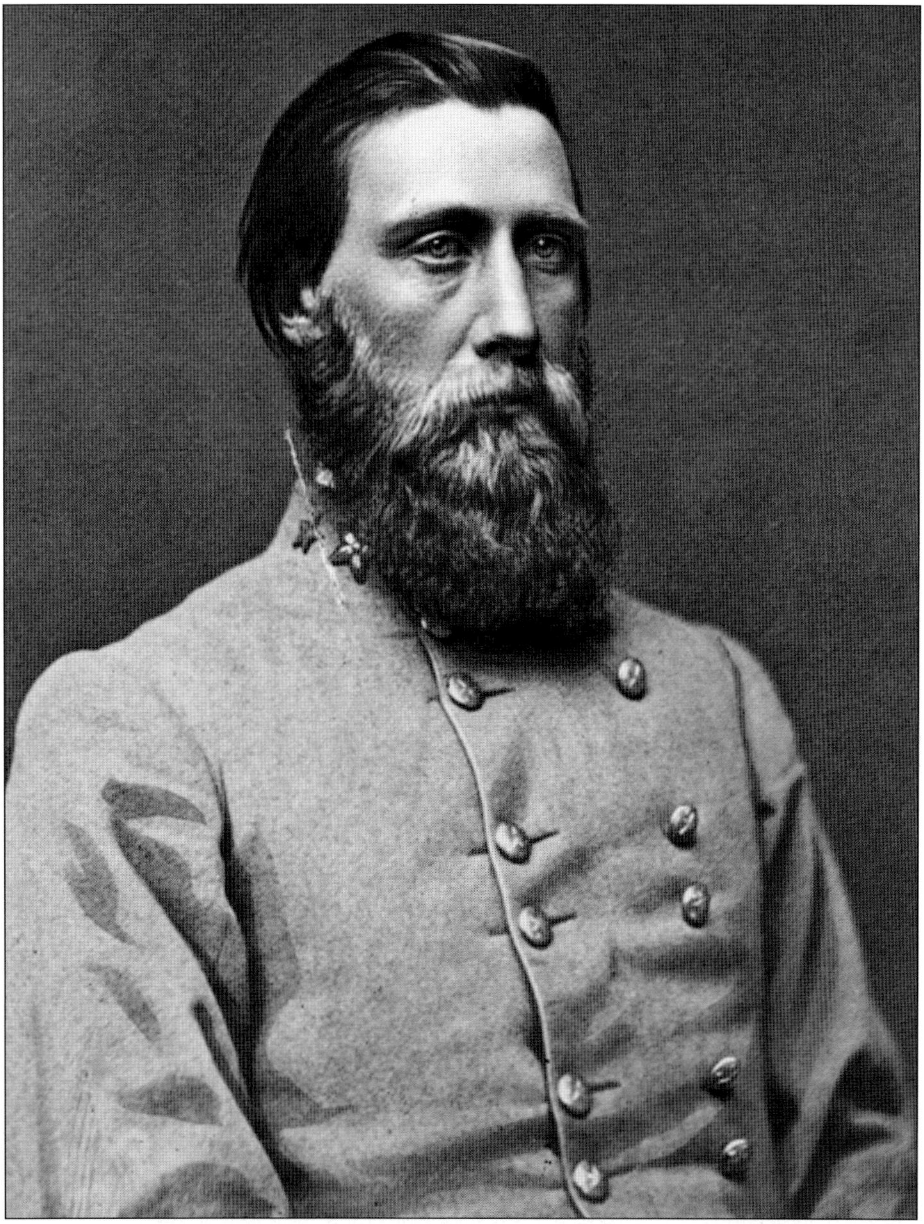

Gen. John Bell Hood commanded the Army of Tennessee, the Confederacy's second largest army after the force led by Robert E. Lee in Virginia. For about a month before the Battle of Franklin, things had been going badly for Hood's command. They had a chance to block Union troops—including Schofield's XXIII Corps, Army of the Ohio—at Spring Hill, and keep them from reaching Nashville, but Hood and his staff made a series of blunders that allowed the Yankees to pass quietly in the night. Then, Hood sent his men into the Battle of Franklin, marching across a broad cornfield, directly into the guns of an equal force of dug-in Union infantry, artillery, and cavalry. Hood had entered the state with a force of about 34,000, but about 7,000 men were killed, wounded, or captured at Franklin. There is no way to measure the demoralizing effect it had on the survivors when they looked out upon the bodies of their friends piled up where they met the Union line and painting the entire field in gray.

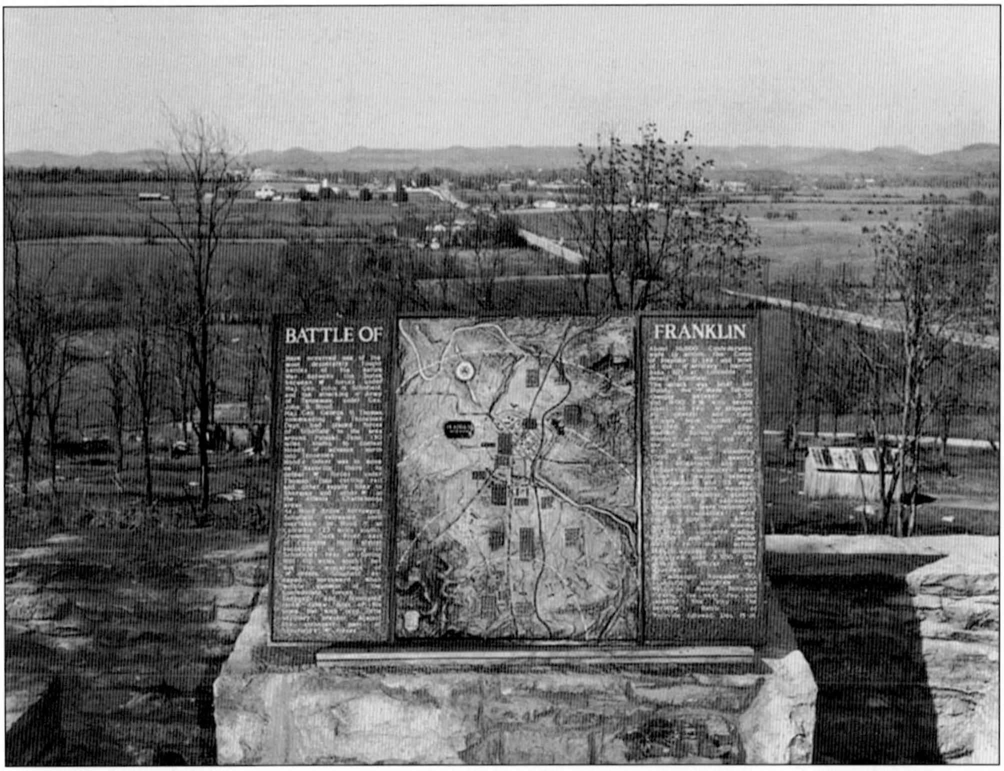

This photograph, taken on Winstead Hill south of the city in 1950, shows the battlefield across which Confederate troops advanced under a withering fire. They had no cover, and those at the rear were soon walking on their fallen comrades. On both sides of the Columbia Pike, Confederate officers led soldiers toward the Federal breastworks, funneling them into the Carter House on the left, and the cotton gin on the right. (TSL.)

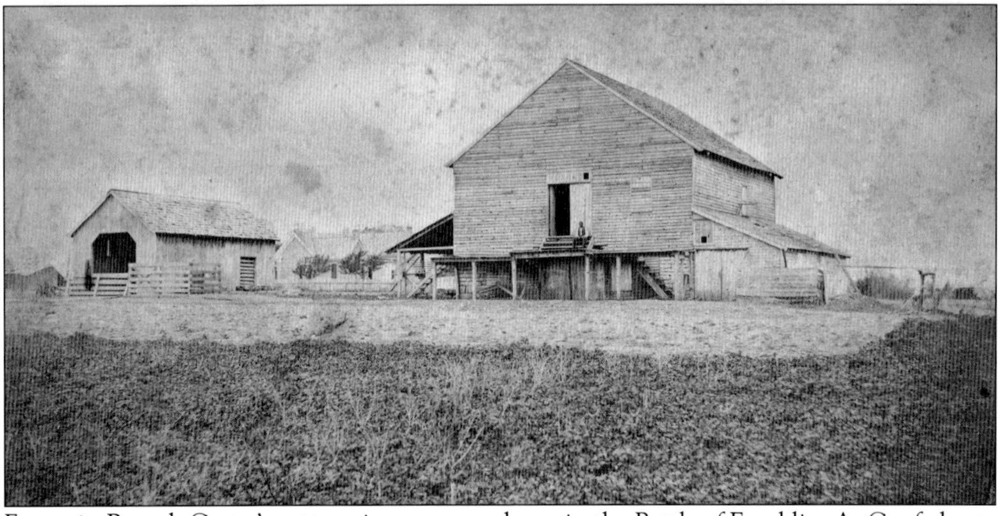
Fountain Branch Carter's cotton gin was ground zero in the Battle of Franklin. As Confederate troops advanced, their right flank was concentrated upon the Federal breastworks before the gin, where the fighting was fiercest. After the war, the gin was repaired and put back in business, though, as this photograph shows, the lower half was riddled with bullet holes. (BFTC.)

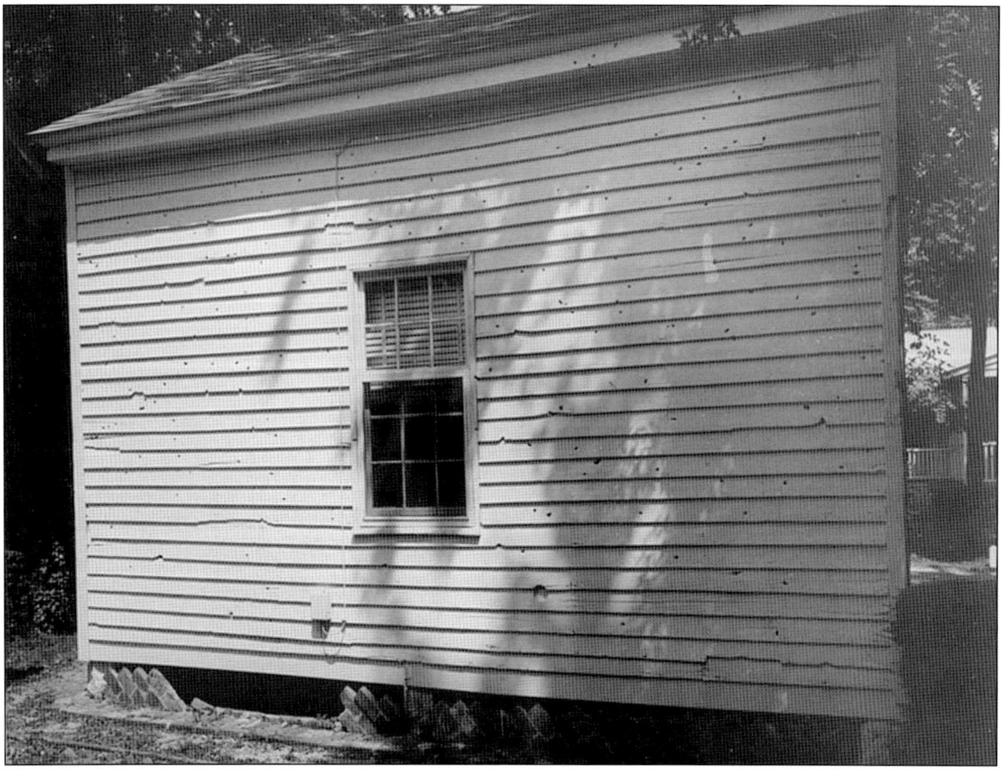

The frame office and brick smokehouse of the Carter House were peppered with bullet holes in the battle, and the damage remains to this day. The Federal breastworks were within yards of the Carter family home. Though thousands of Confederate troops fell dead and wounded on the thousand-yard approach, some made it through the works and engaged in hand-to-hand fighting. With no chance to reload, rifles became clubs, and bayonets, knives, and sabers rattled among the screams, prayers, and oaths of the fighting. Soldiers fought around the buildings while the terrified Carter family heard it all—huddled in the basement as bullets and cannonballs smashed into their home. (Both, TSL.)

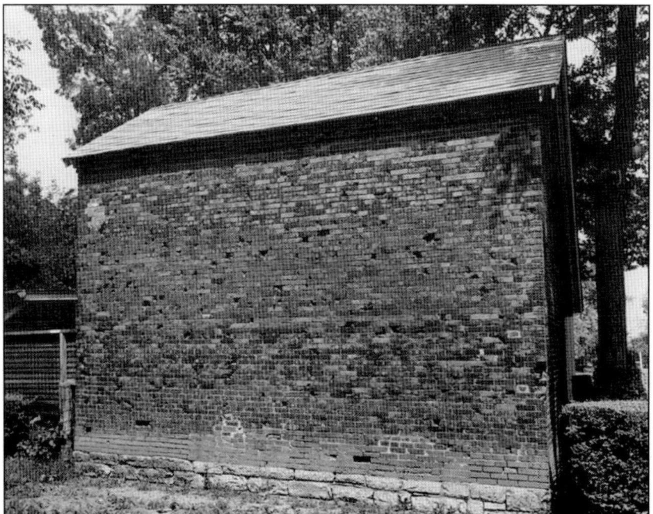

Gen. John Adams, a Nashville native, was one of the six Confederate generals killed in the battle. Leading his men, he jumped his horse over the Federal breastworks and then fell, wounded nine times. After the battle, Union soldiers lifted the dead horse from him, brought him water and comforted the 39-year-old general as he died, saying, "It is the fate of a soldier to die for his country." (TSL.)

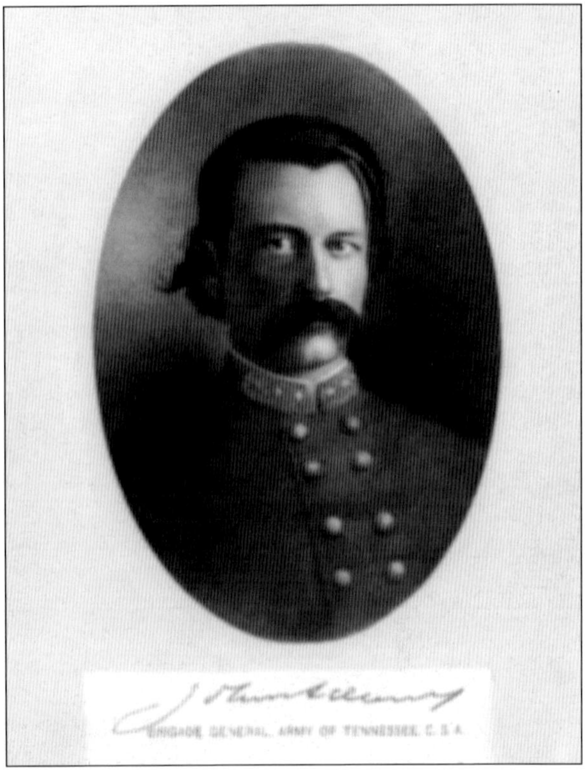

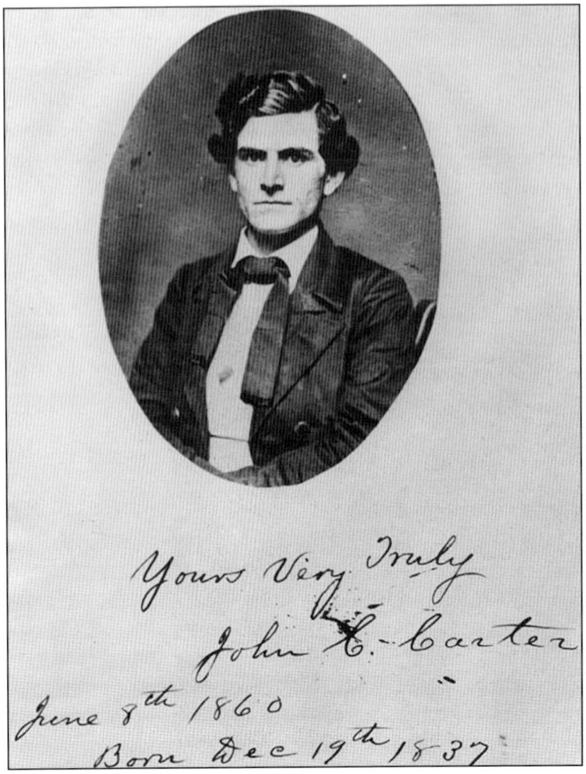

Another of the six generals killed at Franklin was John C. Carter, a Tennessee native and Memphis lawyer who joined the 38th Tennessee Infantry as a captain, quickly rose to colonel, and then brigadier general. After surviving major battles like Shiloh and Stones River, he was mortally wounded at Franklin and was moved from the field to Harrison House, south of the city, where he died three days later. (TSL.)

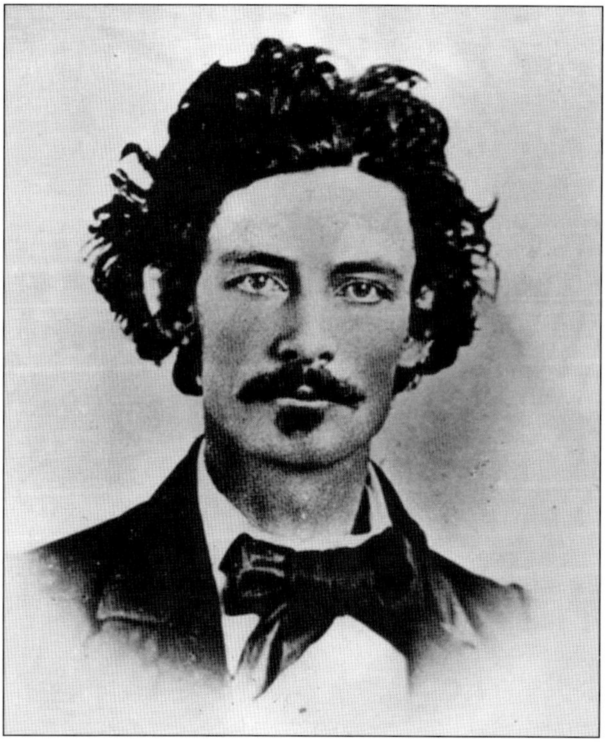

Brig. Gen. Hiram B. Granbury commanded eight Texas regiments, which had been decimated by the time they got to Franklin. He led his men directly into the Federal lines, and died at the breastworks. Like it did for all of the generals killed that day, Franklin later named a street for Granbury. He was eventually reburied in Texas, and the town of Granbury was named for him. (LOC.)

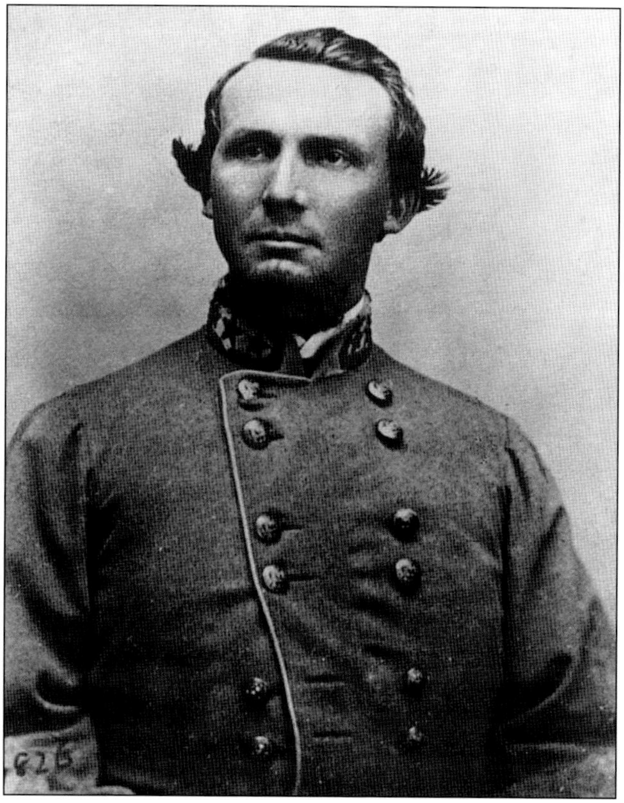

States Rights Gist was a South Carolina lawyer and militia general before rising to the rank of brigadier general in the Confederate army. As he led his men into the Yankee guns at Franklin, Gist's horse was shot from under him and he continued forward on foot. He fell before they reached the breastworks, shot in the chest. (LOC.)

Patrick Cleburne was an Irish immigrant who became an Arkansas businessman and lawyer. He cast his lot with the Confederacy during the Civil War not because he favored slavery, but because he loved the Southern people. He enlisted as a private, rose to the rank of major general, and, when he saw that the Confederate cause was lost, he futilely proposed that the slaves be freed if they would enlist in the Confederate army. At Franklin, he was one of several officers who opposed Hood's plan to march across the 1,000 yards of open ground into the Yankee guns. Leading his men into battle, his horse was shot from under him and he bravely continued on foot—his sword held over his head—until he was mortally wounded. Today, Franklin honors the place where he fell with Cleburne Park, pictured below. (Right, LOC.)

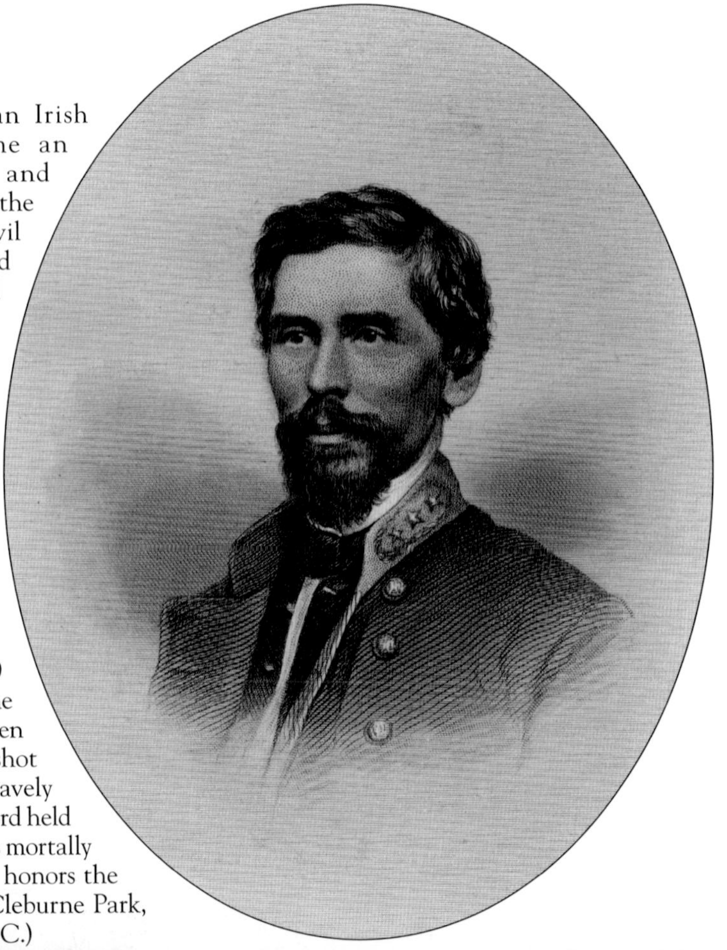

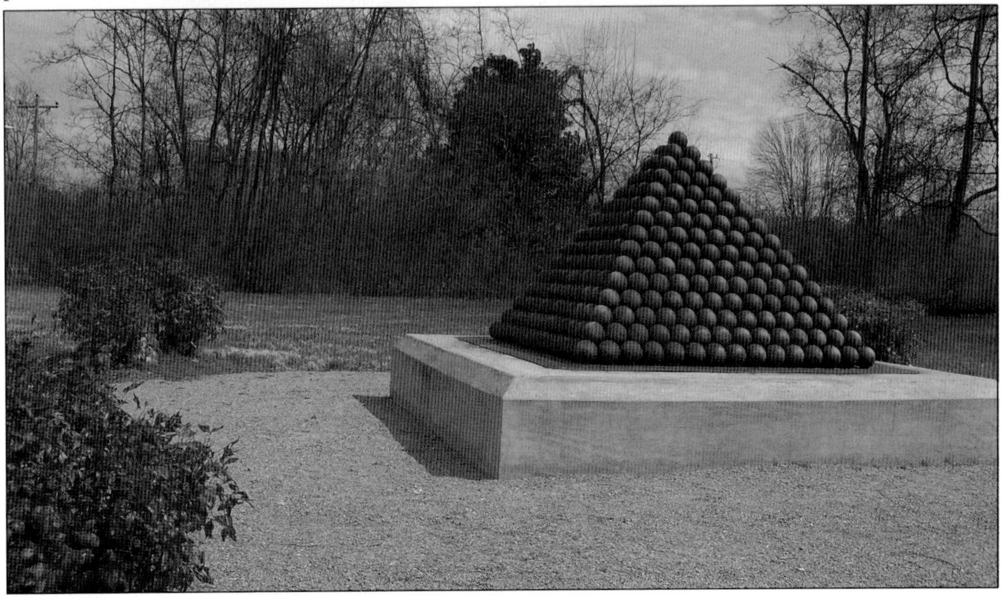

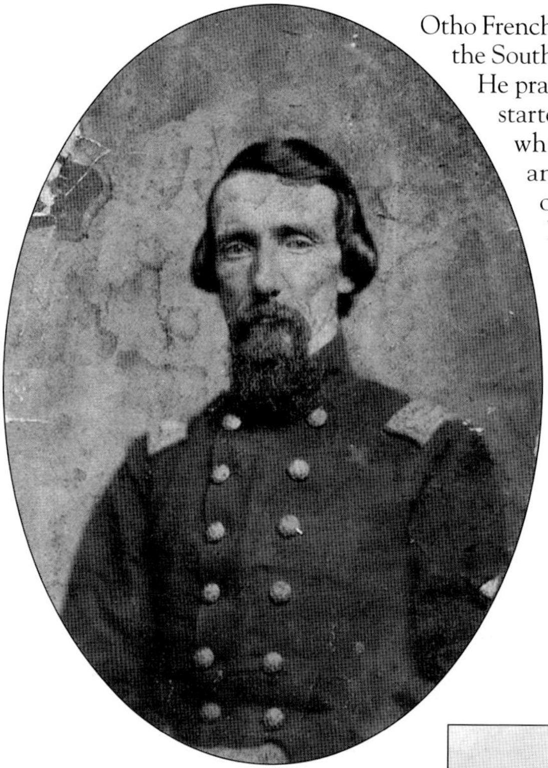

Otho French Strahl grew up in Ohio, but learned to love the South because of his two southern grandmothers. He practiced law in Dyersburg, and, when the war started, raised a Confederate infantry regiment, which he led through battles like Shiloh and Atlanta. At Franklin, he led his men on foot until being shot in the neck and head. (TSL.)

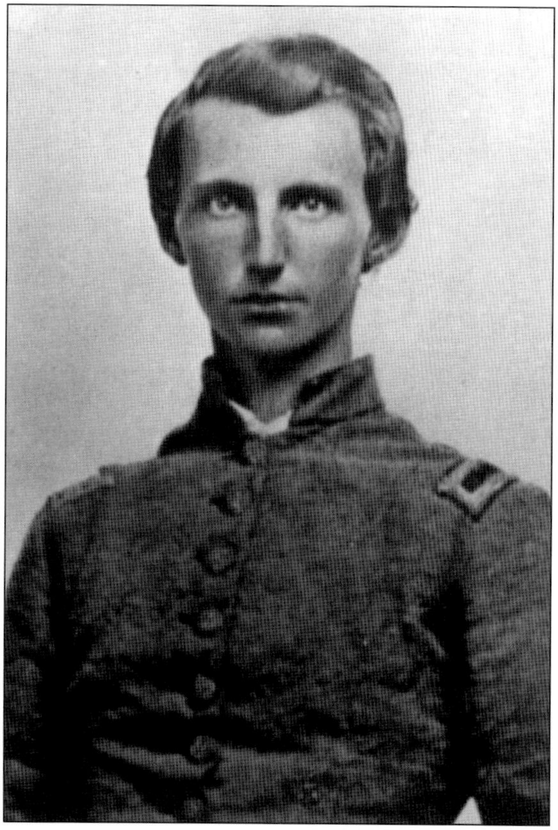

After the Battle of Franklin, 24-year-old Capt. Todd Carter was found wounded, brought to his father, and died in the house where he had been born in 1840. Before becoming a tragic icon of the war, he was an attorney, and, while in the army, served as assistant quartermaster, provost marshal, and newspaper correspondent. Before Franklin, Carter had been captured, escaped, rejoined his unit, and become an aide to Gen. Thomas Benton Smith. (BOFT.)

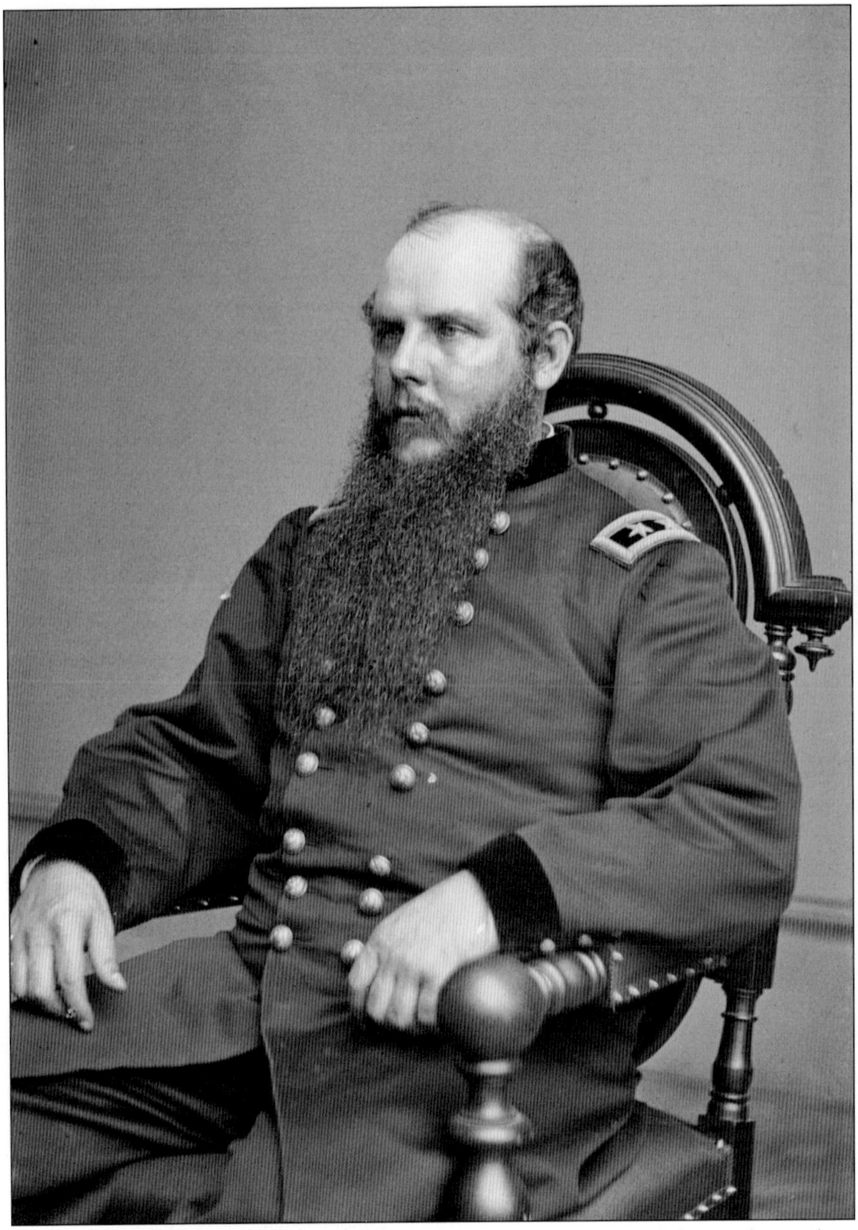

Maj. Gen. John M. Schofield, a New York native, was a controversial figure during his time as the commander of the Department of Missouri. Reassigned under Sherman at Atlanta, Schofield had some success and was sent to join General Thomas in the defense of Nashville against the Confederates under Hood. Slipping past Hood, he turned and prepared a defensive position at Franklin. Though he had only one day to prepare, the occupying Union troops already had works in place, so by the time that Hood attacked, the Union lines were impenetrable. The left was anchored on the Harpeth River, beyond which was Fort Granger, with its batteries that raked the advancing gray line. Before the Confederates reached the Federal breastworks, they had to fight through an Osage orange thicket, where they were riddled with bullets. Finally, the terrain funneled the Southern Army into a narrow front, so that they bunched together and stalled while Union fire rained down on them. The result was an overwhelming Union victory.

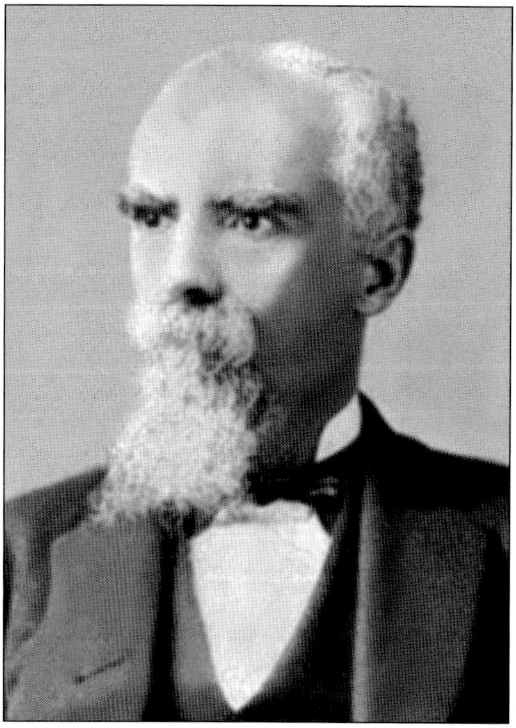

Edward McKendree Bounds was a Methodist minister who served as chaplain for the 3rd Missouri Infantry. Though seriously wounded at the Battle of Franklin, he helped to nurse the casualties and bury the dead. After the war, he returned to Franklin and spent days walking and praying over the battlefield and the city. He pastored the Methodist church until 1869, and went on to become a well-known evangelist and writer.

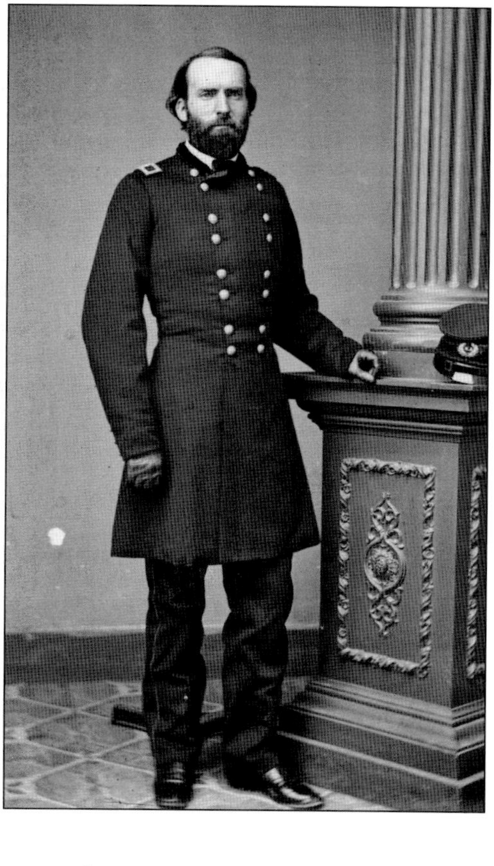

Union Maj. Gen. David S. Stanley distinguished himself in several battles during the war, but his corps was placed under the command of Brigadier General Wagner at Franklin—leaving Stanley with no command. When Wagner was overwhelmed during the battle, Stanley rode to the front and rallied the men to turn the Confederates back. His horse was killed and he was shot in the neck, but lived and received the Medal of Honor for his actions. (LOC.)

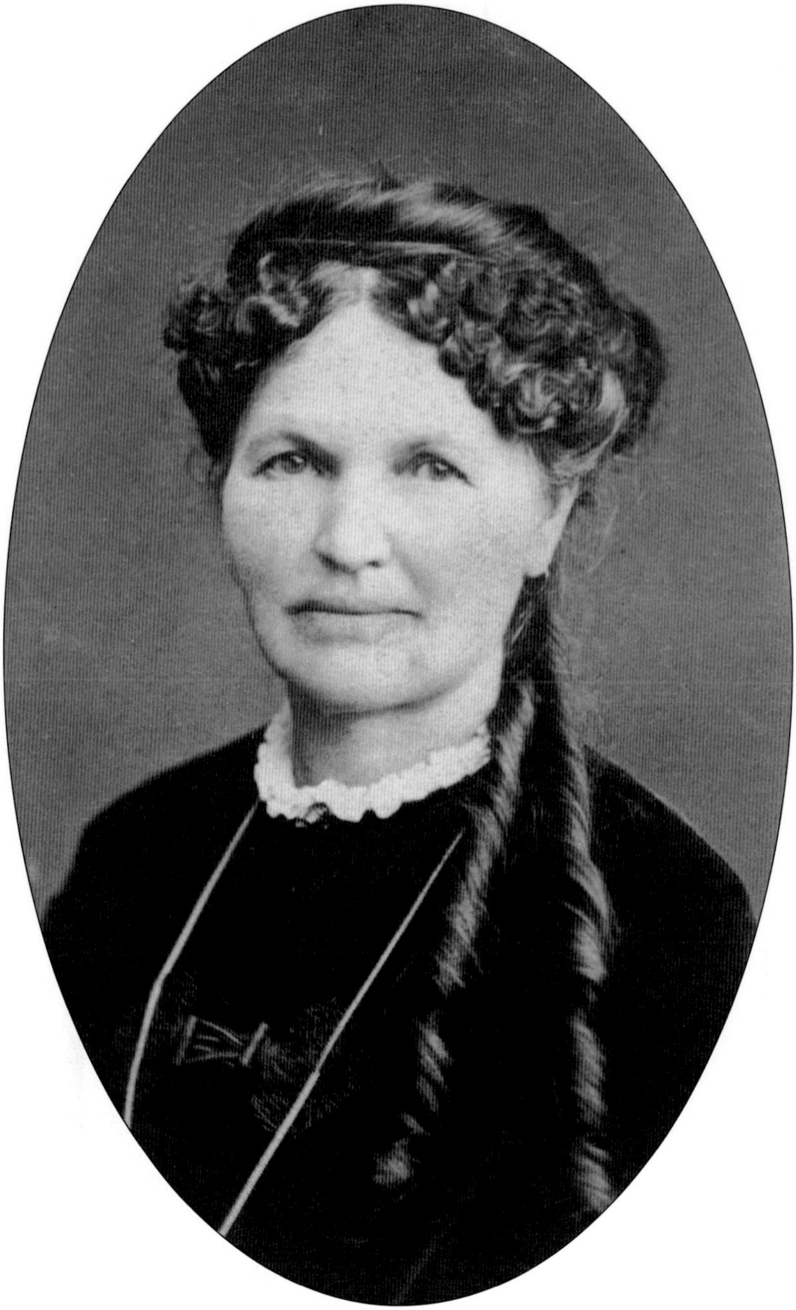

The Lotz House stands across Columbia Pike from the Carter House. As thousands of Union soldiers prepared for battle, the family moved to the home of their neighbors, the Carters. For hours, Margaretha Lotz, her husband, and their children huddled in the basement of the Carter house, terrified by sounds of battle. After the battle, walking the 110 steps back home, they could not set a foot down without stepping on the body of a soldier. Their home sustained damage in the fighting, including a scorched dent in the floor left by a cannonball, and the destruction of most of the south wall. The Lotz family had little choice but to turn to the care of the dead and dying who filled their home. (Lotz House.)

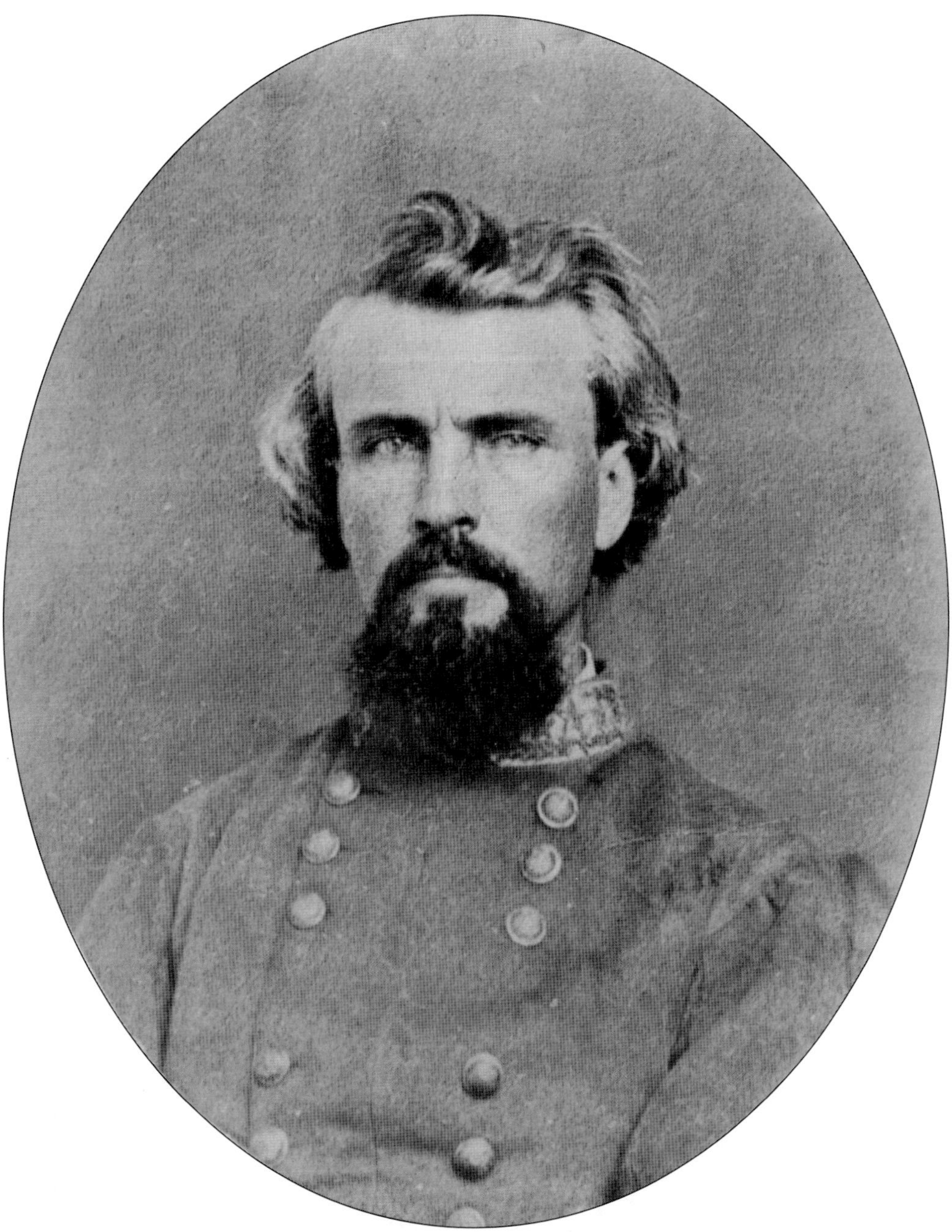

Nathan Bedford Forrest was, arguably, the finest cavalry officer in the Confederacy, but he suffered his worst defeat at Franklin. He was among the generals who protested Hood's plan for a frontal attack. Hood split the cavalry for a poorly coordinated attack, sending Forrest across the river in a failed attempt to turn the Union left. (LOC.)

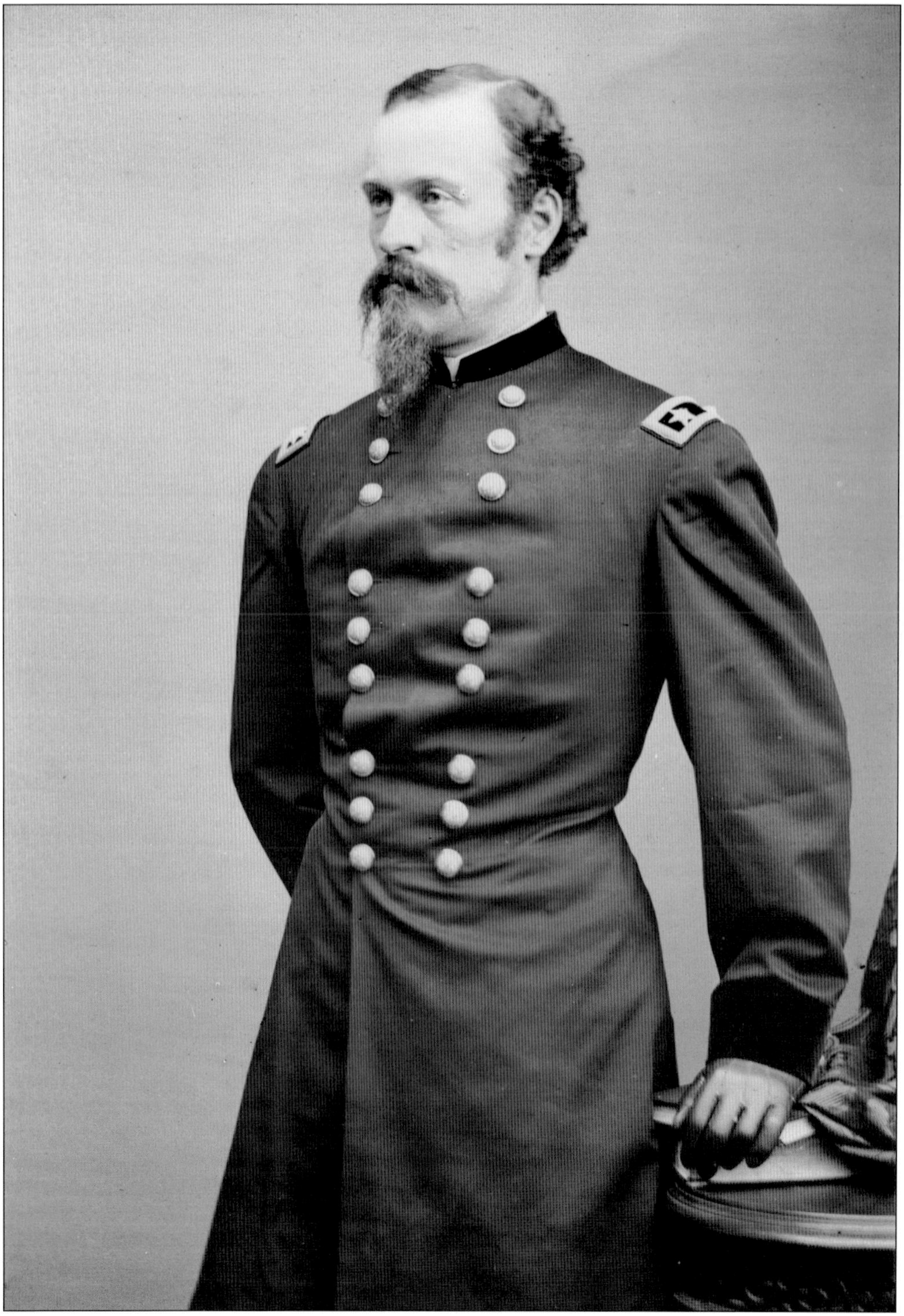

Maj. Gen. James H. Wilson was a Union army engineer who was eminently successful after transferring to the cavalry. He commanded the cavalry at Franklin, and, when Forrest tried to flank the Union left, Wilson became one of the few to ever defeat him in a heads-up fight. (LOC.)

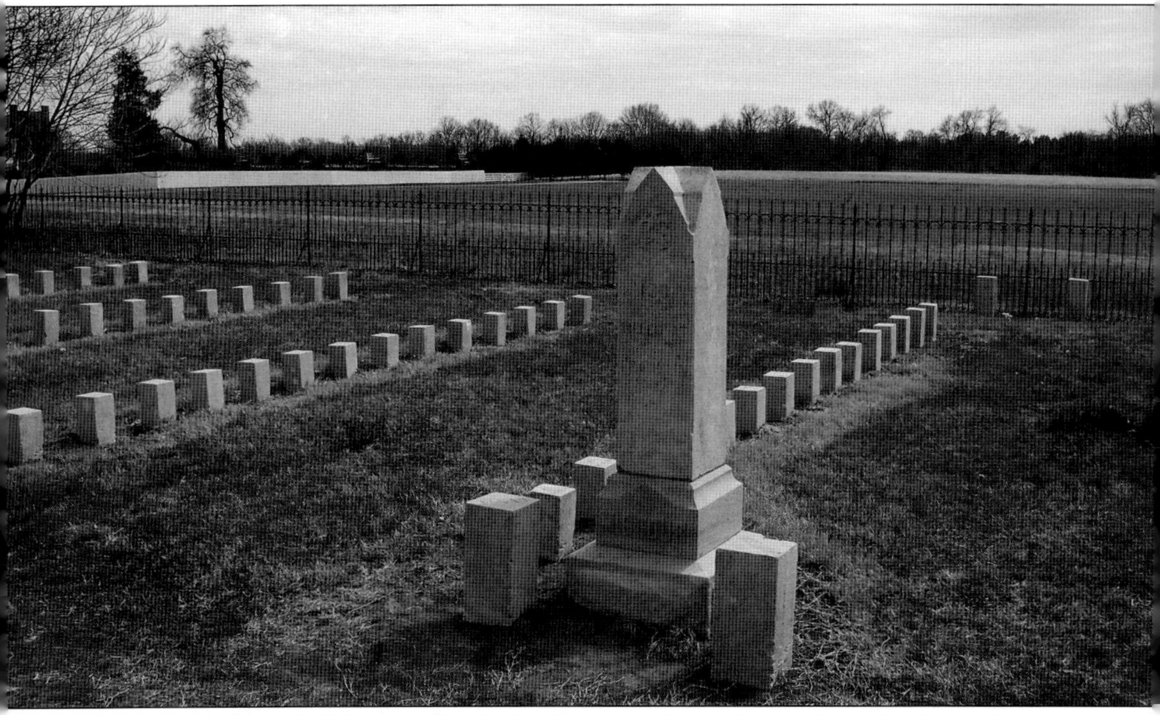

There were almost 2,500 dead after the battle. Local citizens buried the Federal casualties, who were mostly unidentified. On Hood's orders, his troops identified most of the rebels, buried them in quickly dug graves only two to three feet deep, and wrote their names on wooden markers. By the time the war was over the following April and people could turn their attention to proper respect for the dead, many of the names on the wooden markers were gone. Those men became unknown soldiers when they were reinterred in the Confederate Cemetery at Carnton. Today, each Southern state that lost sons at Franklin has a monument like this one, which stands over the graves of 130 Confederate soldiers from Missouri.

Thomas J. Carothers served as captain of Company H, 20th Tennessee Infantry, at the Battle of Franklin. Later, in 1889, he returned to the scene of the battle to buy the Lotz house. There, he and his wife raised their children until his death in 1905. Their descendants still live in the Franklin area. (LOC.)

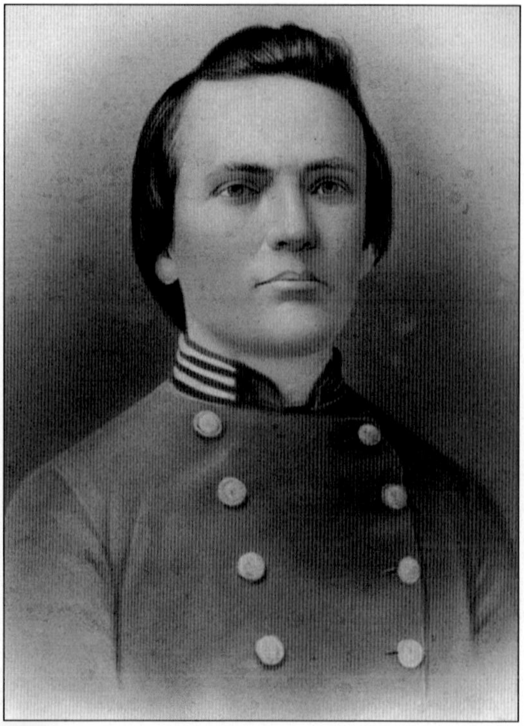

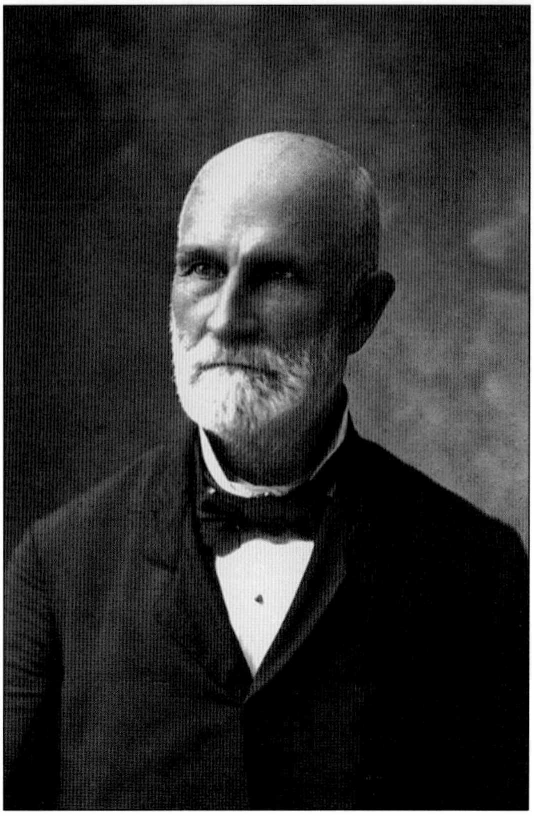

Dr. Daniel B. Cliffe was a prominent Franklin doctor when the war started, and he immediately joined the Confederate 20th Tennessee Infantry as its physician. Following the Battle of Mill Springs, Kentucky, Cliffe resigned his position and returned home to his practice, becoming a staunch and outspoken Unionist. Though his politics were at odds with many in Franklin, his compassionate care for his patients earned him universal respect.

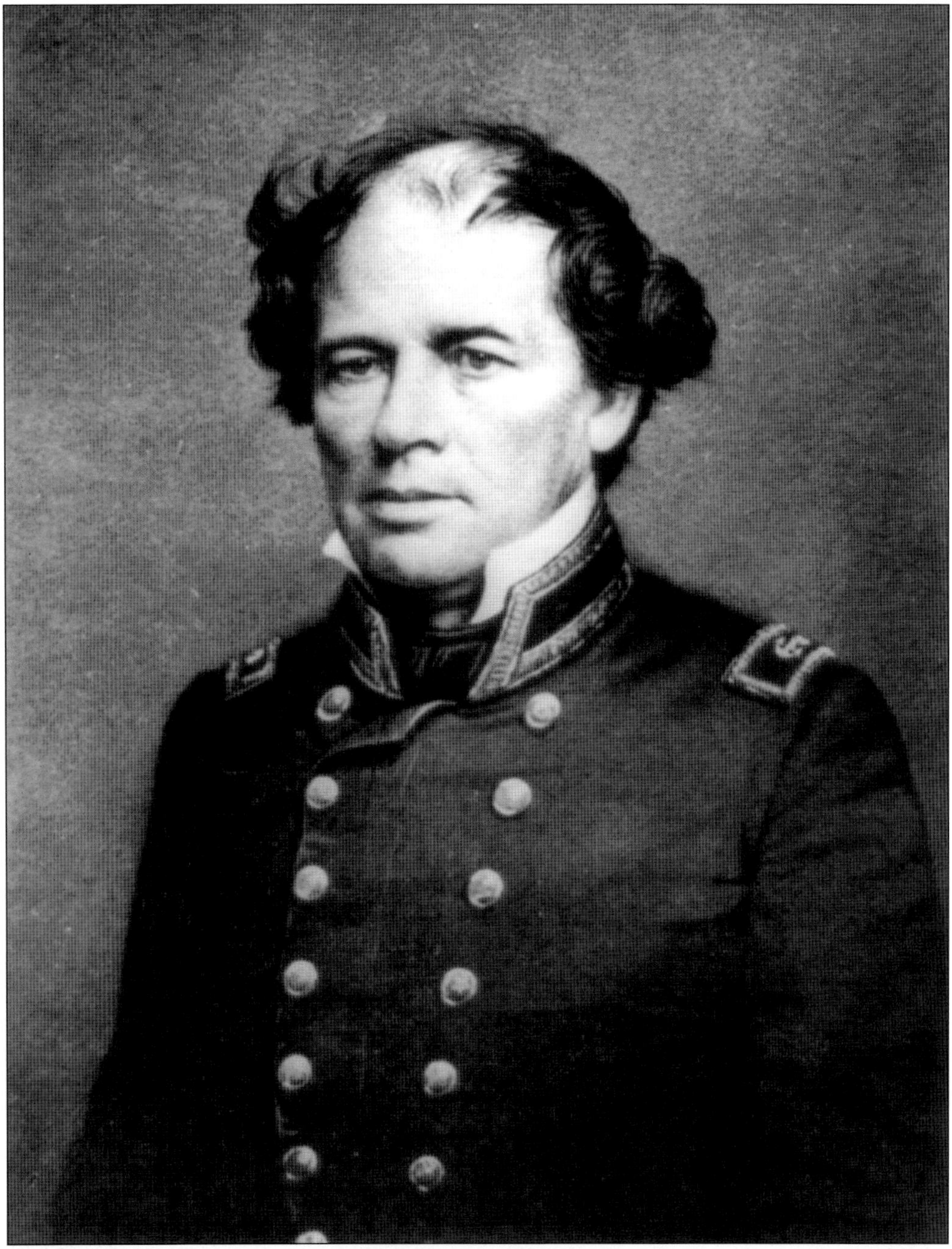

Matthew Fontaine Maury, called the "Pathfinder of the Seas" for his mapping of ocean currents and writings about navigation, also campaigned against slavery. Yet, during the Civil War, he resigned his US Navy commission to serve the Confederacy as commander of the CSS *Georgia*, which he purchased for the Confederate navy. He secured money and arms for the South, and was known as a raider who captured and sank many Union vessels, while letting others that carried no commercial cargo go free. He spent much of the war as a diplomat, negotiating for European pressure to end the war in America. He also perfected a naval mine—which cost the North many ships—utilizing a design that is still in use today. (TSL.)

Matthew F. Maury was the son of Richard L. and Peggy Bon Maury, and was named for his uncle, the Pathfinder of the Seas. He served in Baxter's Artillery during the Civil War. After the war, he returned to his home in Franklin, where he was county surveyor for many years, having been trained in surveying early in life at the insistence of his namesake.

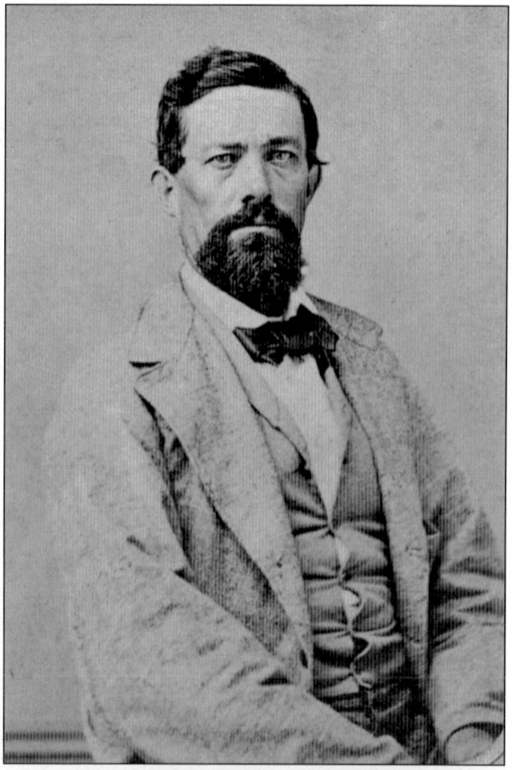

During the battle, Boxmere, the home of 15-year-old Hardin Figuers, was located 200 yards behind the Union front, on Main Street. Hardin climbed a tree to get a better view of the battle, but the family retreated to the basement as bullets and shells hit the house. Boxmere was used as a hospital afterwards, and Figuers helped to care for the wounded. Both the house and the tree are still standing.

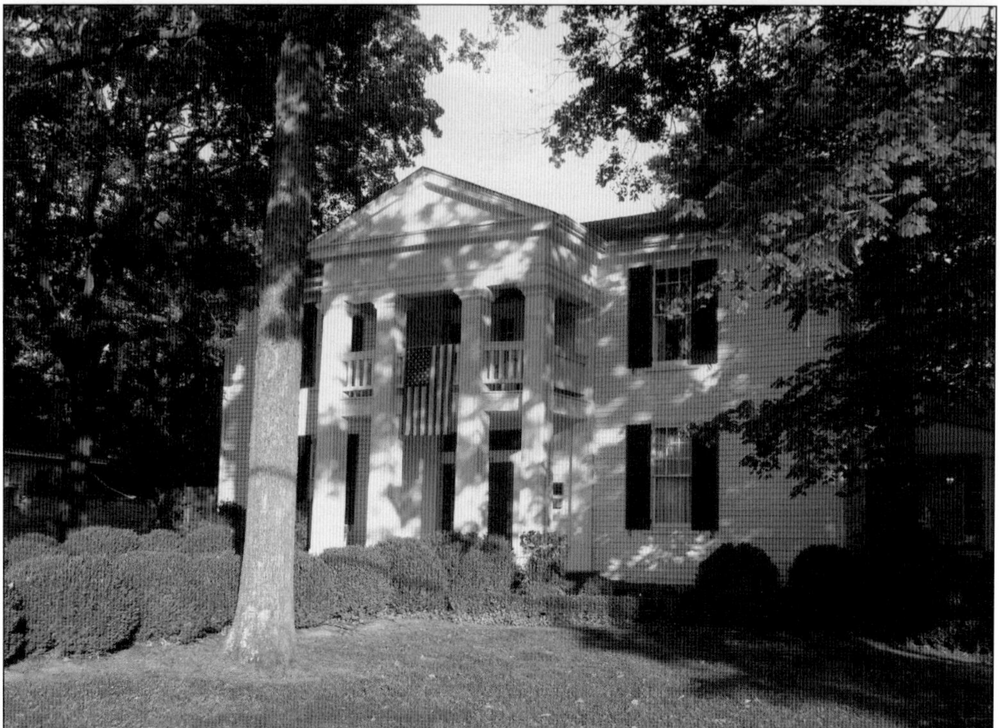

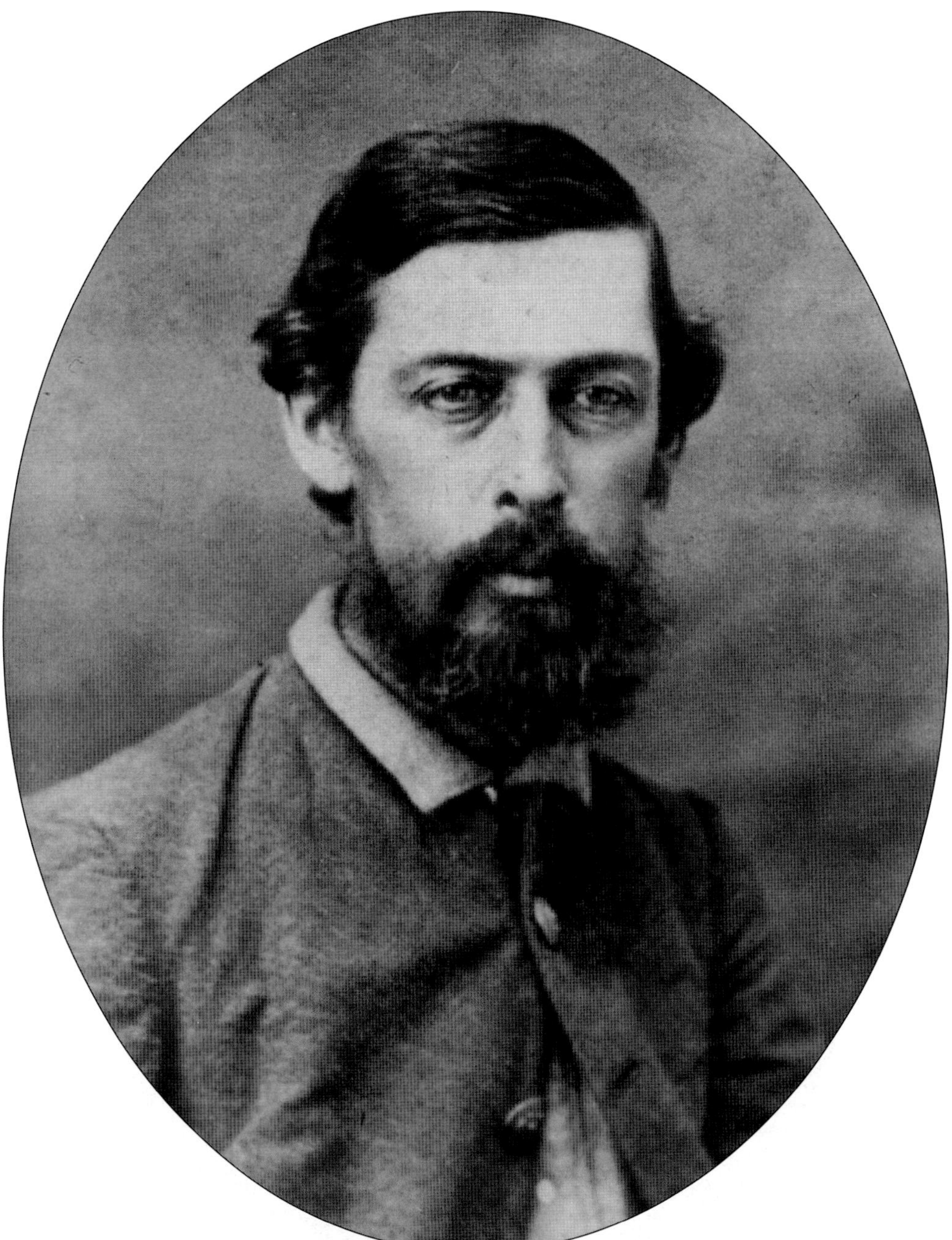

Rev. Moses S. Royce was pastor at St. Paul's Episcopal Church when Union troops occupied the city. He locked the church and joined the Confederate army as a captain in Starnes' Escort, a small cavalry unit. Royce was captured and imprisoned in Nashville, but escaped by digging a tunnel through rain-soaked ground with a spoon. He is said to have spent the rest of the war carrying messages for the Confederacy.

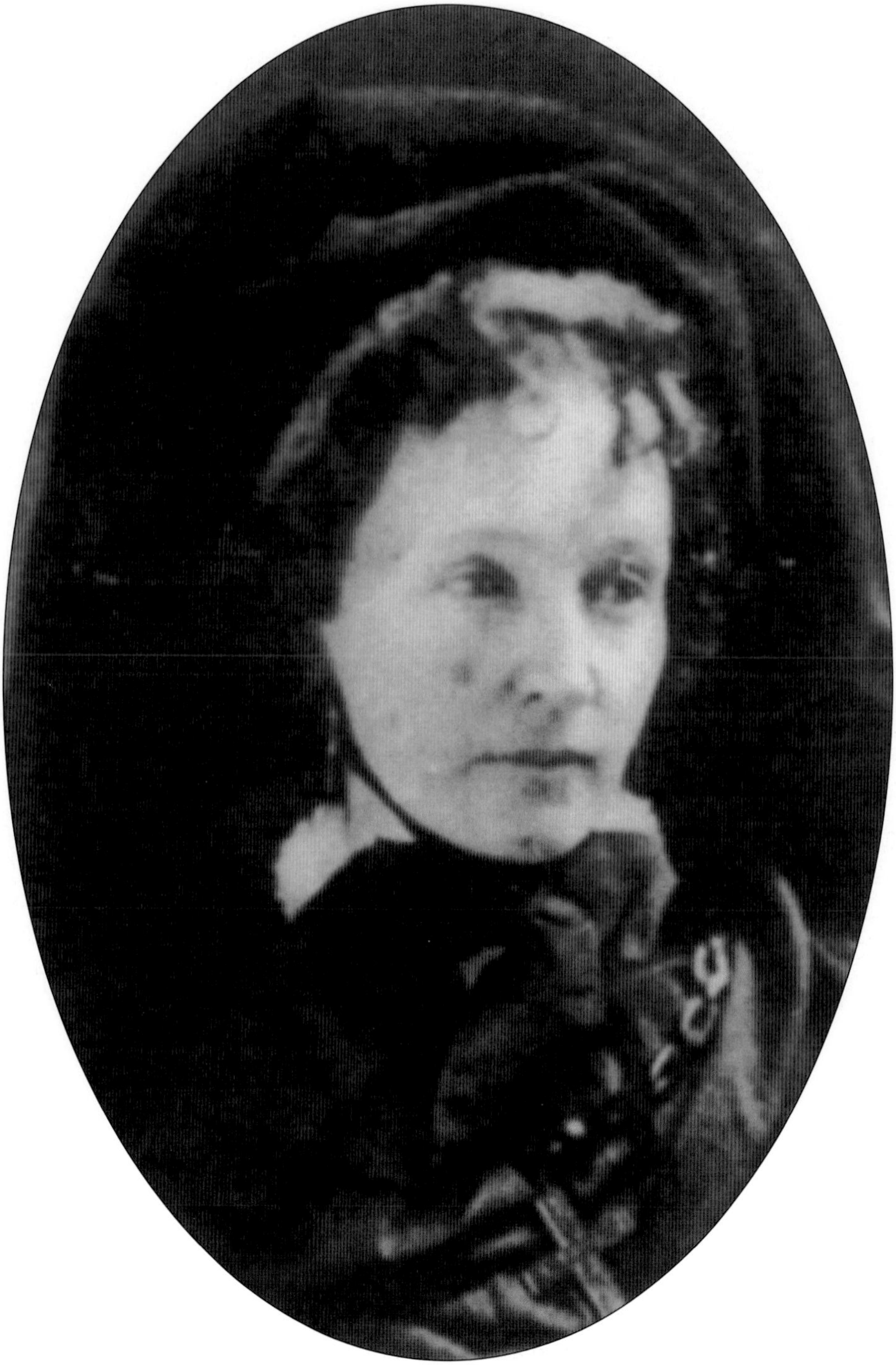

After Pastor Moses Royce went off to war, his wife, Martha Broyles Royce, and their two daughters were forced from their home. Martha was reported to be spying for the Confederacy, writing down the things she learned about Union troop movements and plans, and sewing the notes inside the hem of her daughter Betsy's dress. Betsy would later write a book detailing their struggle to survive the conflict.

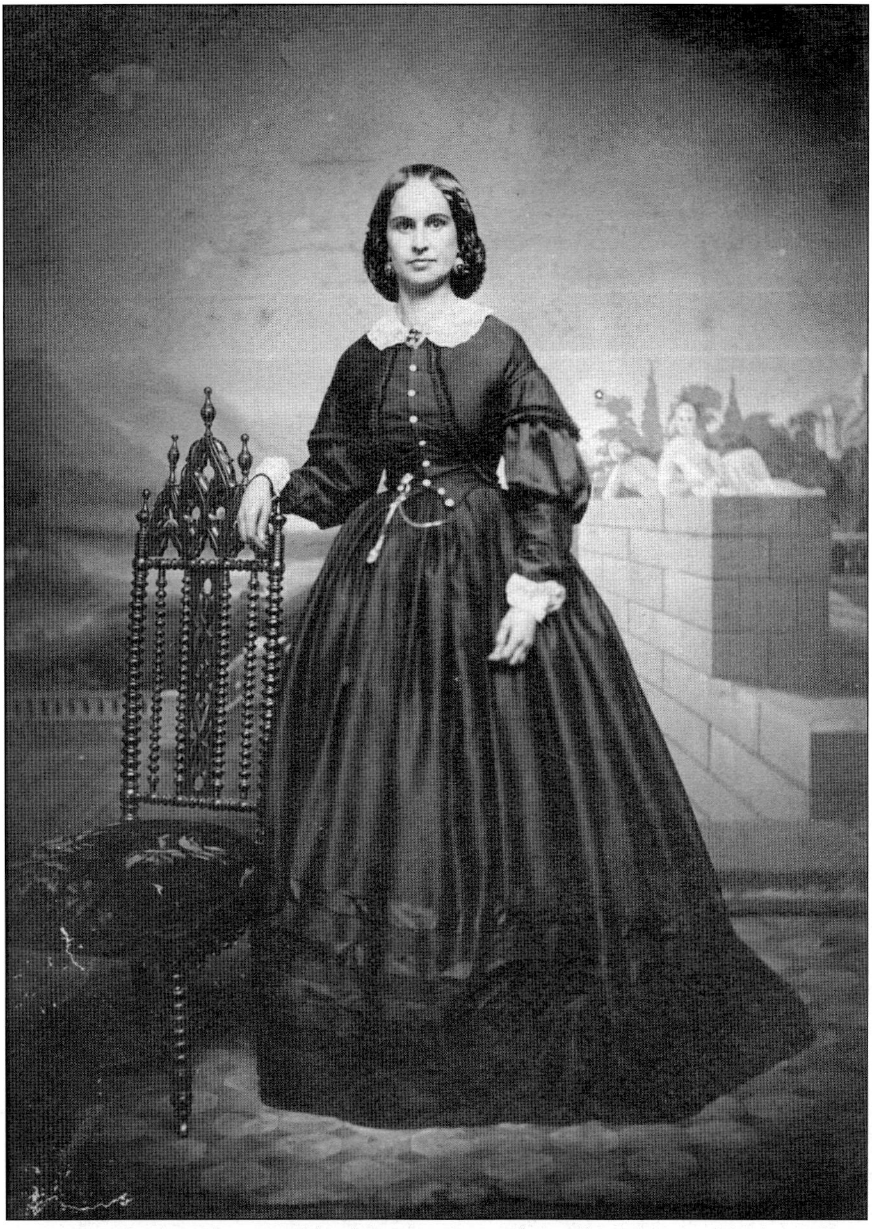

Sara Ewing Sims Carter was a Franklin heroine. An orphan who was raised by her relatives, the McGavocks, she had been widowed twice and had given birth to five children by the start of the Civil War. She flew the first Confederate flag in Franklin, and, after the Battle of Franklin, cared for the wounded of both armies. She also accompanied her wealthy Nashville cousin Adelicia Aklen to Louisiana to rescue Adelicia's cotton crop. The cotton was in Confederate hands, and General Polk planned to burn it to keep it out of Union hands. When Adelicia fell ill, Sara continued to make a total of eight trips, and finally persuaded Polk to let the women have the cotton moved near the river. She then persuaded the Union army to help ship it to New Orleans, where it was released for shipment to Europe. The two women traveled to New York and sold the cotton in England. After the war Sara remarried, was widowed again, and lived out the rest of her life in her Franklin home. (BNTC.)

Four

Franklin's Business Life

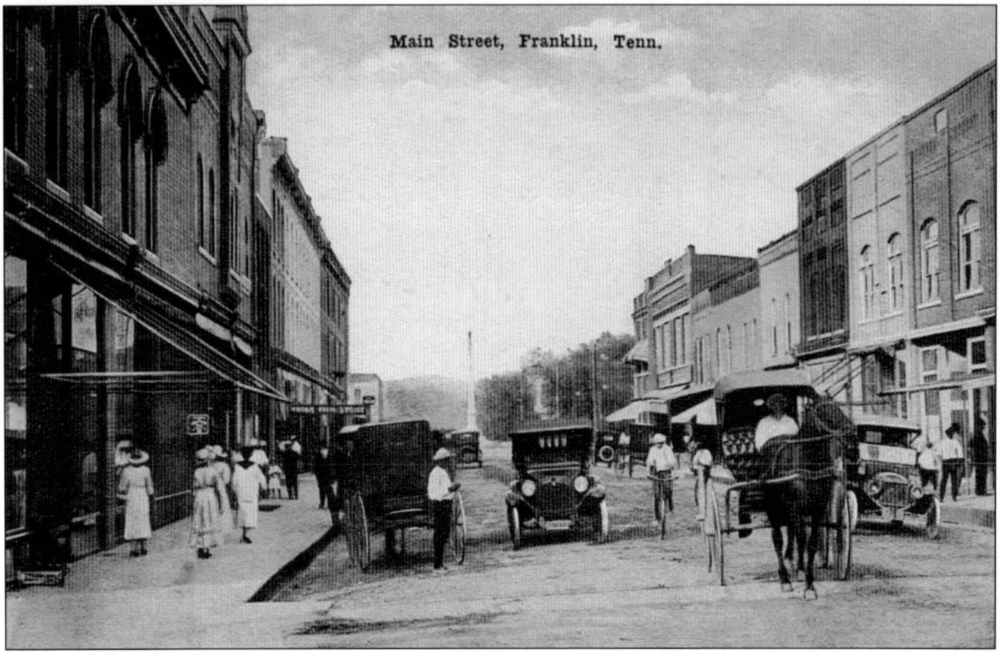

A variety of modes of transportation all share Main Street in this postcard, looking north in the early 1900s. The car at center, probably an early Dodge, goes around the parked horse and buggy, while a boy on a bicycle weaves his way between the vehicles. The only electric service visible is near the courthouse, to the right of the monument.

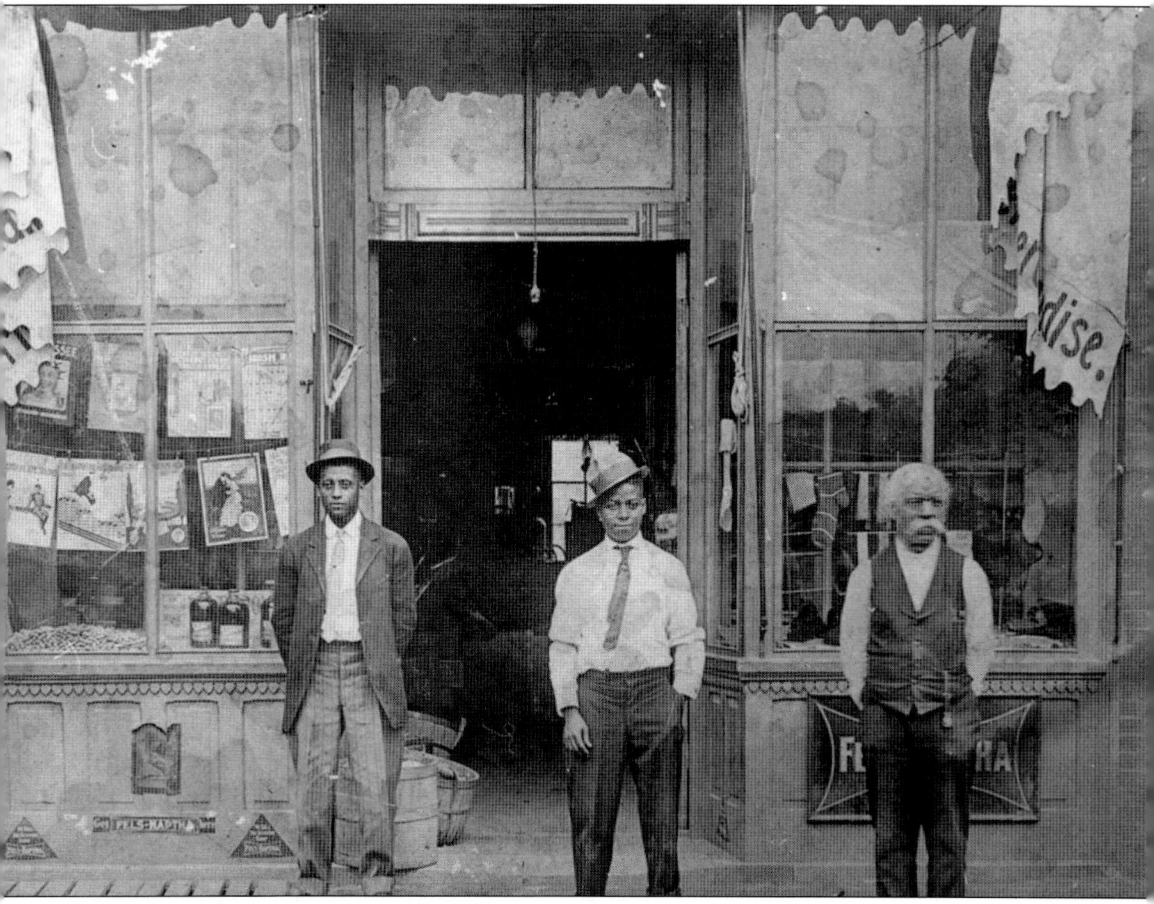

Allen Nevils Crutcher (A.N.C.) Williams was born into slavery, sold, and eventually brought to Franklin when he was six years old. He opened his first store, a shoe store, in 1863 following his emancipation while the Civil War was still going on. He is pictured here (at right) with his sons, Fred (left) and Ostrander, in front of the mercantile that he operated on Main Street for nearly 65 years. An early advocate for civil rights, Williams worked to cool tempers on both sides in the wake of an 1867 riot. Williams also donated the land for Cummins Street Church of Christ and occasionally preached there, as well as investing in other real estate and helping many families buy their homes. Of the many former Franklin slaves who became successful in commerce, farming, and service occupations, Williams was possibly the most successful and influential. When he died in 1930, his obituary was carried on the front page of the newspaper. (Courtesy of Bob Canaday.)

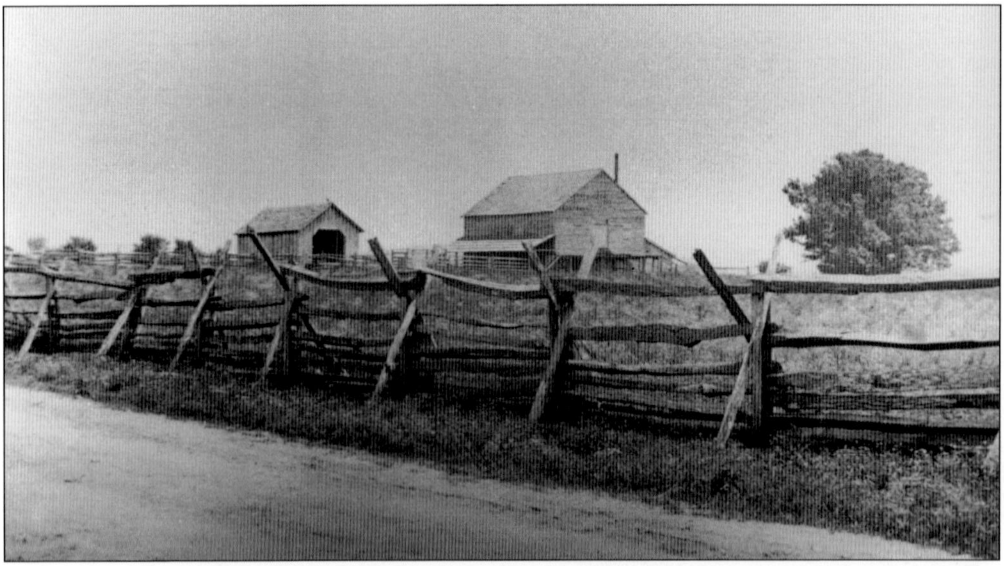

When Fountain Branch Carter built his cotton gin—visible here beyond a rail fence that runs along Columbia Highway—it was a landmark event in Middle Tennessee. Farmers from miles around could bring their raw cotton to Franklin and have it cleaned, weighed, pressed into bales, and even sold before it was shipped out on the nearby railroad. (BFTC.)

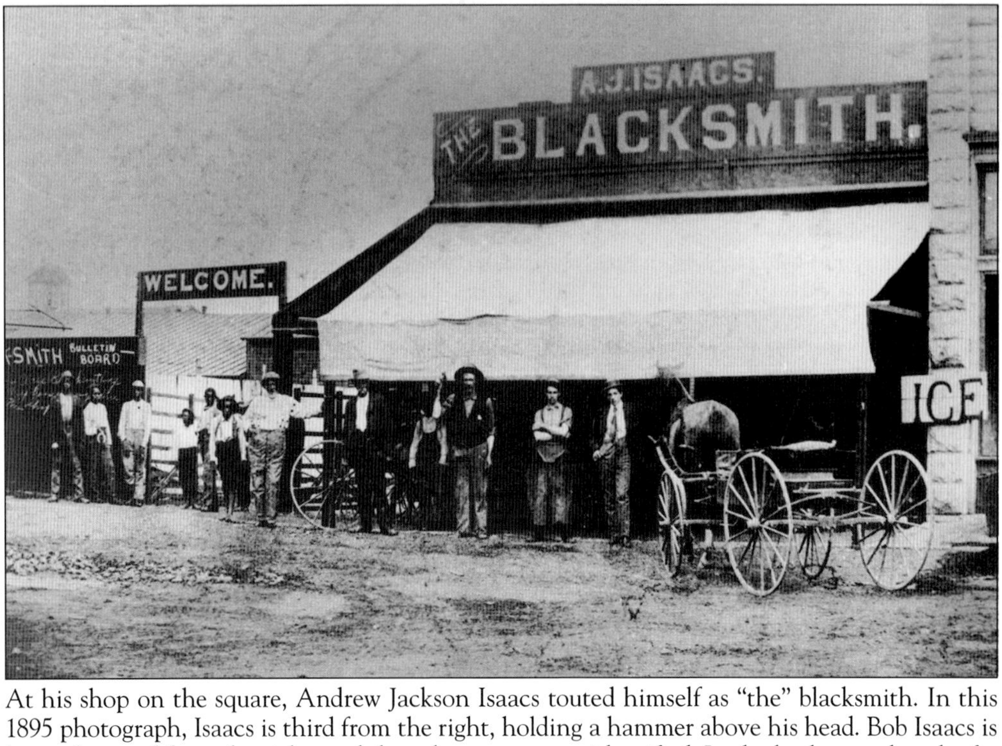

At his shop on the square, Andrew Jackson Isaacs touted himself as "the" blacksmith. In this 1895 photograph, Isaacs is third from the right, holding a hammer above his head. Bob Isaacs is located second from the right, and the other men are unidentified. In the background to the far left, the steeple of the Wiley Memorial M.E. Church on Second Avenue can be seen.

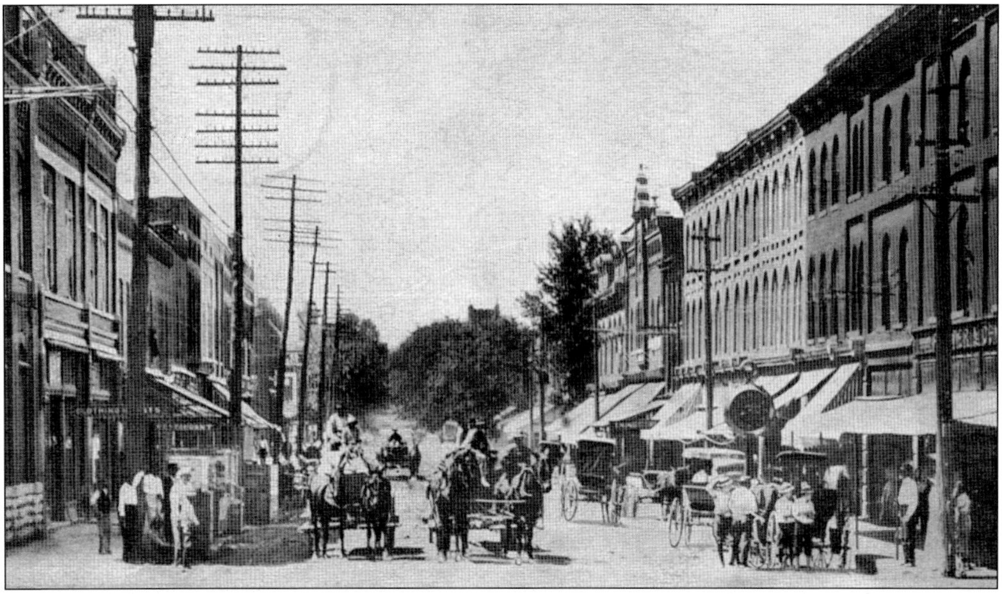

Main Street is alive with pedestrians, wagons, and electric lines in this postcard. The tower of the Episcopal church can also be seen in the background. Even before the Civil War, Franklin's downtown was lined with strong and beautiful brick buildings. These bricks were often made from local clay, dug from nearby hillsides and fired in kilns built right on the construction site.

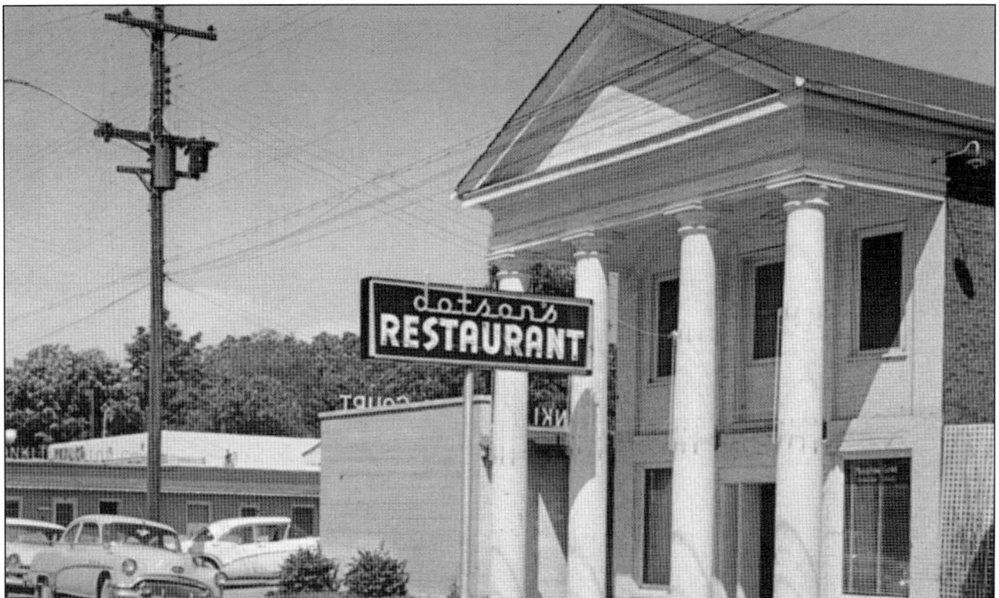

The Factory Store on East Main Street was built about 1825 and sold household goods to employees of the grain mill. Later, Chester and Clara Dotson opened Dotson's Restaurant, which flourished in the building from 1954 to 1978, before moving to another location where it is still known for its fresh-baked pies and family-style seating. The building then housed a bank, a coffee shop, and a jewelry store before becoming home to Landmark Booksellers. (TSL.)

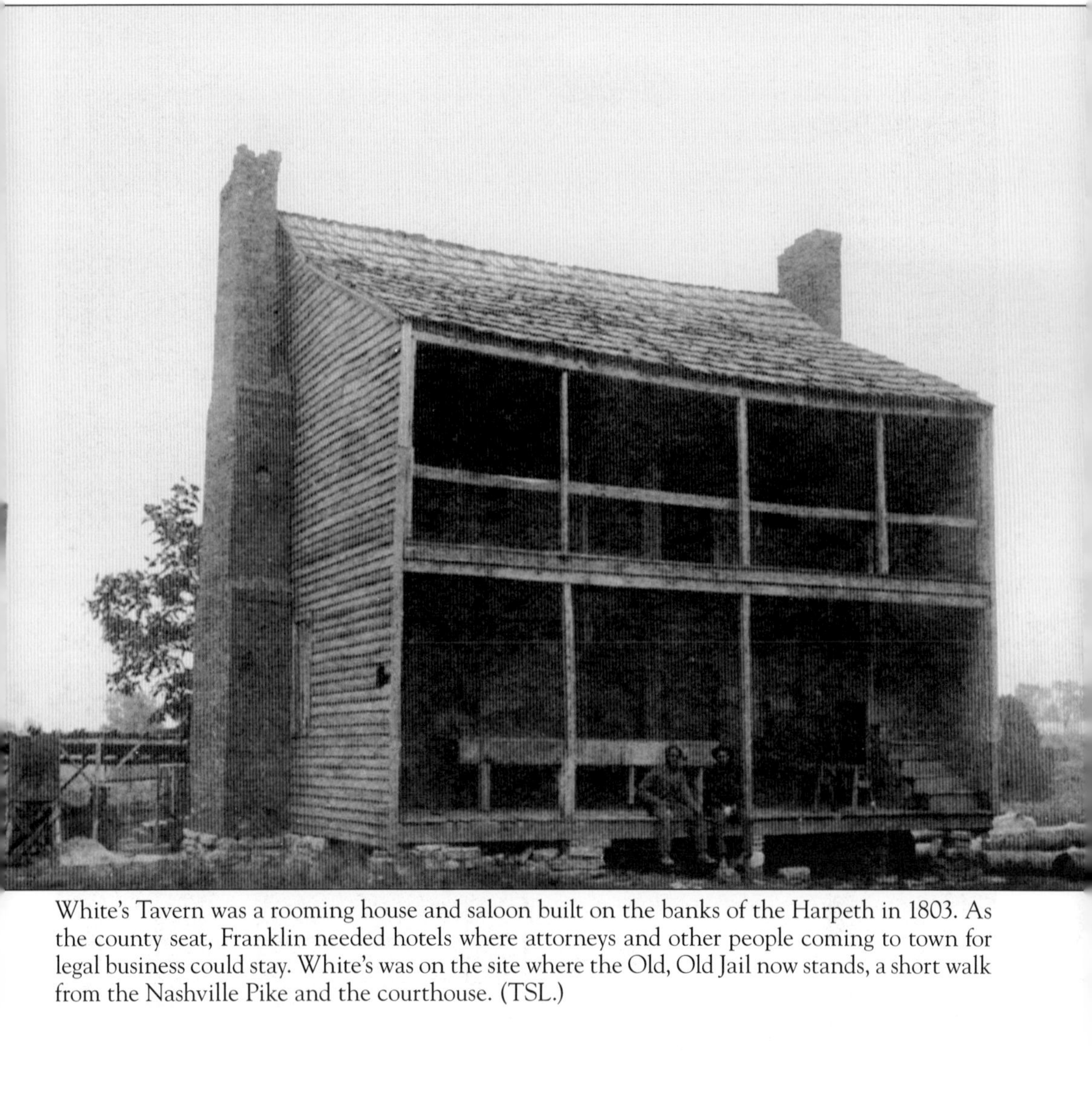

White's Tavern was a rooming house and saloon built on the banks of the Harpeth in 1803. As the county seat, Franklin needed hotels where attorneys and other people coming to town for legal business could stay. White's was on the site where the Old, Old Jail now stands, a short walk from the Nashville Pike and the courthouse. (TSL.)

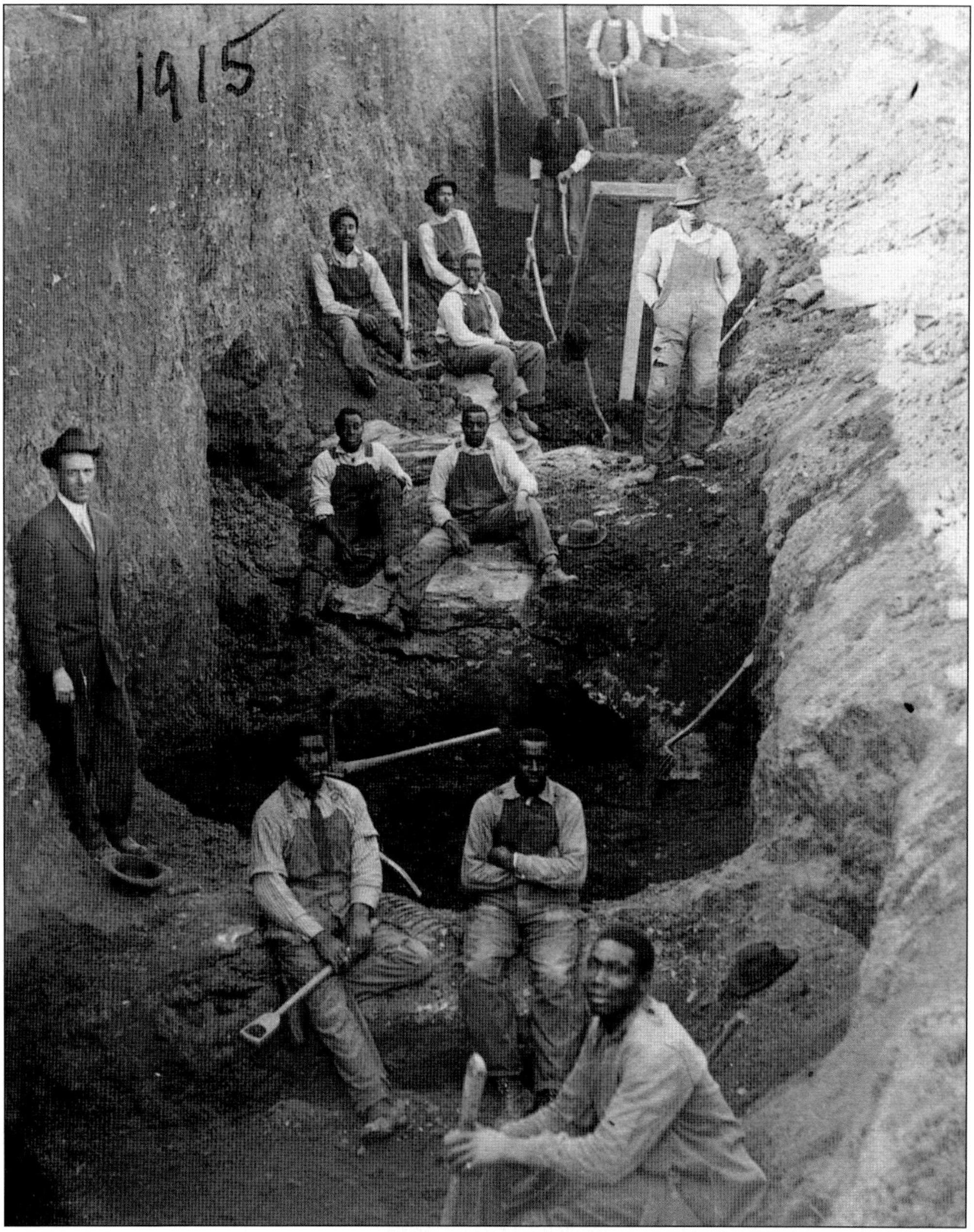

By 1915, mining phosphorus and paint pigment was big business in and around Franklin. Phosphorous was in high demand for fertilizers, matches, and other uses. W.A. Johnson, pictured here at far left, watches a foreman and workers in this phosphorus mining operation. Such hard labor was later replaced with power machinery as mining expanded throughout Williamson County. Later, Johnson would build and manage the Carbsil pigment processing plant. (TSL.)

The Lillie Mill Co., founded by Joshua B. Lillie in 1869, was Franklin's biggest business for nine decades. The company was sold to C.H. Com and W.F. Eakin in 1909, and then to Dudley Casey in 1945. Featuring its main brand, Franklin Lady Flour, the plant shipped over 300 railcars of flour per year at its peak. A testament to the agricultural power of the Franklin area, the granary and mill were busy until they finally burned in 1958 in a heartbreaking fire that was beyond the capability of Franklin's volunteer firefighters. The silos, which were built in 1925, can still be seen on First Avenue South. (Right, RHC.)

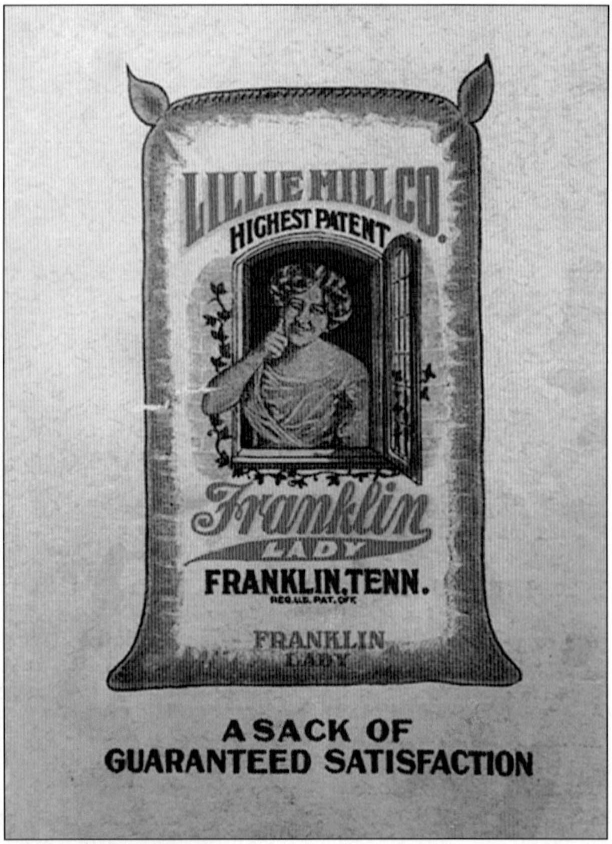

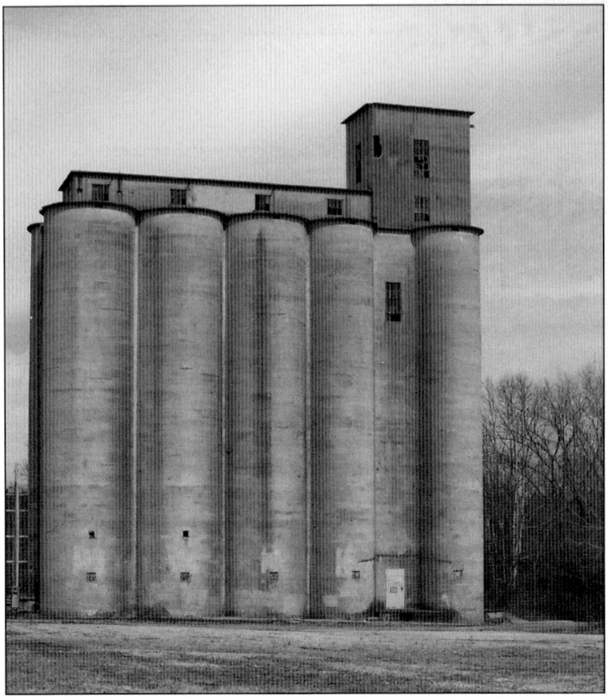

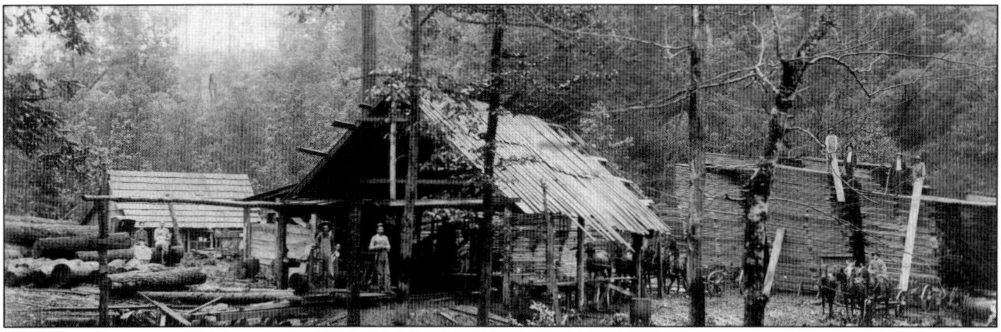

Brothers Mack and W.A. Southall managed sawmills in Franklin and Leiper's Fork. They owned large tracts of timbered land, and multiple steam engines that powered the saws, turning them with canvas belts. The local lumber industry thrived because the Tennessee woods offered vast stands of walnut, maple, hickory, oak, and poplar, and supplied builders both locally and across the country. (TSL.)

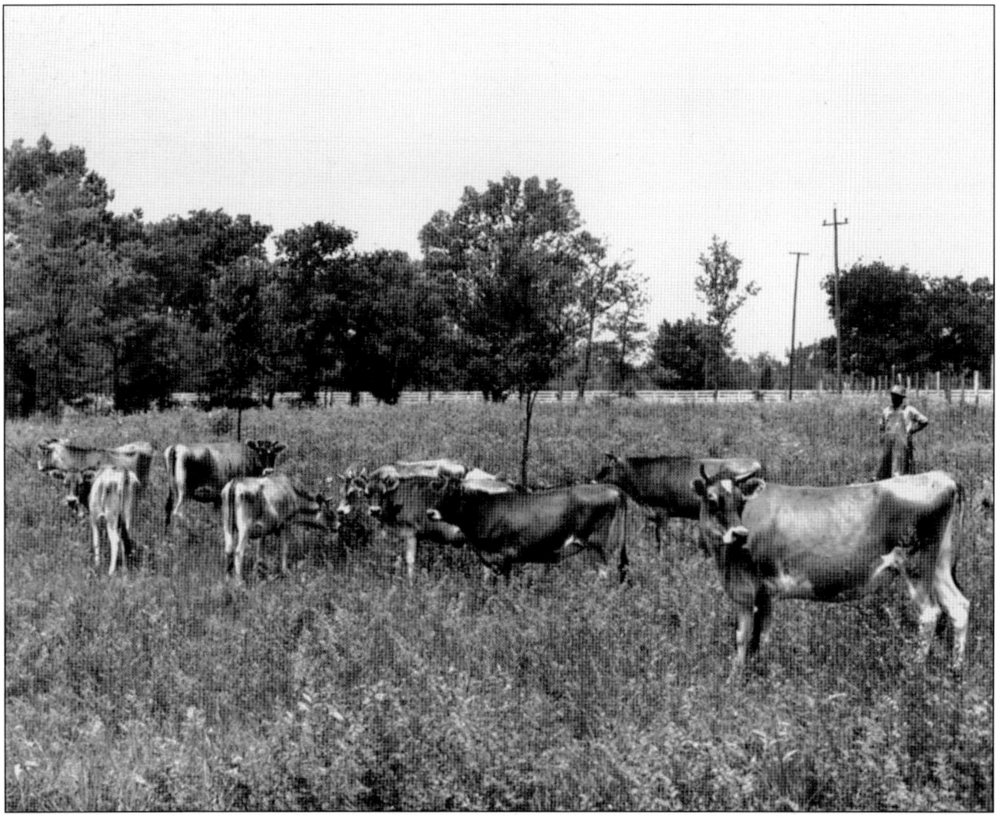

Dairy products were once a family enterprise. The need for refrigeration made it impossible to ship milk, butter, and cheese very far, so virtually every farm had a milk cow, and storage in a springhouse or a stone-lined box in the ground, which stayed at a steady temperature. As more people moved into town and owned refrigerators, local dairies boomed, taking advantage of breeds like the pictured Guernsey cattle. (TSL.)

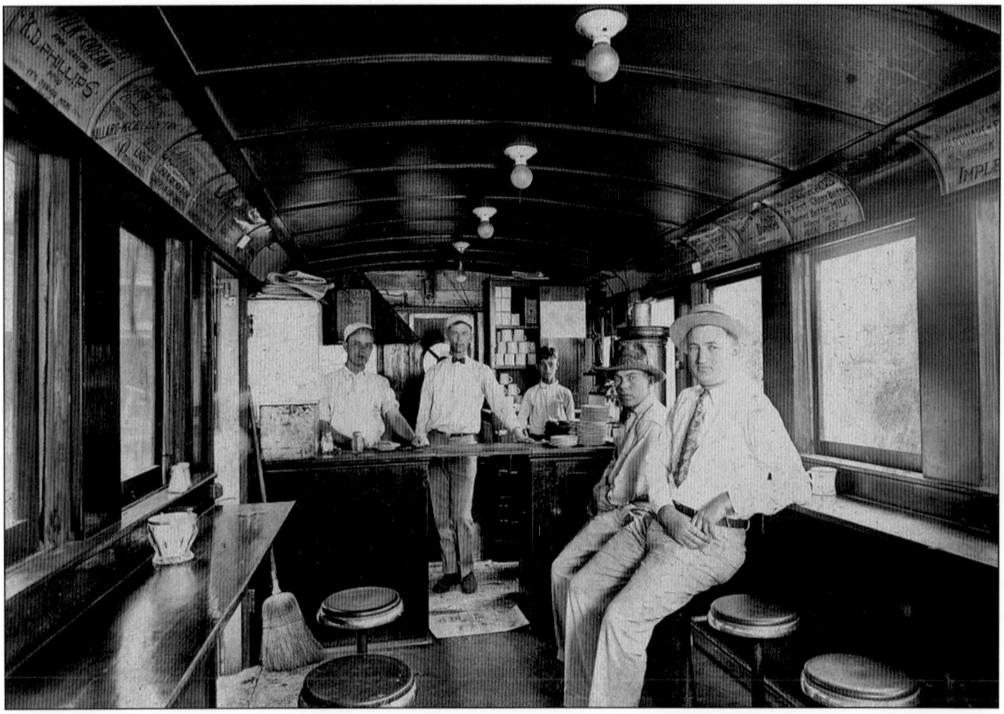

Jim Chapman, seen second from the left above, served Franklin diners at his steel-wheeled Chapman's Pie Wagon from 1922 to 1946. Chapman's design featured portable wooden stairs, bare light bulbs, a kitchen at one end, counters along the inside walls, and seating on stools. In an era when traffic congestion was unheard of, the Pie Wagon became a landmark. It can be seen, parked on the square and surrounded by cars, on the right in the postcard below. With hamburgers and fresh pies as its specialties, the Pie Wagon was a popular meeting place for coffee, lunch, supper, or snacks after movies at the Franklin Theater. Chapman's was a remarkably successful and long-lived business, especially for such a tiny establishment. (Above, RWC; below, TSL.)

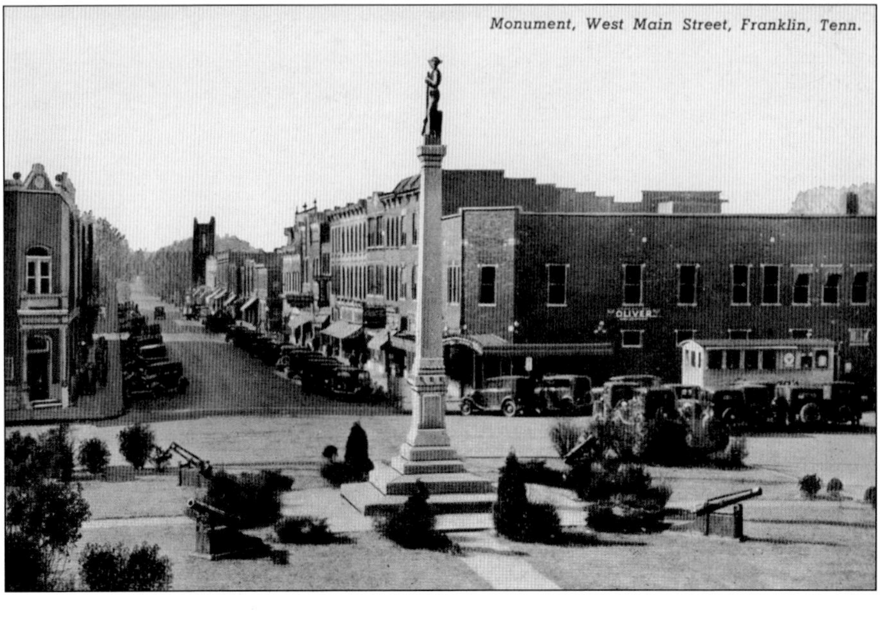

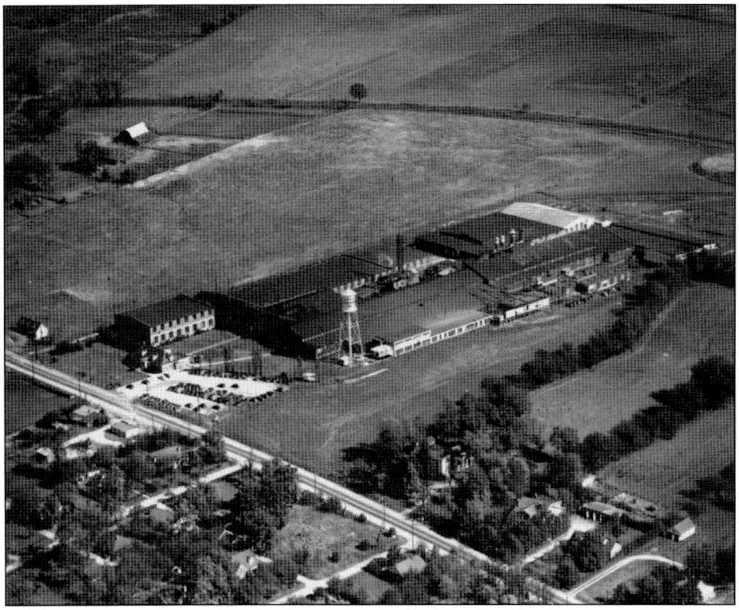

This massive factory, which was built in 1929 on the Nashville Highway, was home to Allen Manufacturing, a stove company. Allen fell victim to the Depression, and the Dortch Stove Works prospered at the site until 1955. The plant, pictured here in 1947, was surrounded by farmland and featured its own water tower, a sizeable employee parking lot, and plenty of office space. (WCA.)

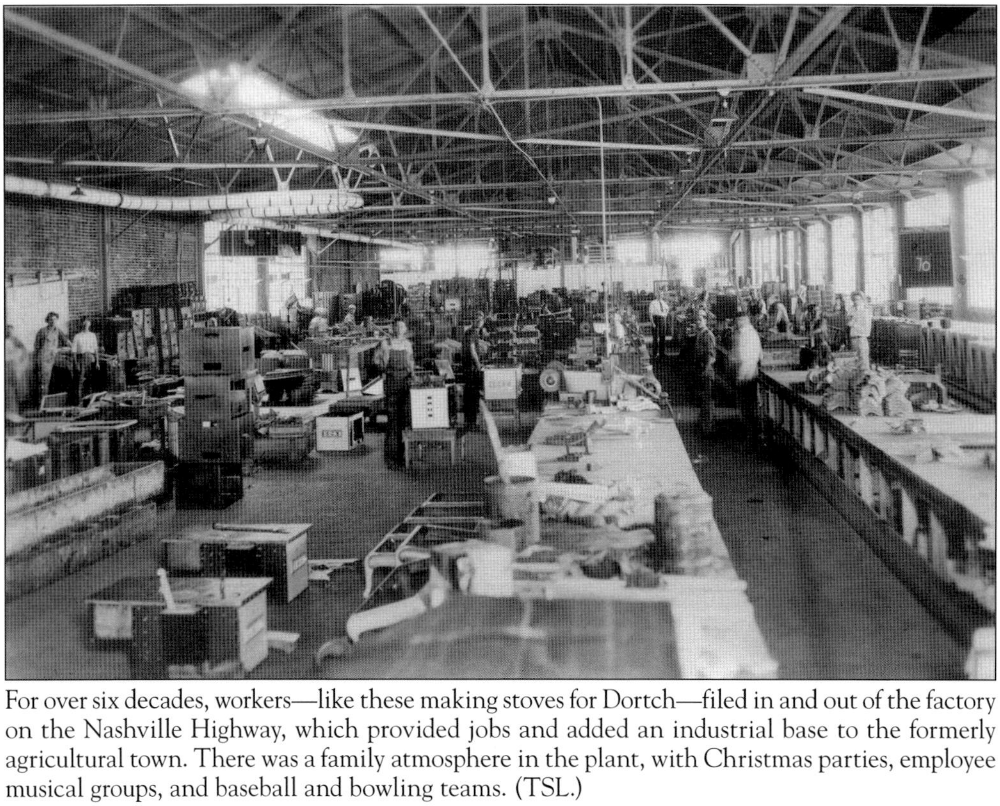

For over six decades, workers—like these making stoves for Dortch—filed in and out of the factory on the Nashville Highway, which provided jobs and added an industrial base to the formerly agricultural town. There was a family atmosphere in the plant, with Christmas parties, employee musical groups, and baseball and bowling teams. (TSL.)

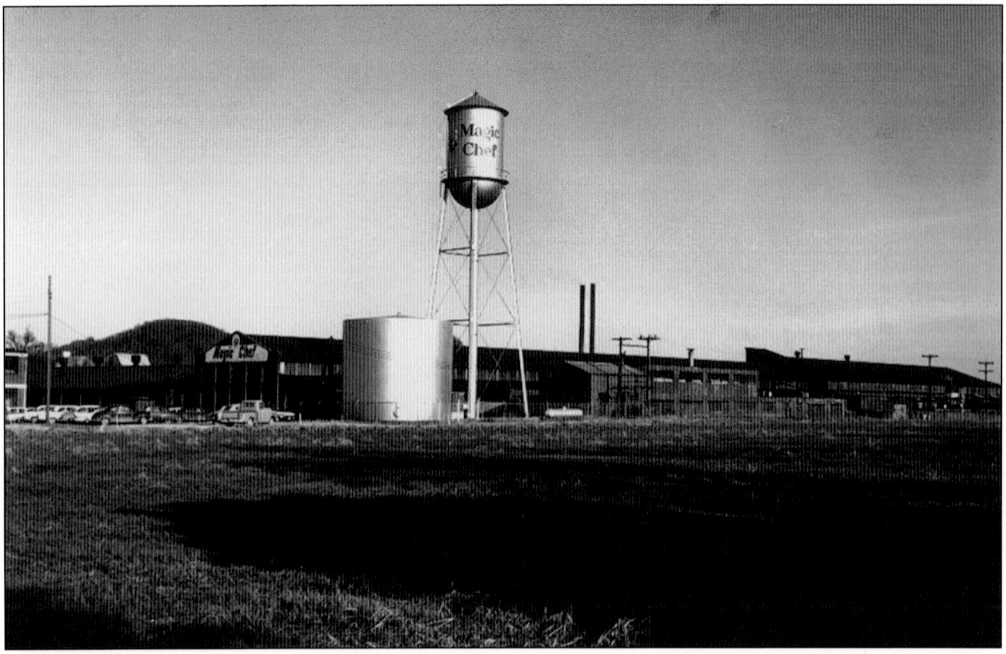

Magic Chef was already a successful national stove manufacturer when it was acquired by a small Cleveland, Tennessee, company, and moved into the former Dortch factory in 1955. Magic Chef operated there for five years, followed by Jamison Bedding for another 30. The factory was the largest employer in Franklin for generations. (TSL.)

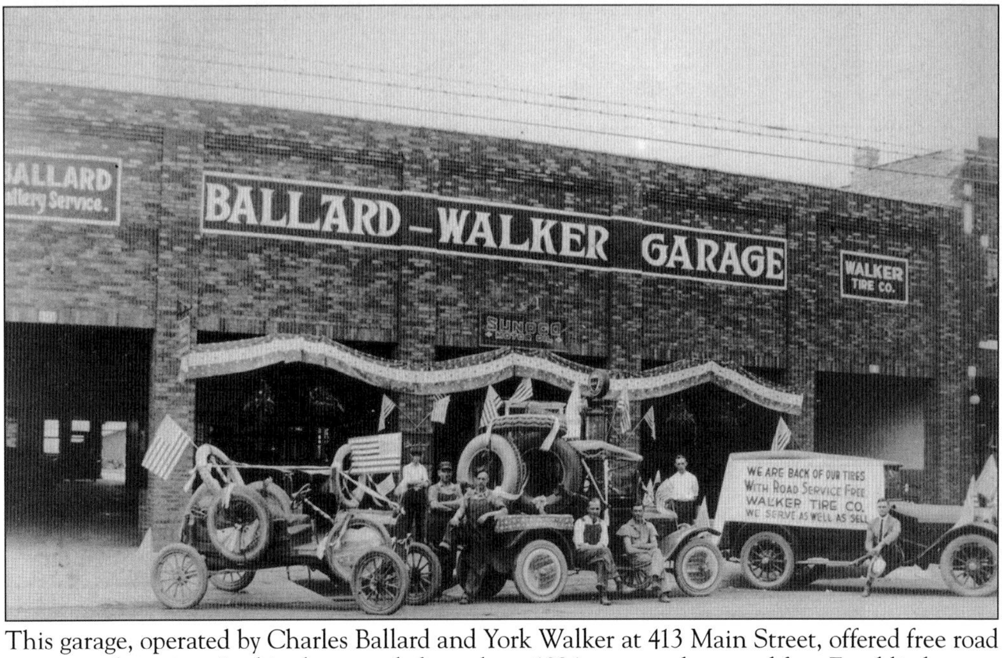

This garage, operated by Charles Ballard and York Walker at 413 Main Street, offered free road service with its tires. In this photograph from about 1924, cars are decorated for a Franklin booster tour. Posing with the vehicles are, from left to right, an unidentified teen, Leon Evans, George Hamer, John Henry Givens, Cortez Isaacs, Ballard, and Walker. Today, the building is a busy arcade. (Courtesy Bob Canaday.)

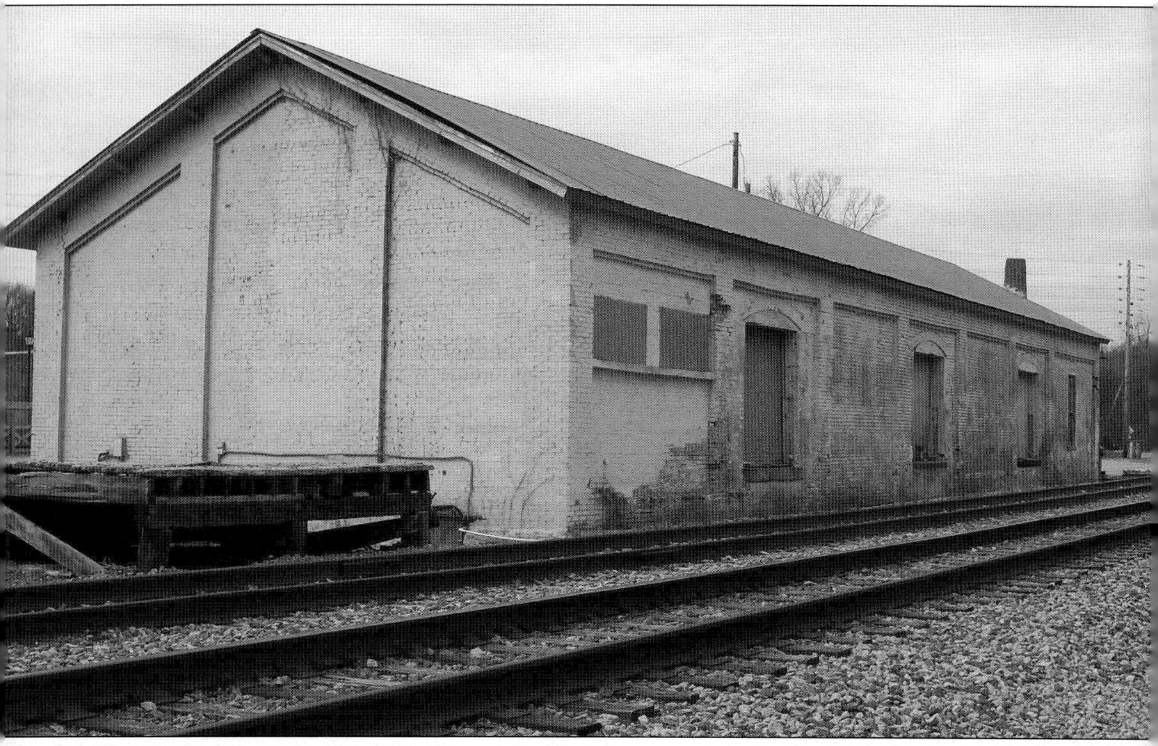

The combination of railroad service and the Carter cotton gin was a boon to everyone in the area, as manufactured goods could be brought for the growing Franklin population, and agricultural goods could be shipped out. There was even a short rail line to Leiper's Fork that brought lumber and other goods to the Franklin depot. When Federal forces occupied the city during the Civil War, they also seized the railroad. The engines were in Confederate hands, and the cars had all been taken elsewhere. After the war, in 1866, rail service was restored by the Nashville and Decatur Railroad, which was leased and then purchased by the L&N Railroad, which later became part of the CSX system. Passenger service faded over time, and the passenger depot was demolished in 1959. The brick and concrete freight depot (pictured), built in 1858, is one of two antebellum railroad buildings remaining in Tennessee.

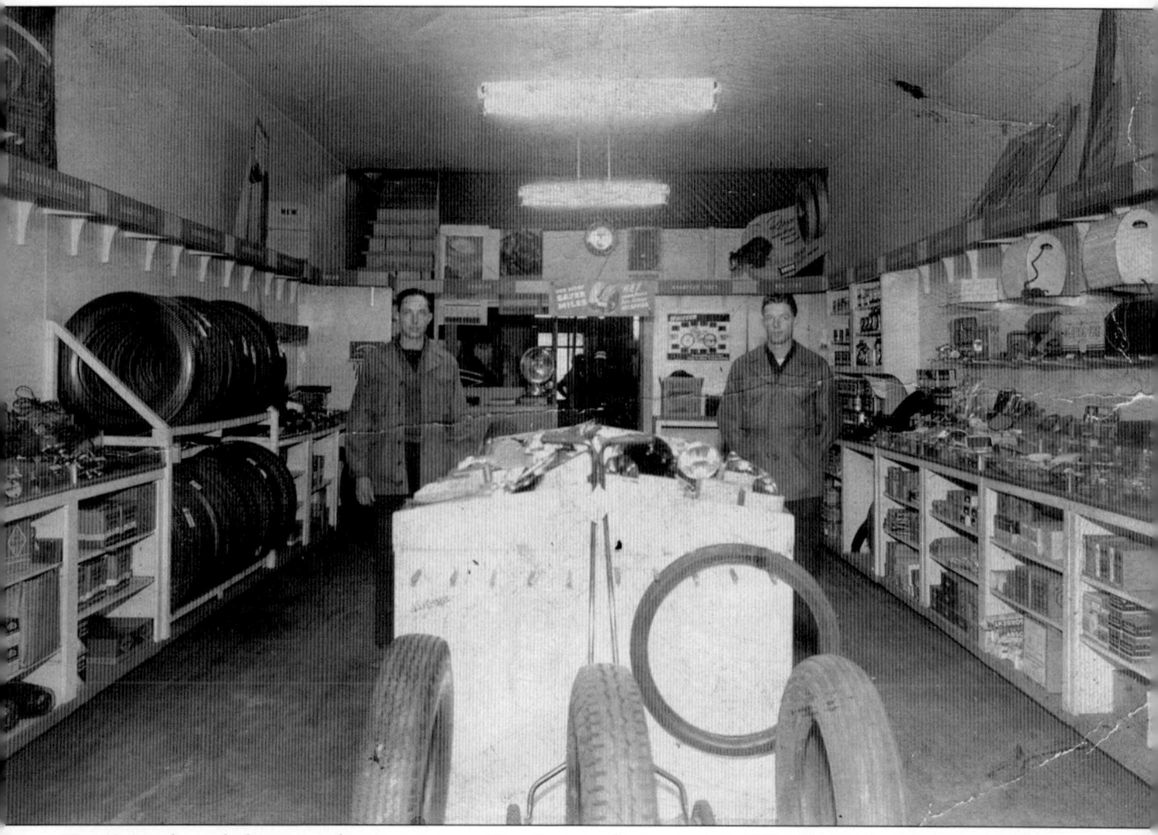

Tom Moody, at left, opened a tire store at Five Points during World War II. At the time, tires were rationed, so most of his business consisted of recapping tires and selling and servicing bicycles. His brother Ed joined him in the store upon returning from military service, and the company eventually moved to Columbia Pike, where it is still in business today.

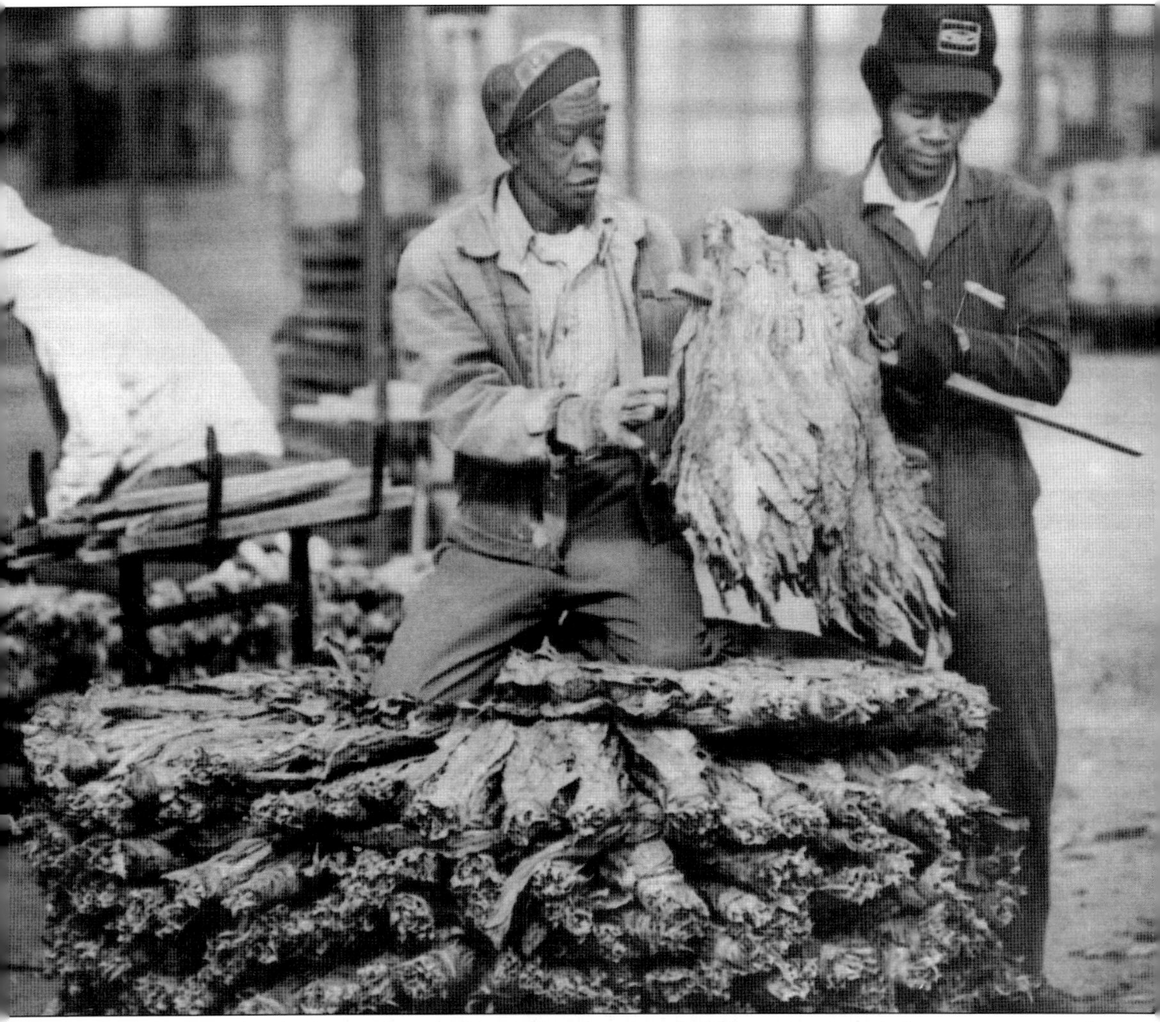

Two men work tobacco at a warehouse in this photograph. Tobacco was an early season crop, and well suited to the growing conditions around Franklin. The plants were cut when they dried, then finished curing in warm, vented barns with smoldering fires. Tobacco buyers graded and bought tobacco at the railroad for shipment to manufacturing plants. (WCA.)

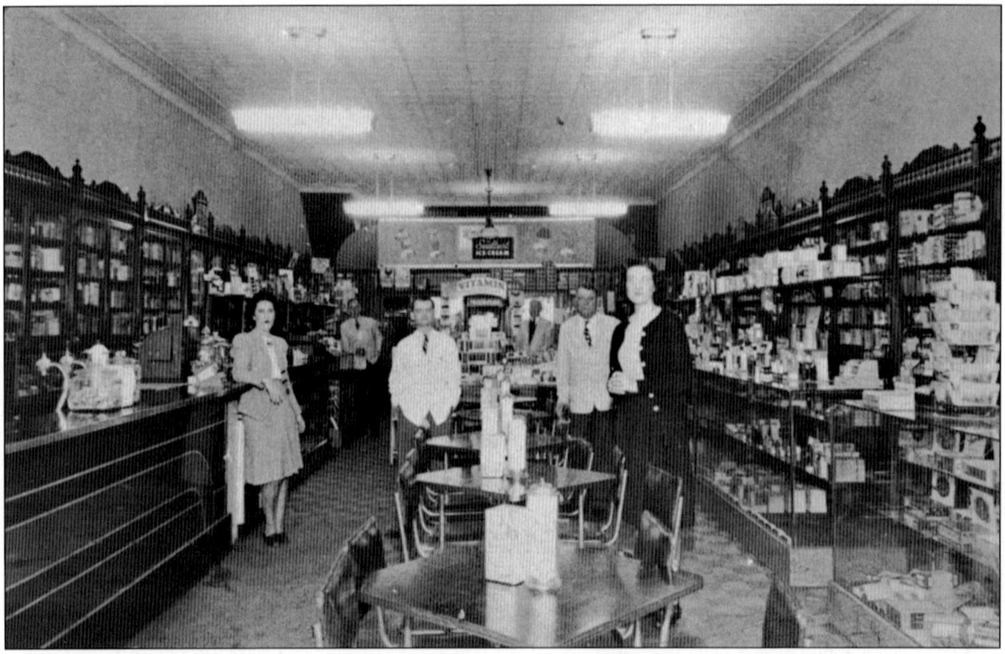

Pictured above from left to right, Francis Hay; pharmacists William "Will Bo" Miller, Duck Locke, Frank Gray Sr., and John McMahon; and Ida Mai Johnson, pose inside Gray's Drug. Taken in 1943, this photograph shows the store's embossed tin ceiling, the Art Deco–style soda fountain to the left, and open cigar boxes on display to the right in the case beside the cosmetics. When John Moran opened the store in the late 1920s as the Moran Drug Company, it quickly became one of Franklin's go-to gathering places and was a thriving pharmacy. Frank Gray, who bought the store in 1930, is pictured below with a floral arrangement, celebrating 50 years on Main Street. Visible on the shelves behind him are items ranging from mouse poison to mastitis remedies. (Above, WCA.)

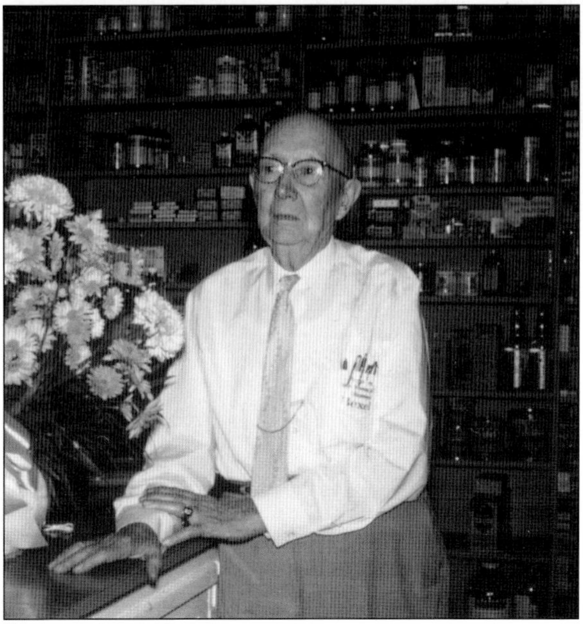

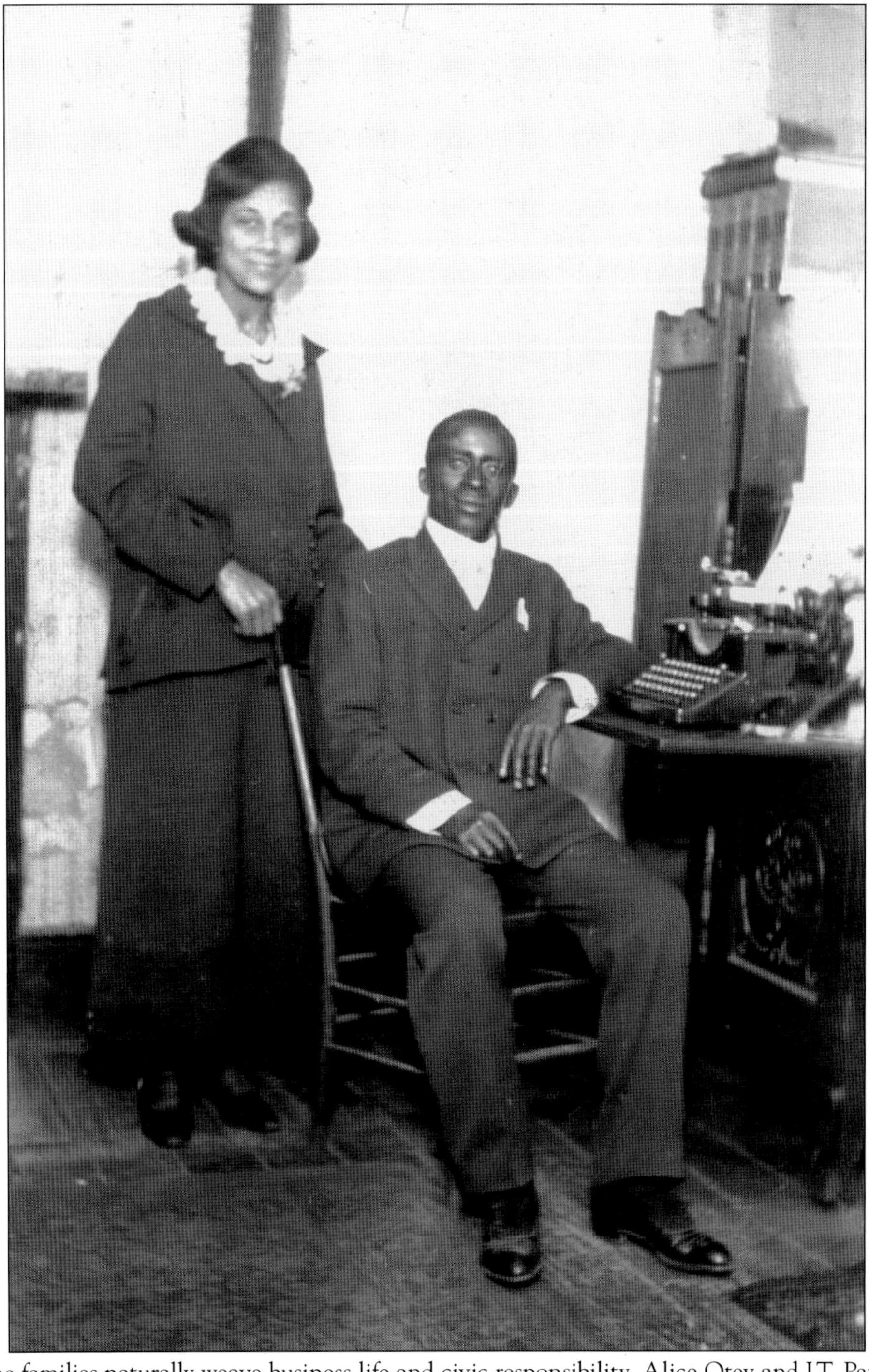

Some families naturally weave business life and civic responsibility. Alice Otey and J.T. Patton, their sons, and other members of their family, were operators of the Patton Brothers Funeral Home. Their son Thomas was a Tuskegee Airman during World War II, returned to Franklin and the family business, and married Louise Beale, who was the first African American public school teacher to teach white students in Franklin.

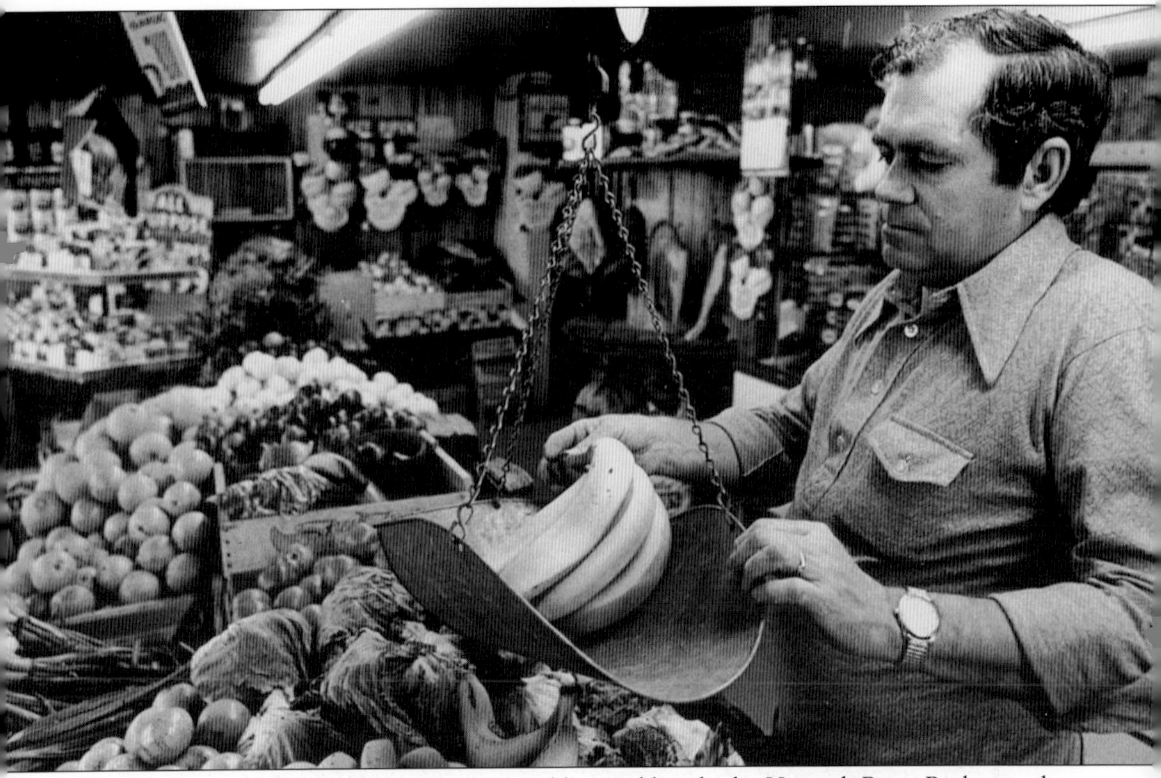

Earl Tywater operated a fresh fruit and vegetable stand beside the Harpeth River Bridge on the Franklin Pike. Patrons recall Earl doing a booming business in local watermelons during the summer months. For over 40 years, he greeted regular customers by name and hired schoolboys to help him with chores around the store, often paying them in soft drinks.

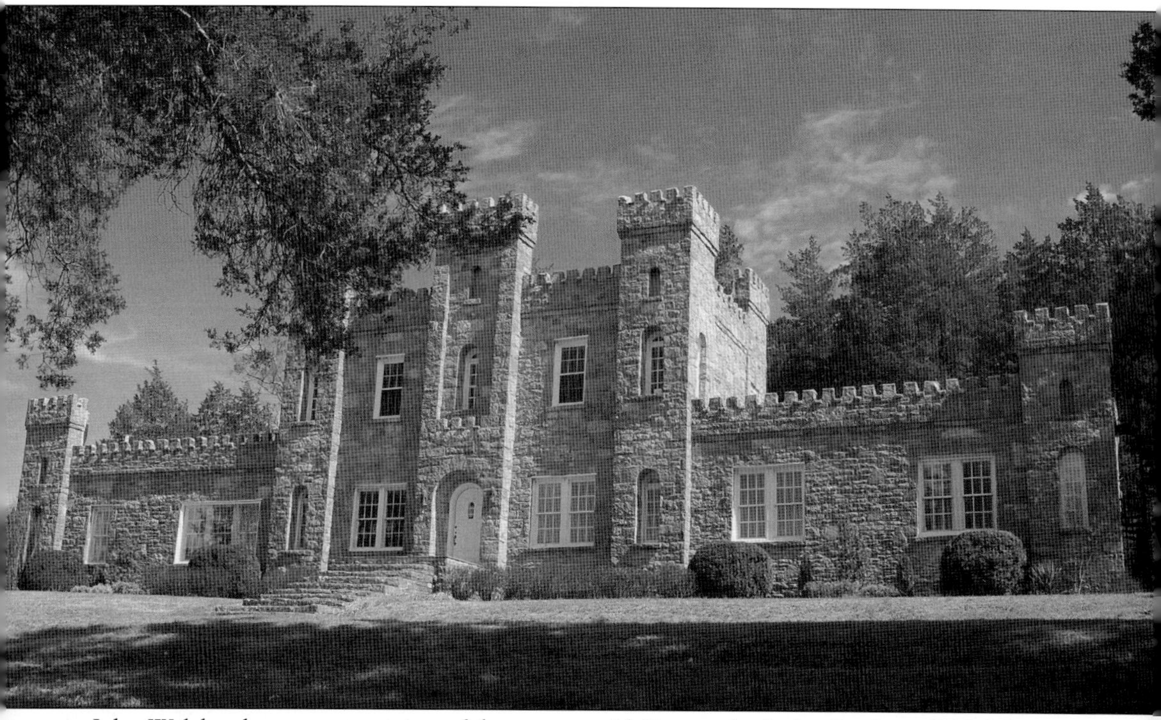

John Welch, who was an associate of the gangster Al Capone, built the Castle in 1930. It became a favored destination of Capone and others of the Prohibition era. Legends say that it was a liquor distribution center, that it houses escape tunnels that emerge miles away, and that the grounds hide unmarked graves. In 1981, the Nuyens family restored the Castle into one of the world's premier music recording studios.

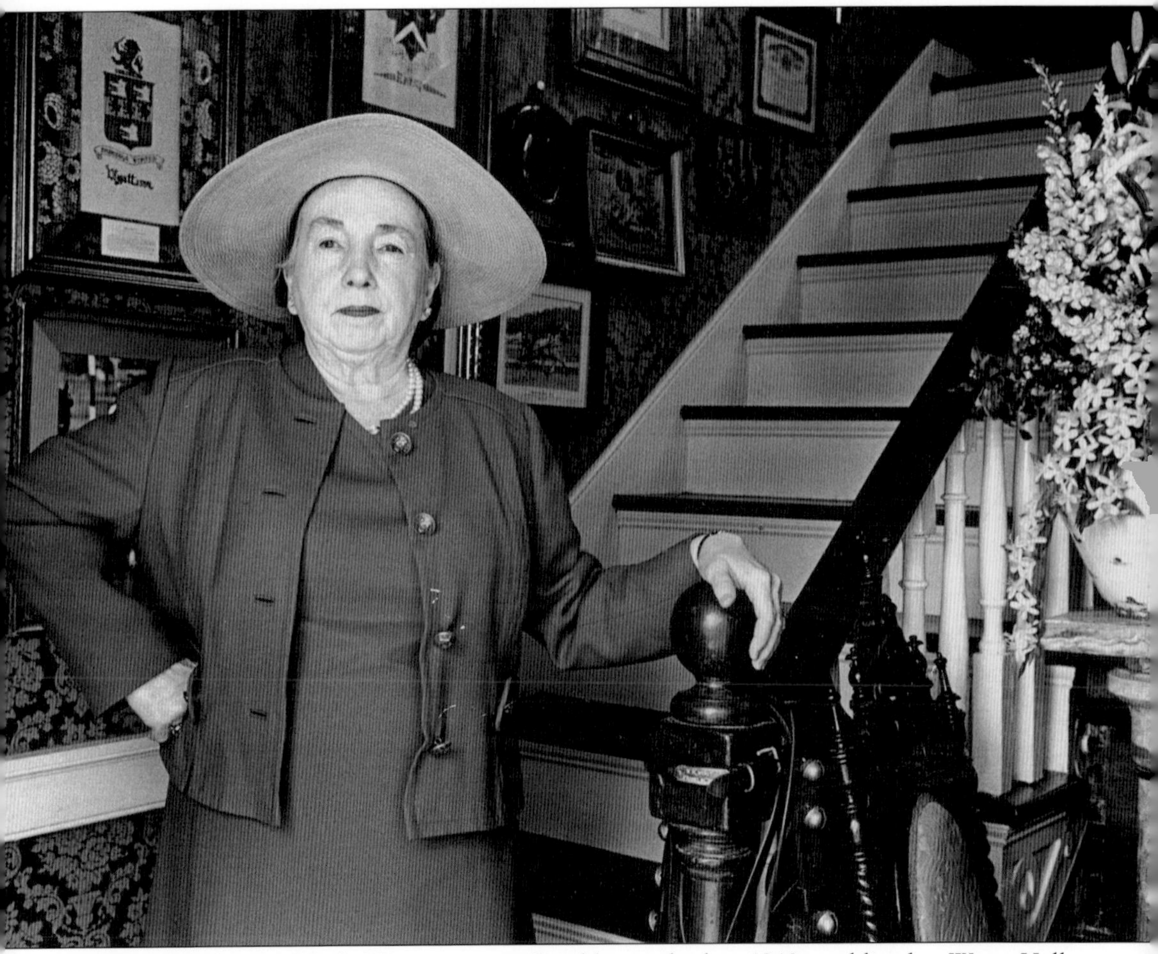

Hubert and Margaret Early Wyatt came to Franklin in the late 1940s and lived at Wyatt Hall on the Nashville-Franklin Pike. Margaret established a stable with a practice track, and became active in harness racing to the point of training the horses herself. In the 1950s, she was devoted to Southern tradition and was active in early preservation efforts, including those for the Carter House. (Courtesy of Dennis Wile.)

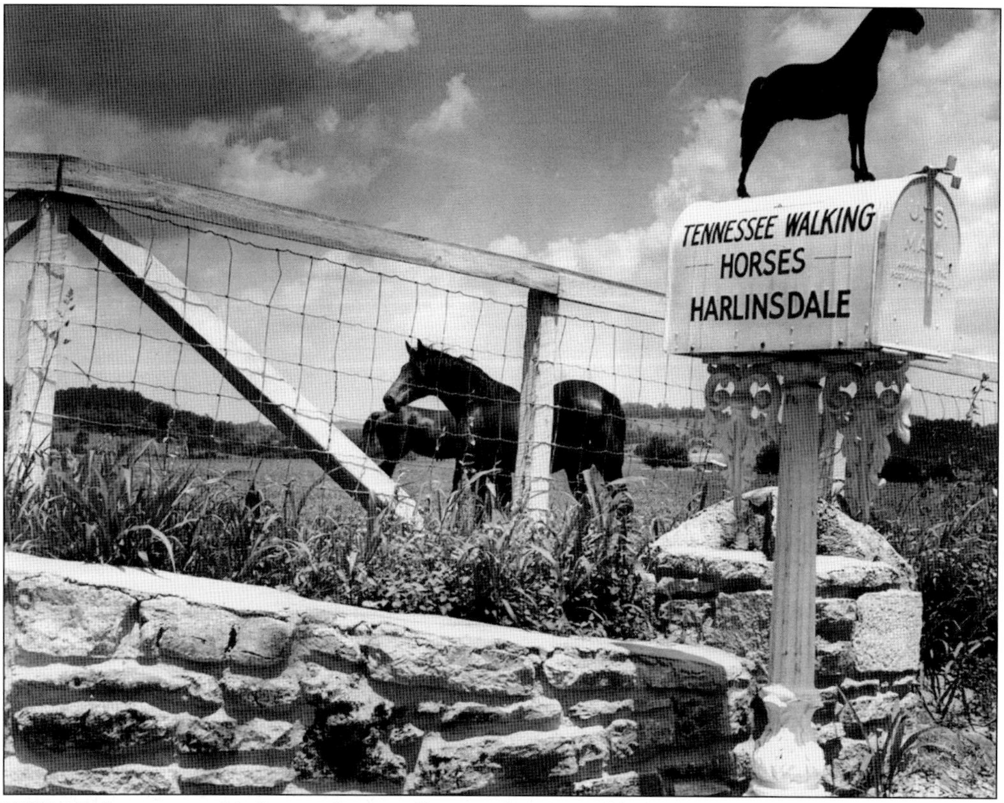

W.W. Harlin, pictured below with one of his yearlings, established Harlinsdale Farm as a premier horse breeding operation in 1933, when the Tennessee Walking Horse breed was still being established. The Tennessee Walking Horse Breeders Association was formed in 1935, and the first Walking Horse Celebration was held in 1939. For 21 years, Harlinsdale was the home of Midnight Sun, a magnificent black Tennessee Walking Horse sire who was the first repeat world champion in 1945 and 1946. The horse's record in the ring and as a breeding sire has never been matched. The farm remained in the Harlin family until the 21st century; today, the majority of champion Tennessee Walking Horses can trace their lineage to Midnight Sun. (Both, TSL.)

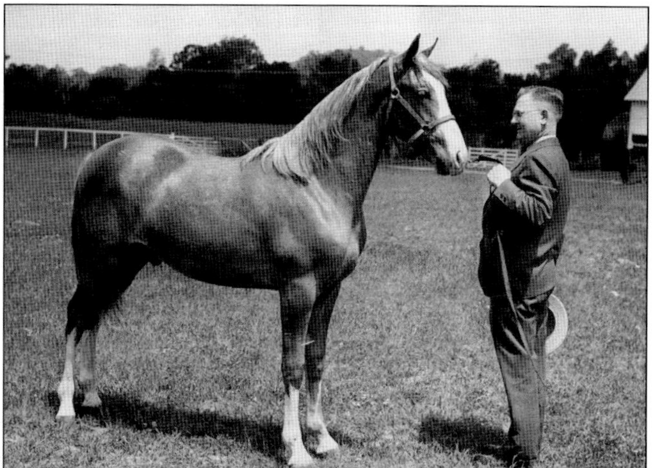

Five

HOME, SCHOOL, AND FRIENDS

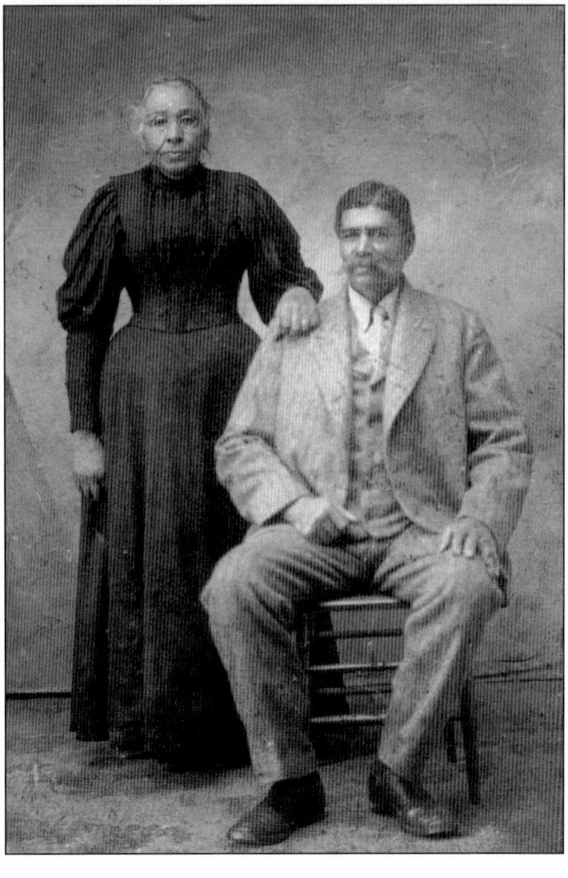

Mariah, a McGavock family slave, was born in 1838 and married Harvey Otey in 1852. She gave birth to eight children, including two sets of twins. After Harvey's death during the Civil War, the McGavocks sent her to Montgomery, Alabama. There, she married Bolen Reddick—pictured with her here—who returned with her to Franklin. Bolen was Franklin's trash collector, and their son John Watt Reddick became an African American community leader. (BFTC.)

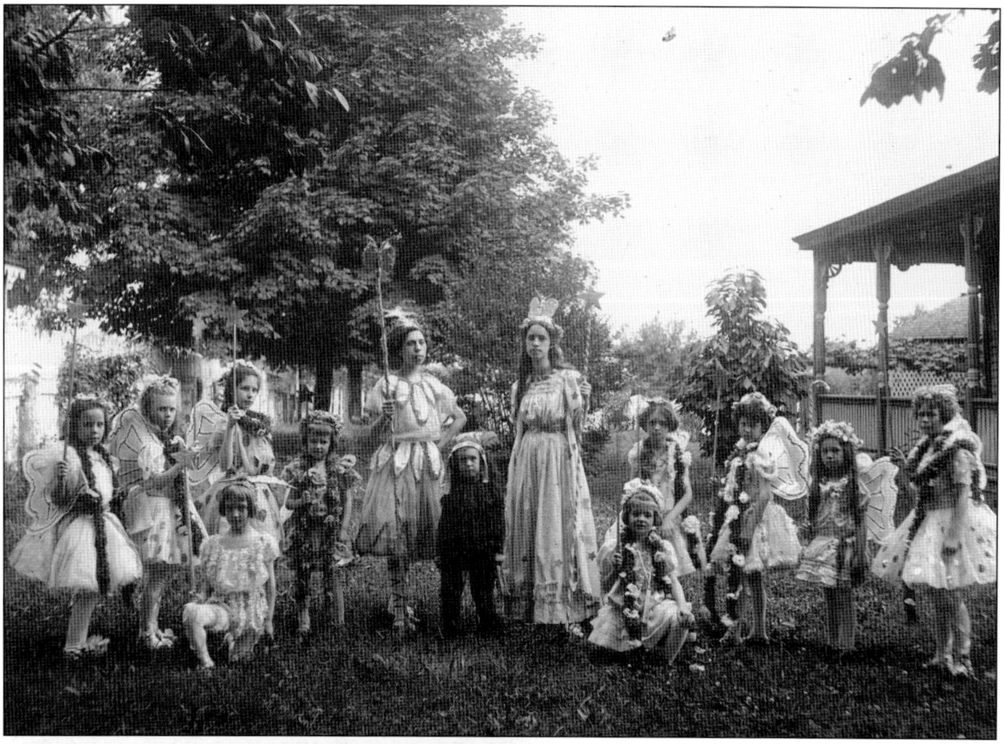

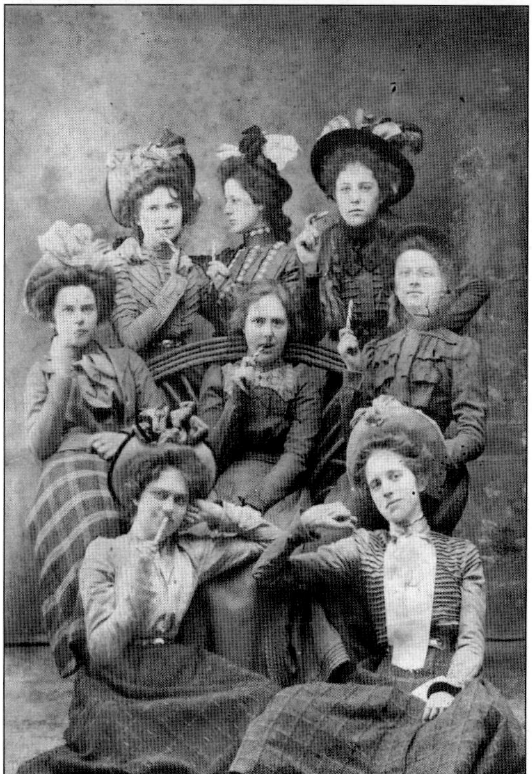

Like most dramatic productions put on by Franklin students in the first half of the 20th century, this 1908 production of *A Midsummer Night's Dream* was directed by Mrs. Pryor Lillie. Mrs. Lillie was a beloved and devoted teacher of public speaking and drama to private students, and in public and private schools, including Battle Ground Academy. She taught until her death at the age of 64. (RWC.)

With the somber faces in most old photographs, it can be easy to forget that people have always been people, and friendships have always been precious. These cousins and friends sharing the sweet joy of peppermint sticks are, from left to right, (first row) Hattie McGavock and Annie Compton; (second row) Sallie McGavock, Virginia Fitts, and Pattie DeGaffenried; (third row) Theresa Henderson, Margaret Douglas, and Carrie Cowan, granddaughter of John and Carrie McGavock. (BFTC.)

"Mammy Nancy" Vestal was 10 years old when Seth Sparkman, a Leiper's Fork farmer, bought her at a Franklin auction in 1845, saving her from an abusive owner. She learned to read, and was so loved by the family that they had this portrait made. After emancipation, Nancy continued to serve members of the Sparkman family until her death in 1903. (BFTC.)

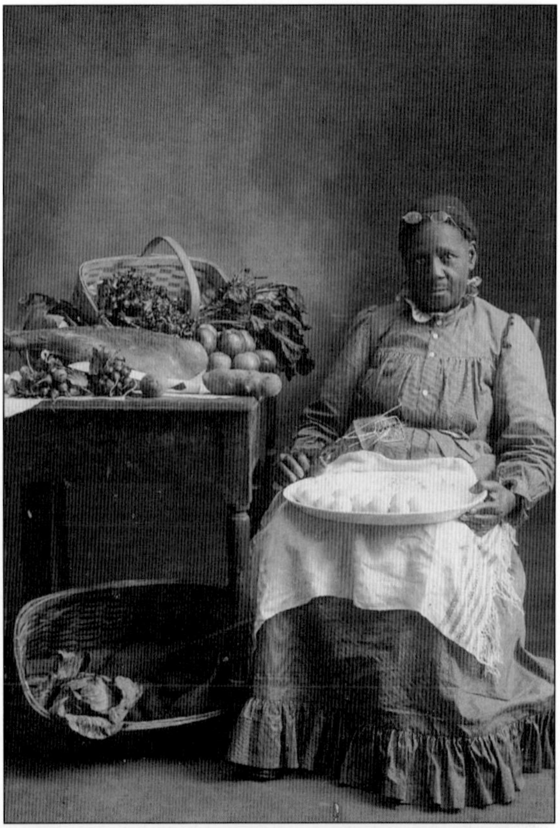

The Boy Scouts started in England and came to the United States in 1910. Battle Ground Academy had a troop as early as 1913, and the troop in this photograph started meeting at St. Paul's church shortly thereafter. They are pictured with their adult leaders, standing in front of the church in about 1920. Today, there are four active Scout troops in Franklin.

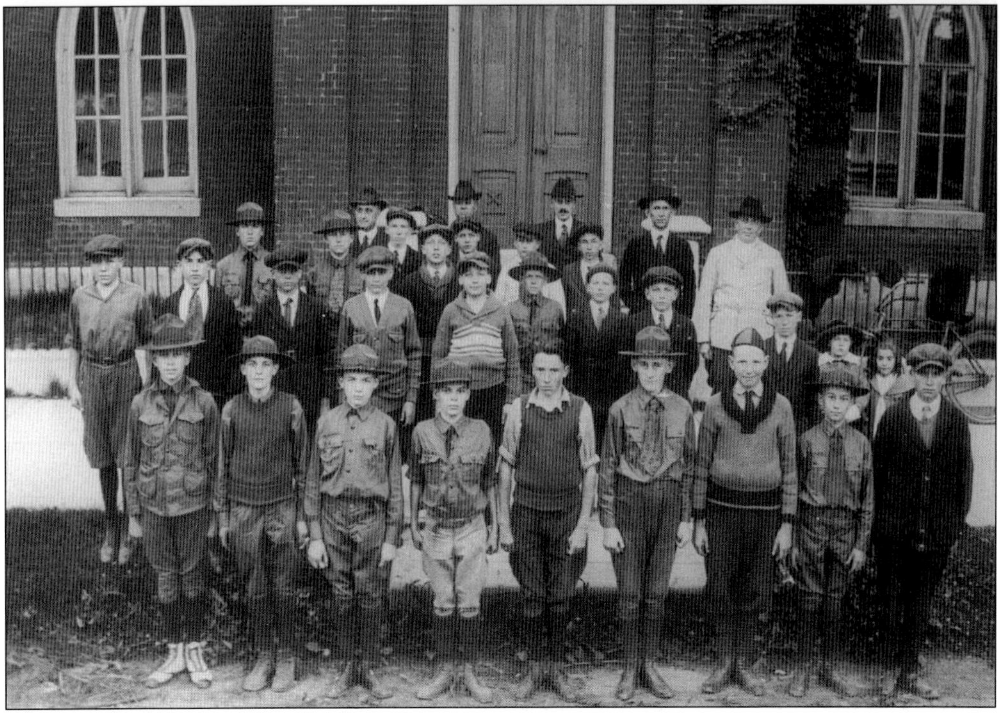

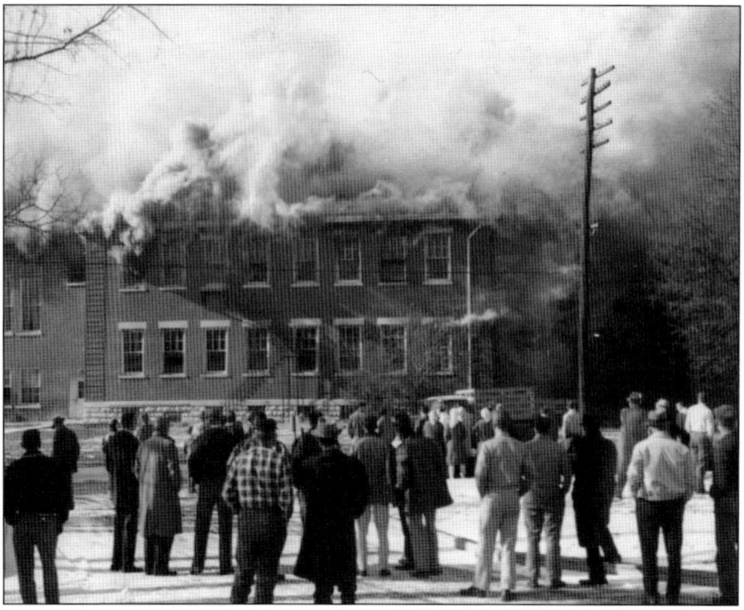

Franklin Elementary School, located at Five Points, was once the pride of the city. It was built in 1907, with an auditorium added in 1911 and other additions that kept pace with the growing city. Finally, in the spring of 1961, a new school building opened on Cannon Street. The original building burned two years later. (WCA.)

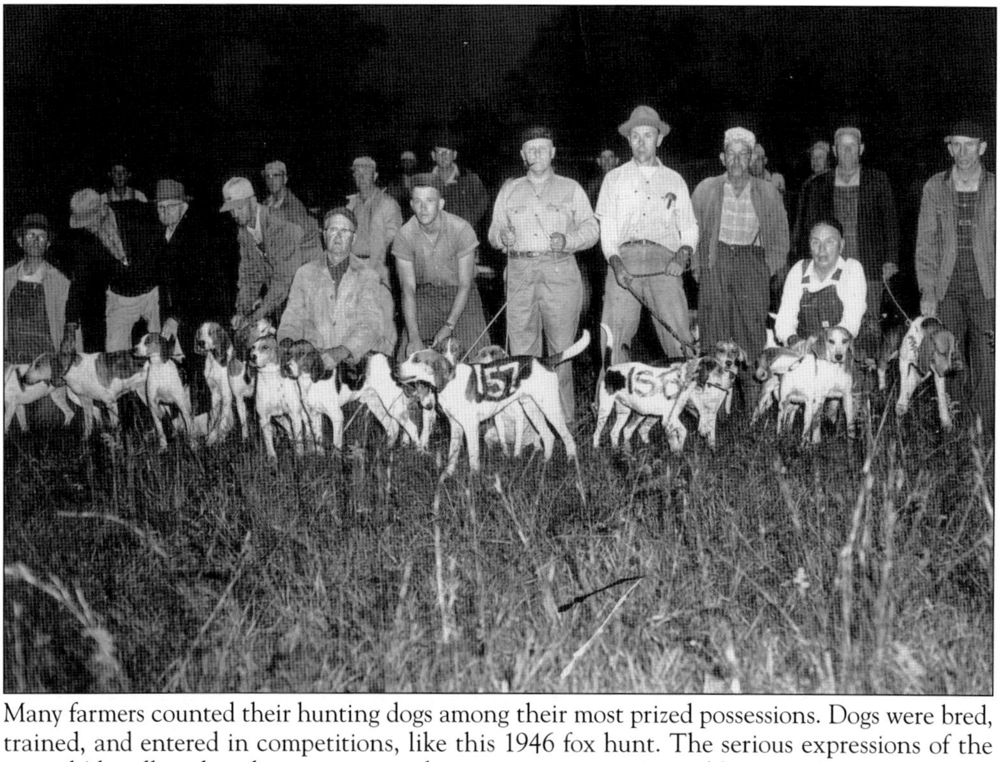

Many farmers counted their hunting dogs among their most prized possessions. Dogs were bred, trained, and entered in competitions, like this 1946 fox hunt. The serious expressions of the animals' handlers show how important these contests were. A good hunting dog not only sold for a good price, but could also help to keep the family fed. (RWC.)

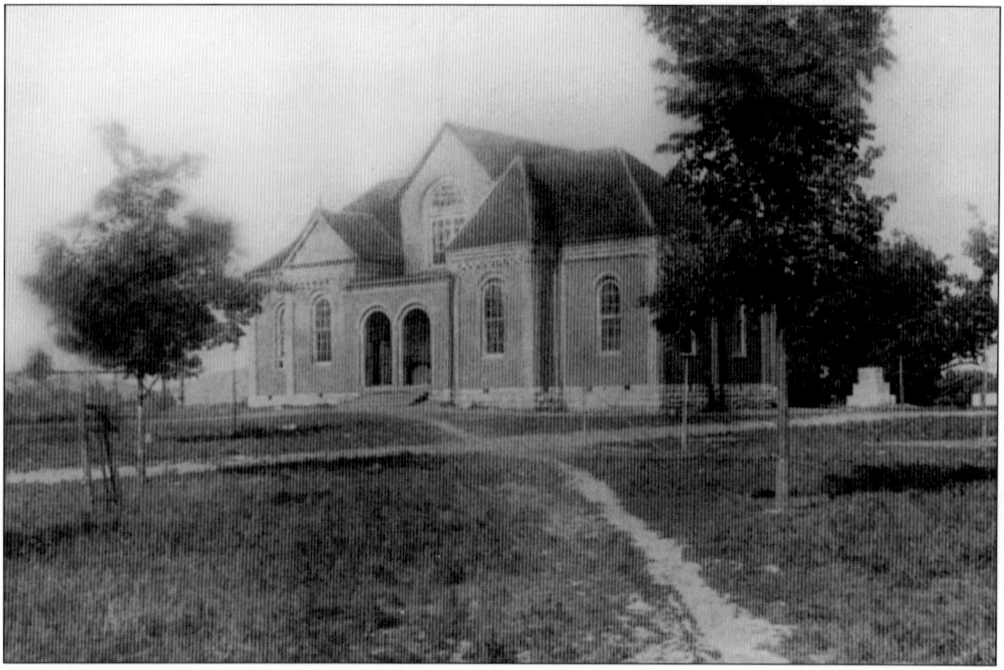

Battle Ground Academy (BGA) was built on the battlefield at the site of Fountain Branch Carter's cotton gin in 1889. The building (above), with its gabled roof, burned just a few years later, in 1902. It was soon replaced with the newer school (below), which still stands on the west side of Columbia Pike. With the addition of a dormitory in 1922, it became a boarding school, and, a few years later, entered a 50-year stretch as a male-only campus. BGA endured at this location on Franklin Pike until it moved in the late 1990s to a beautiful new campus north of the city, designed to include the lower, middle, and upper schools as well as athletic fields and other facilities.

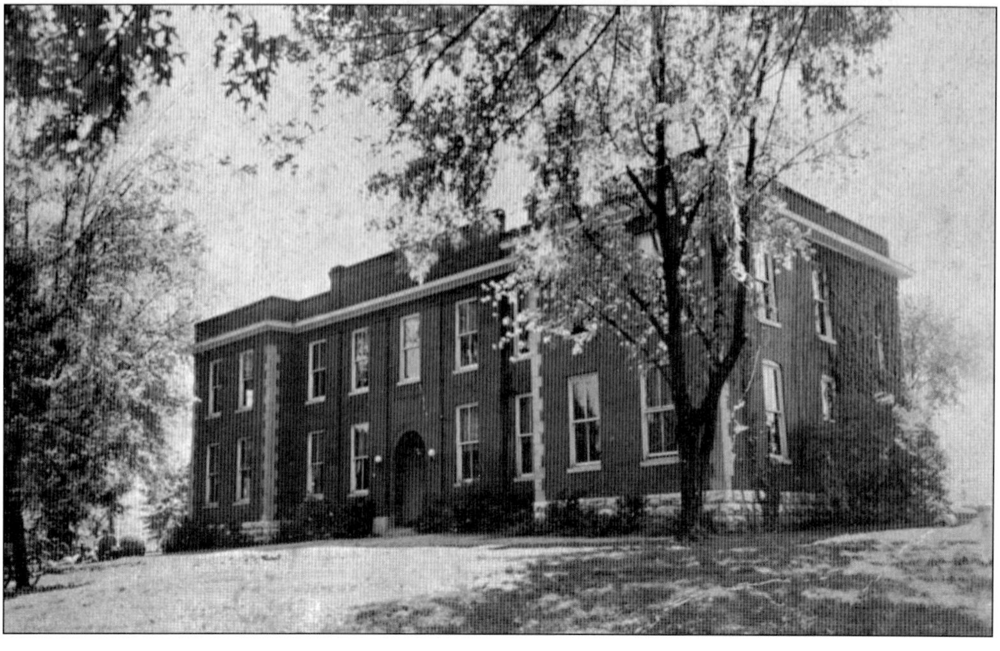

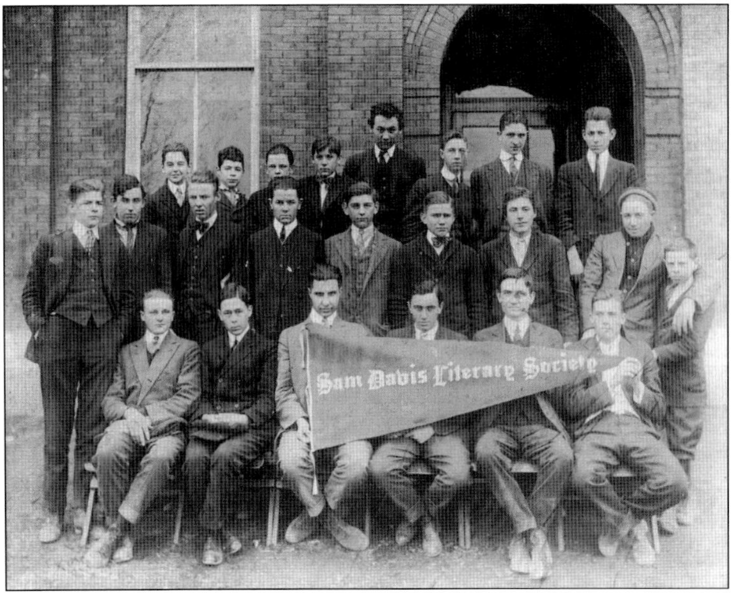

Among Battle Ground Academy's long-standing traditions are its literary societies, in which members unite for friendship, academics, and sports. The best-known groups were the Greers and the Platos, but there have been others. In this photograph, the members of the Sam Davis Society, named for a hero of the Confederacy, pose with their banner on the steps of the school. (WCA.)

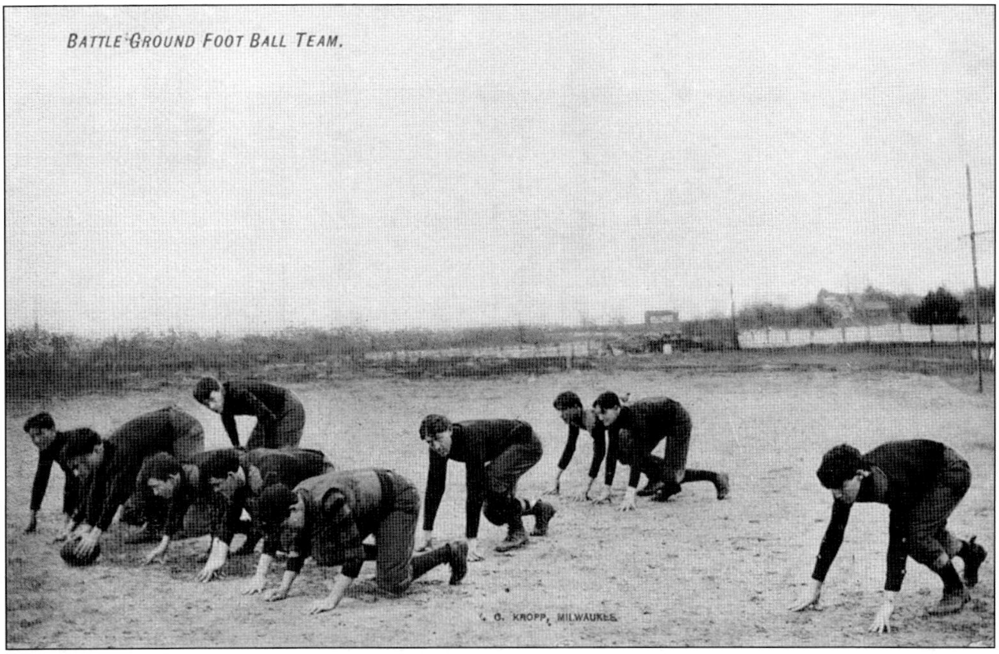

The Battle Ground Academy football team is pictured here, at practice on a cool fall day. The date of the photograph is unknown, but BGA's first football team was organized in 1891. The school went undefeated in 1945, and won the state championship in 1960, 1995, 1997, 1998, and 2003. Alumni include NFL players Darrius McCord and Troy Fleming. (TSL.)

The Tennessee Female College began as a school for girls in grades 1 through 12. It burned down in 1886, and was replaced a year later with this striking building—three stories tall, with a five-story tower. The building served from 1887 to 1916, and the site was used for dormitories for students who lived outside of Franklin.

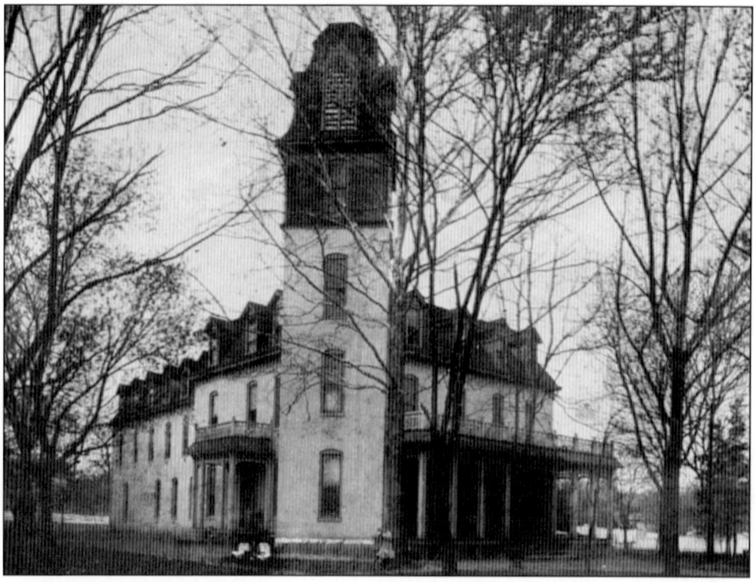

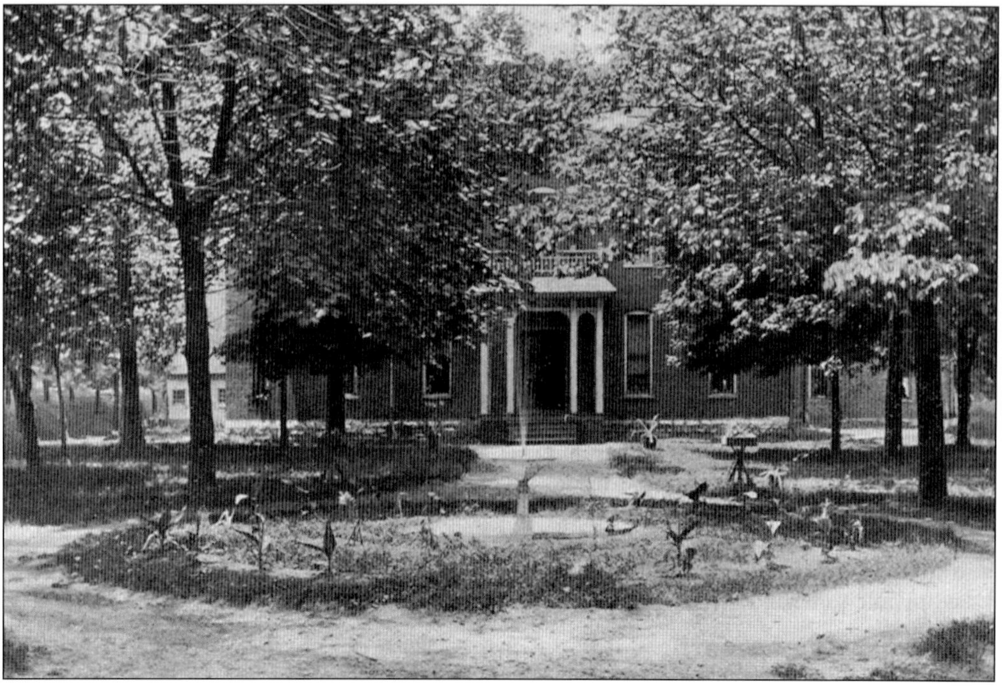

The beautifully landscaped campus of the Tennessee Female College extended from Fourth Avenue to Fifth Avenue on Margin Street. Along with a classical education, a part of every student's "finishing" was classical musical training. The faculty included many graduates of the school, though it was customary at the time for young women to teach only until they married.

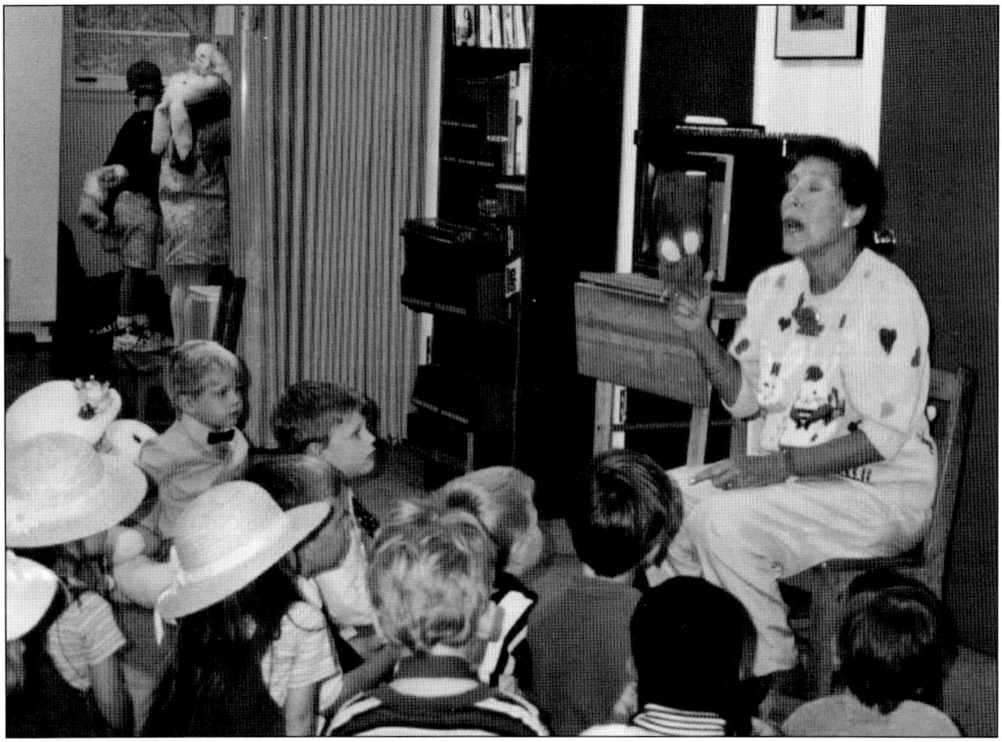

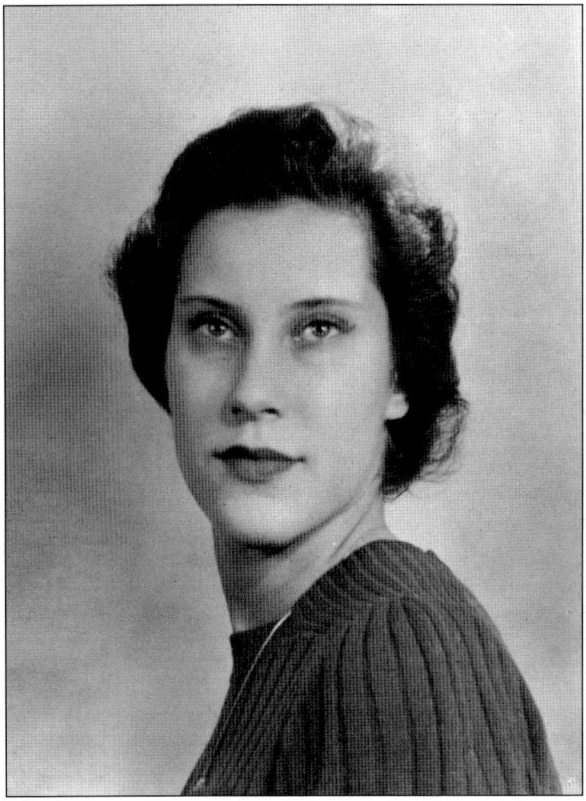

Smith Preschool has been giving children a good start in Franklin for over six decades. The school is still led by its founder, Inge Myering Smith, who is pictured above speaking to students and at left in her twenties. Smith's Jewish family left Germany to escape persecution when she was 15. She and her husband, Paul, came to Franklin in 1946, and in 1952, Smith started Franklin's first kindergarten at First Presbyterian Church—welcoming children of all races and genders. Later, after moving the school to her home, where it still meets, she earned a master's degree from Peabody University, helped establish Head Start in Tennessee, and supervised its teachers throughout the region. She then founded the Harpeth Academy, which became the lower school for Battle Ground Academy. Smith is the subject of a book and a documentary film, and, now in her 90s, is still a teacher and leader in her profession.

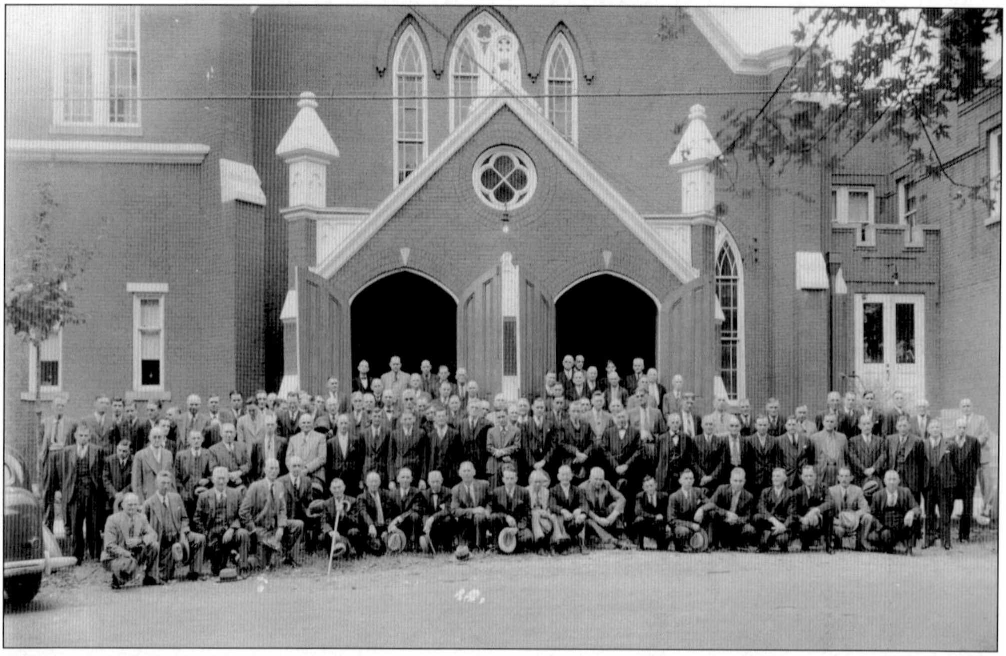

The Hal Peoples Bible Class reunites at the First Methodist Church in this 1937 photograph. Peoples and his brother R.G. "Daddy" Peoples were headmasters of Battle Ground Academy from 1903 to 1912, until Hal's death. Daddy continued there until 1925, continuing an era when BGA was known as "The Peoples School." The Sunday school class was taught by George I. Briggs, who succeeded the Peoples brothers as head of BGA. (WCA.)

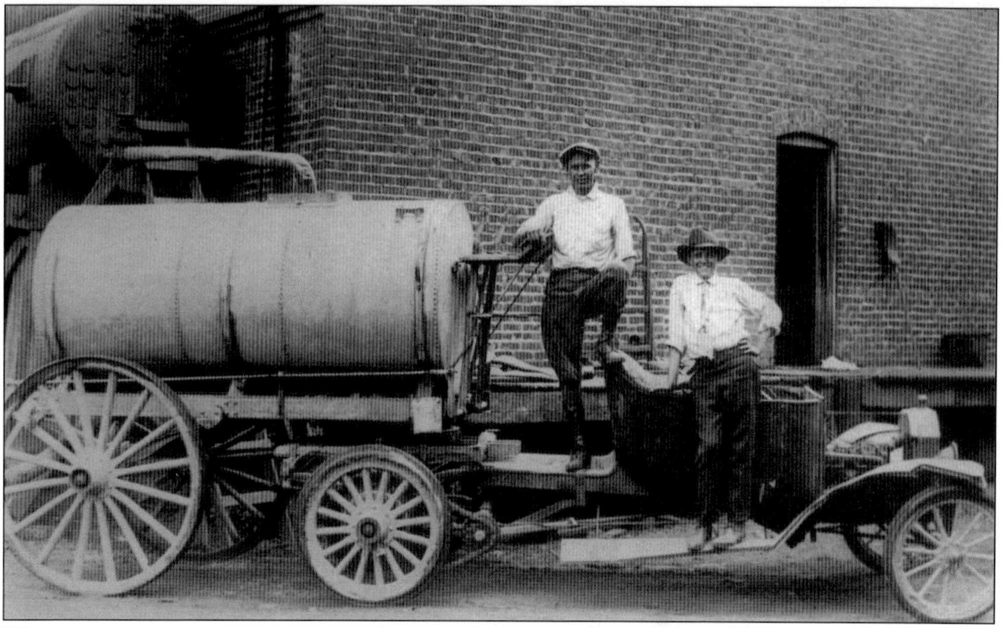

These young men appear to enjoy their work at the icehouse. Everybody in town appreciated the service that they provided. Even in the modern era of telephones and cars, the iceman came around with his horse and wagon, and homemakers depended on a big block of ice in the top of their icebox to keep the food cool. (TSL.)

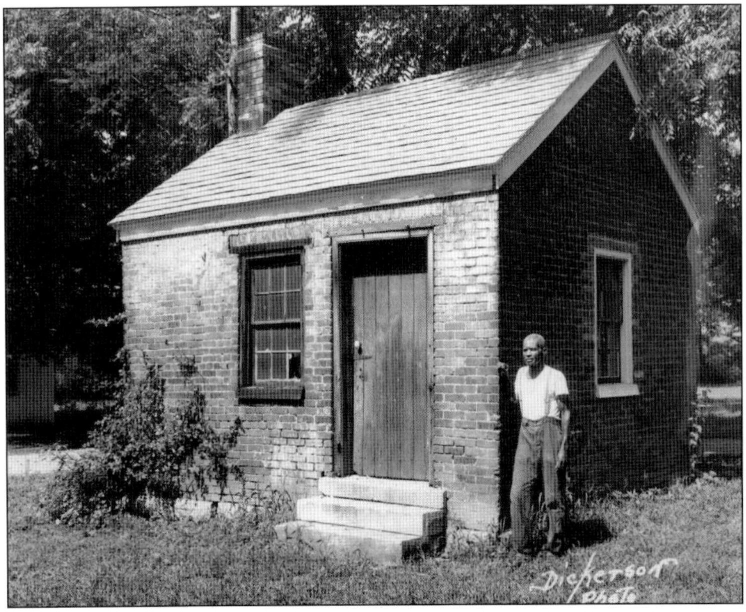

Eugene Scruggs was a caretaker at the Carter House in 1951, before it was restored. In this photograph, he poses beside the kitchen, where damage from Civil War shelling can clearly be seen. In the era when the house was built, it was common to build a separate kitchen, which helped keep the house cool in summer and reduced the danger of fire from the wood stoves. (BFTC.)

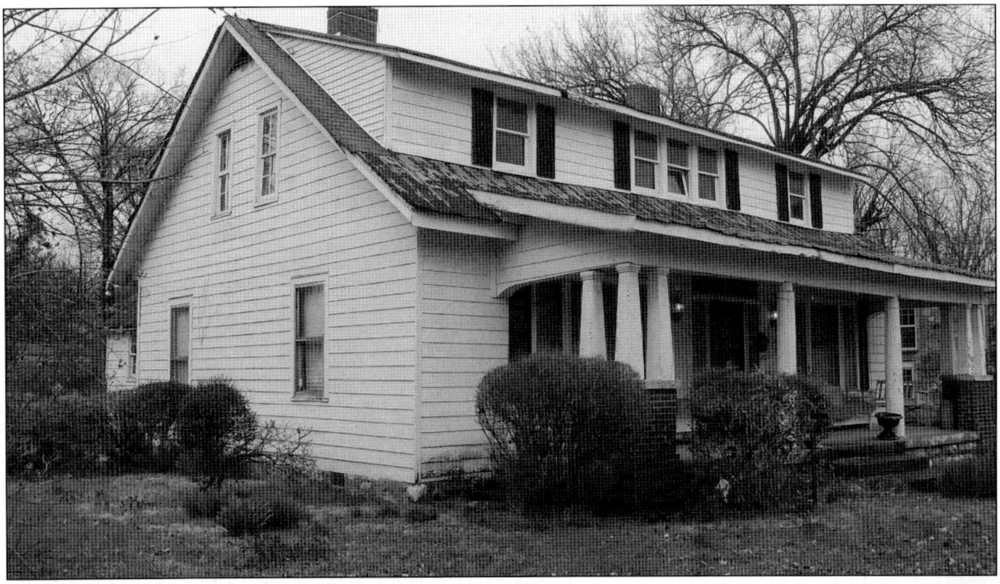

Former slave Moses Merrill built this home on Natchez Street in 1881. In 1892, he sold it to A.N.C. and Malissa Williams, who raised their 11 children there. In the 21st century, the house is still in the Williams family, and the neighborhood is now a Historic District listed in the National Register of Historic Places.

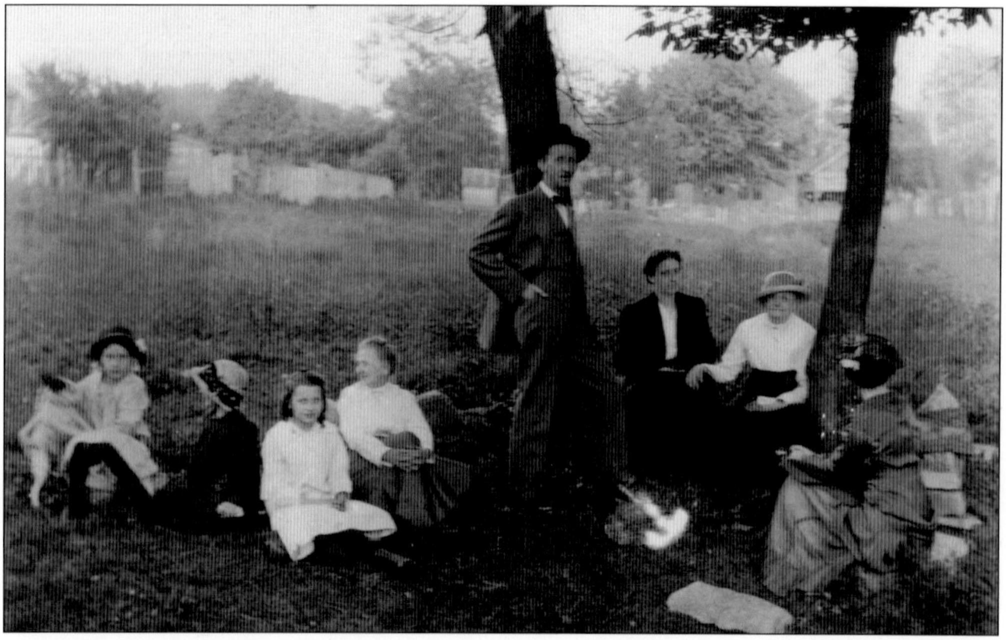

The Carter family is all dressed up for a picnic in this photograph from 1908. The little girl in the white dress third from left is the future Dr. Rosalie Carter. Standing beside her is her father, Franklin dentist Dr. Moscow B. Carter, and at the far right is Rosalie's mother, Lucy. The others are unidentified. (WCA.)

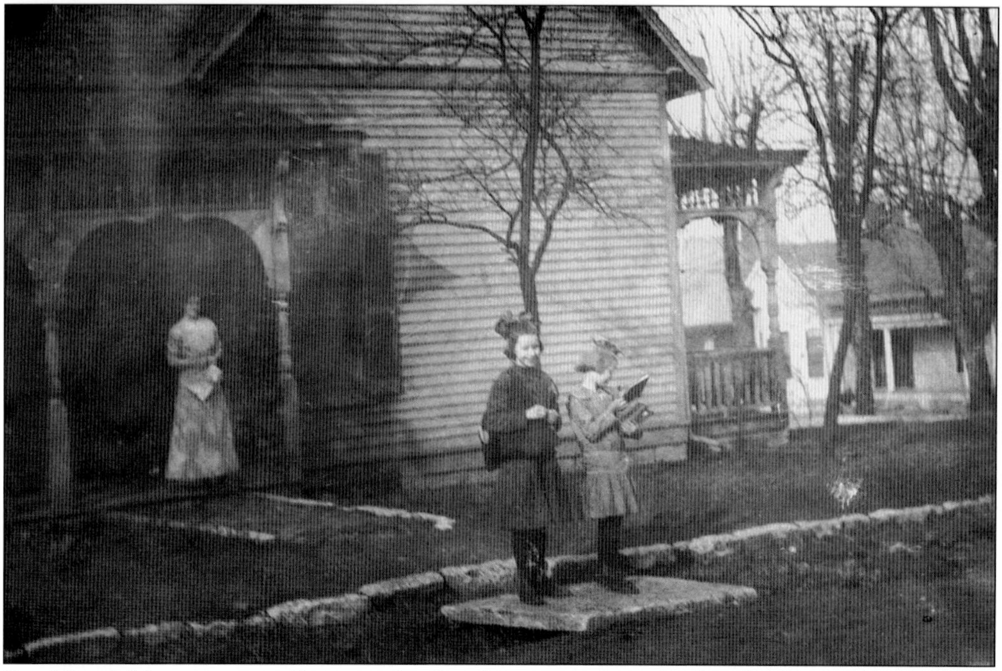

Franklin children set out walking to school each morning carrying their books and their lunches. The smiling girls in this photograph are the Carter sisters, Rosalie (left), who would grow up to be a dentist like her father, and her sister Corine. Their mother, Lucy, watches from the porch.

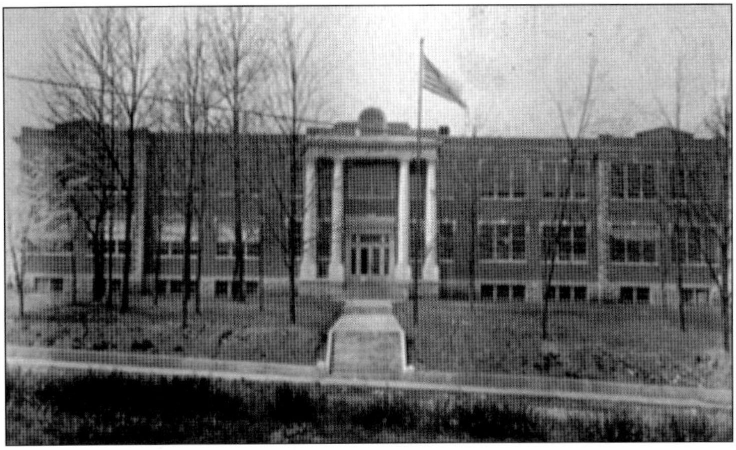

Franklin High School, which stood next door to the Carter House, was built in 1927, and its students were bused in from all over the county. It served the community until a lightning fire destroyed it in 1956. Classes met in local churches until the new school opened, and that building was finally replaced in 2004.

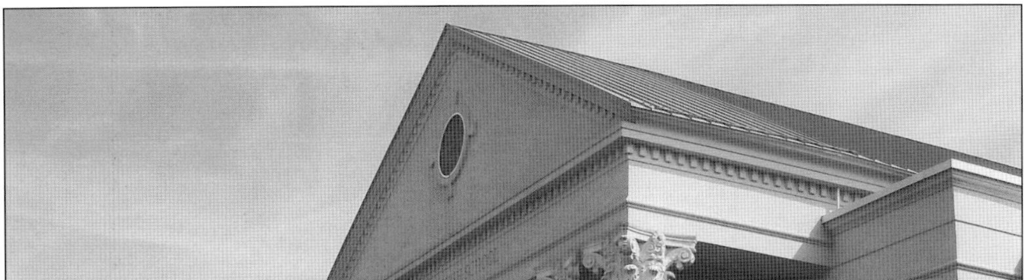

When Franklin High School burned down, it was replaced with a one-story brick building west of town on Hillsboro Road. In 2004 the school was renovated, without stopping classes, by replacing half of the old building at a time. The new school features a classical design and broad, open common areas. Franklin High's alumni include professional athletes, Miss Tennessee winners for 2009 and 2010, singer Wynona Judd, and actress Ashley Judd.

Starting in 1908, workers and shoppers rode the Franklin Interurban—an electric trolley with overhead wires. Cars ran all the way to a terminal in downtown Nashville on a route that was dotted with stops with sheltered benches. The line's route basically followed Franklin Pike, and it was converted to buses in the 1940s. (Courtesy of Bob Canaday.)

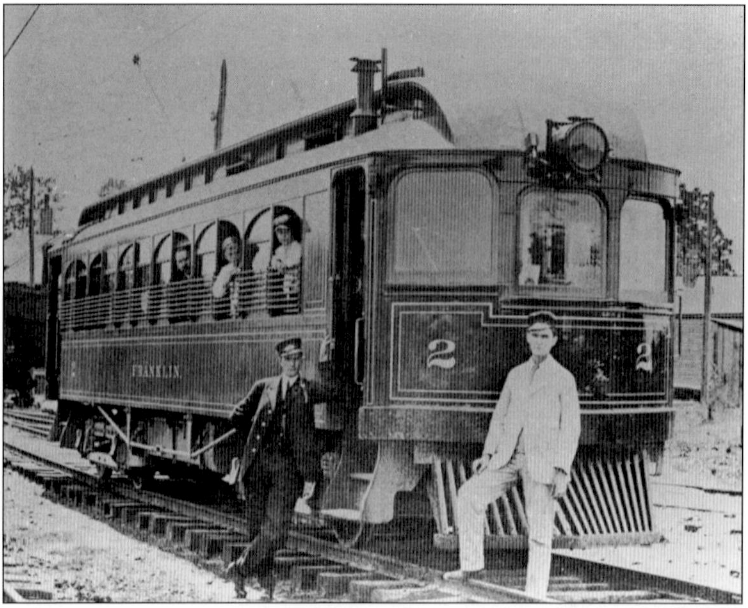

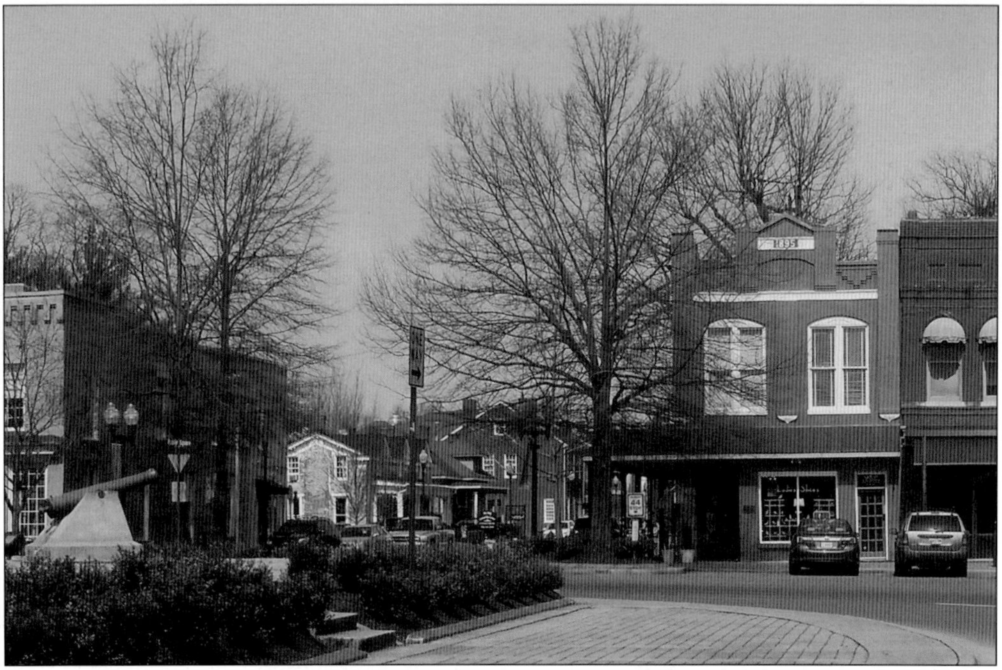

The ladies' shoe store in the pictured corner building (constructed in 1895) was once the ticket office for the Franklin Interurban, which was also called the Nashville-Franklin Railway. The line's electric street cars ran from a depot on Third Avenue North, around Franklin Square, north along Franklin Pike, and entered Nashville on Eighth Avenue South. The line was so busy that cars ran almost hourly, from 6:00 a.m. until midnight.

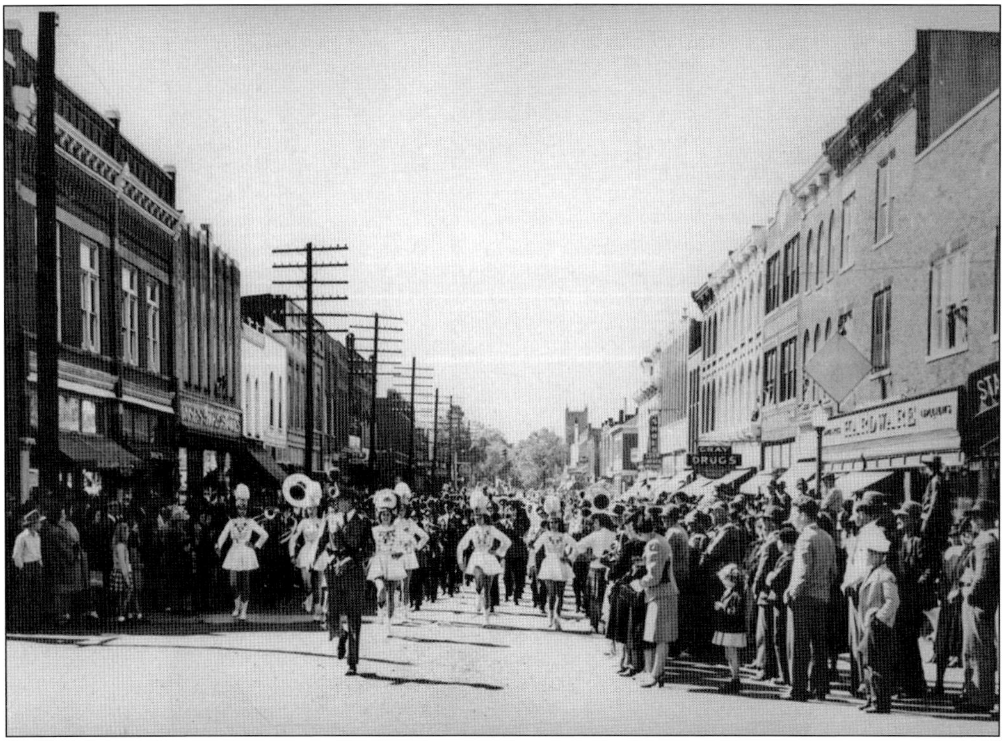

Downtown Franklin has always been the scene of well-attended parades, ceremonies, and celebrations. In this photograph, members of the Franklin High School Band, in their military-style uniforms, march north on Main Street during a parade in the late 1940s, with the streets so crowded the band barely had room to pass. In the distance, beyond the stores, the tower of St. Paul's Episcopal Church is visible. (WCA.)

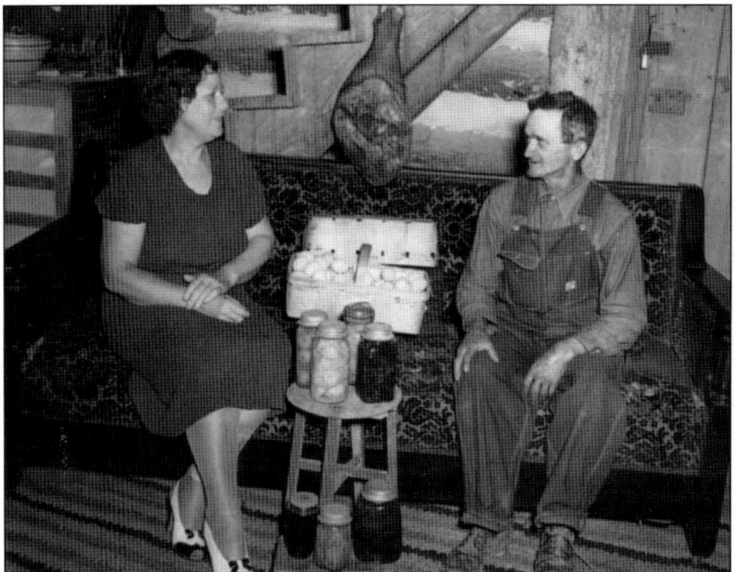

In this photograph, Mr. and Mrs. W.H. Morris pose with a ham, eggs, and canned goods, all produced on their 72-acre farm. Their farm was one of several featured in educational materials produced during the state's food supply program, which was an effort to teach farm families about getting the most agricultural production from their land during World War II. (TSL.)

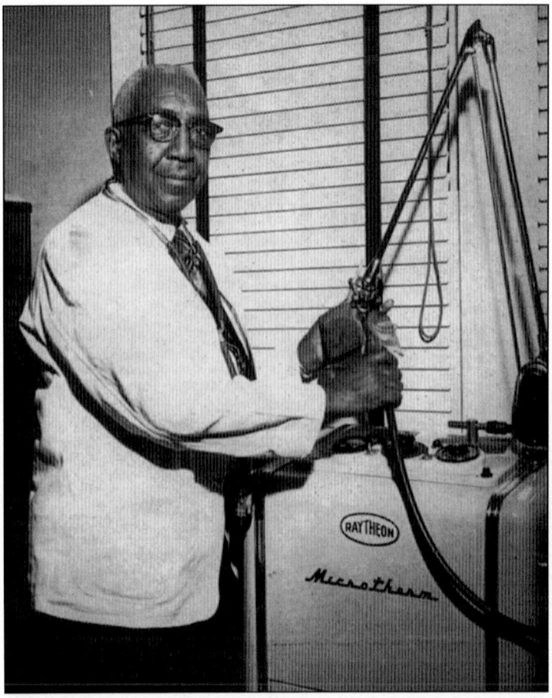

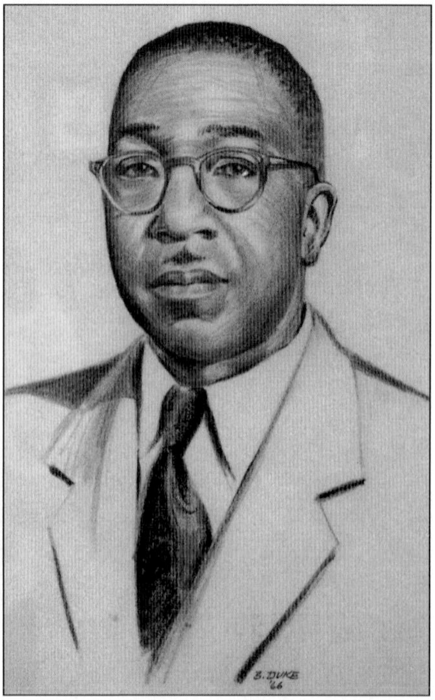

The Charles Johnson Elementary School was named for Dr. Charles C. Johnson, who moved from Iowa to Franklin with his wife in 1917. Learning that African Americans—even women delivering babies—were not allowed to spend the night in the county hospital, he opened the first hospital for African Americans in Franklin. The school opened to African American students in 1956 and was fully integrated in 1971.

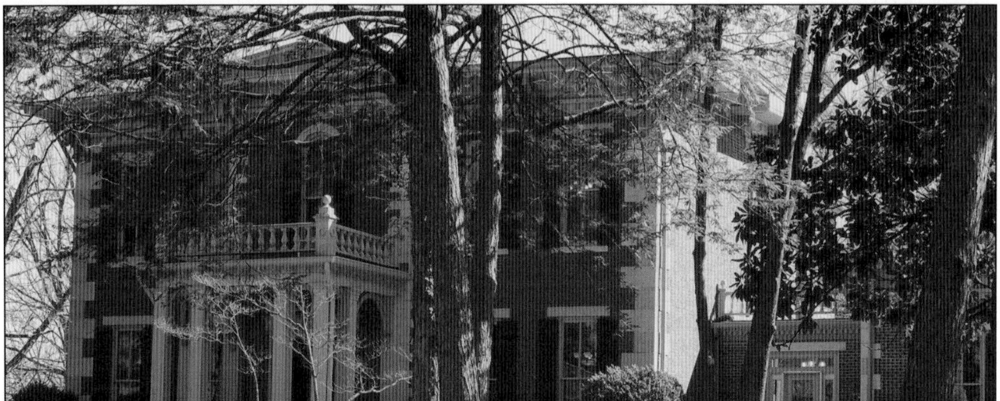

Tennessee native Eloise Pitts O'More was educated in Paris and New York and settled in Franklin, where she taught dance and interior design classes before founding the O'More College of Design in 1970. The administration offices are housed in the historic Abbey Leix Mansion (pictured), and some 200 students attend classes on the seven-acre campus just off the square. O'More became a four-year college in the 1980s.

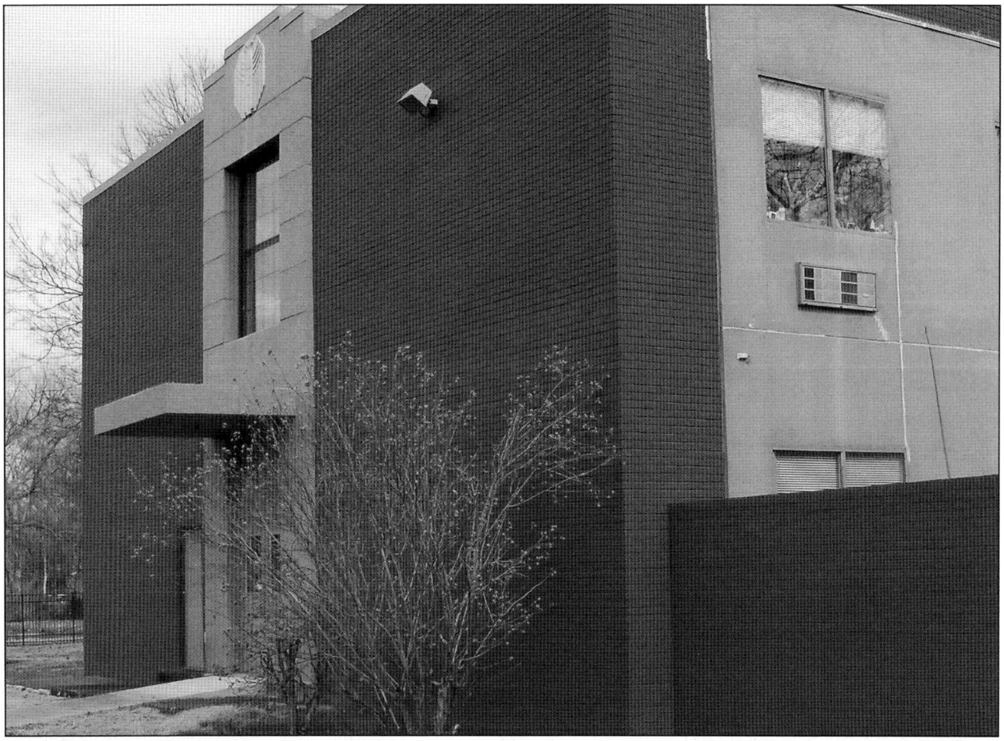

For 90 years, African American children were educated at the above location on Natchez Street. Claiborne Institute, the first school at this site, was founded by citizen action in 1888 and named for the first principal, Willis Claiborne. It was rebuilt in 1907 as the Franklin Colored School, and then, in 1925, more space was added, along with more vocational and technical classes, and the name was changed to the Franklin Training School. The Training School football team is pictured below in 1956, with coach Henry Hardison (far left), and principal J.R. Watkins (far right). The name changed to Natchez High School in 1962, emphasizing the school's excellent, long-standing academic and extracurricular programs over its vocational training. The school system adopted an integration policy in 1964, and Natchez graduated its last class in 1967, as Franklin High was integrated that fall.

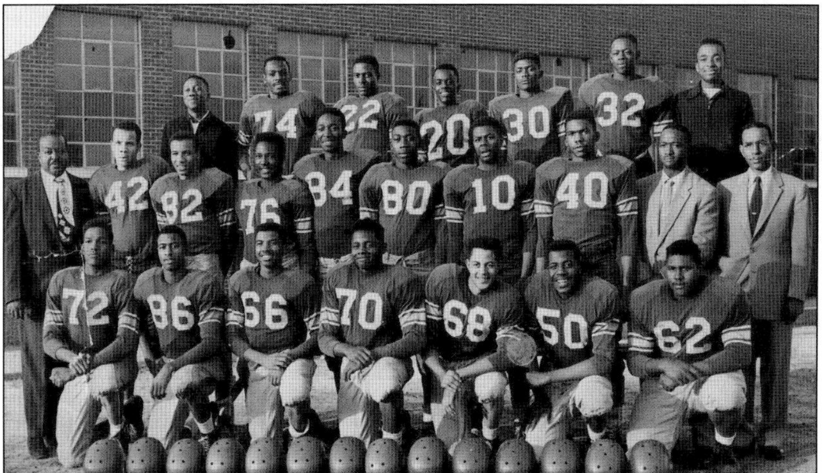

Six

Building a Community

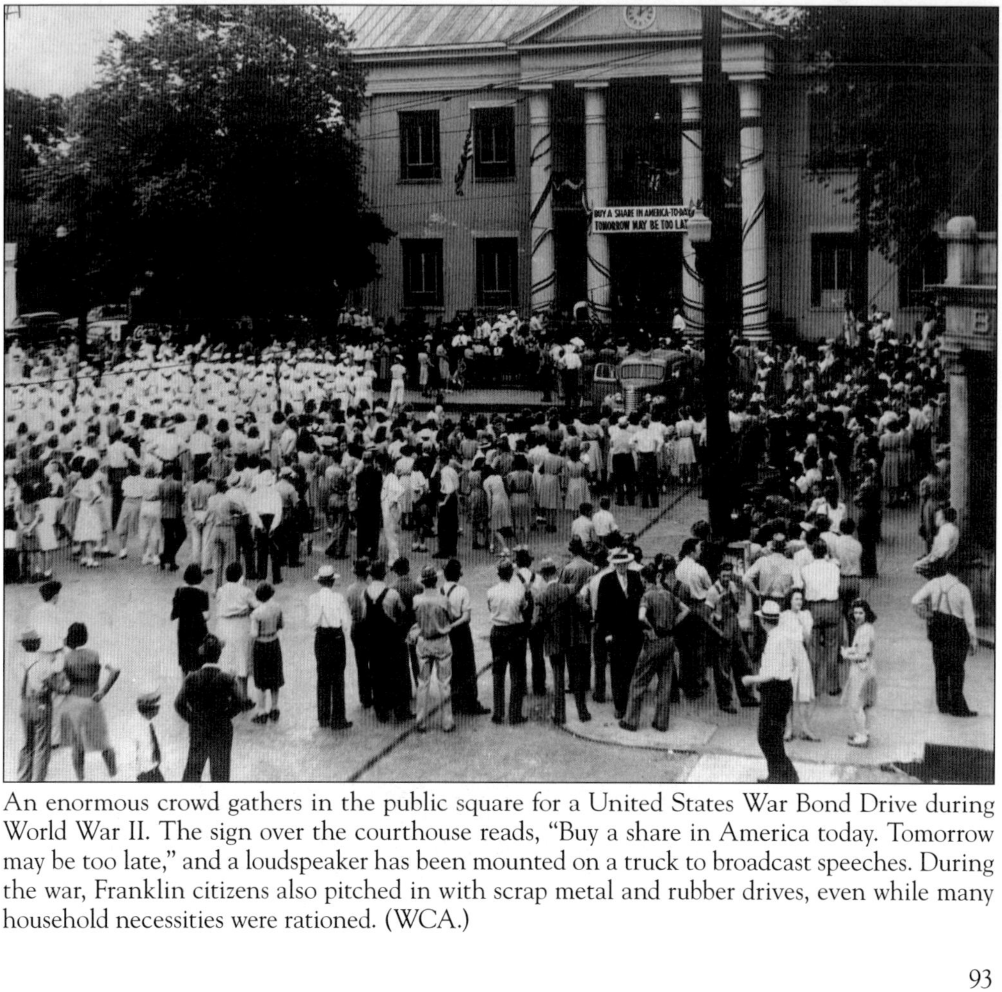

An enormous crowd gathers in the public square for a United States War Bond Drive during World War II. The sign over the courthouse reads, "Buy a share in America today. Tomorrow may be too late," and a loudspeaker has been mounted on a truck to broadcast speeches. During the war, Franklin citizens also pitched in with scrap metal and rubber drives, even while many household necessities were rationed. (WCA.)

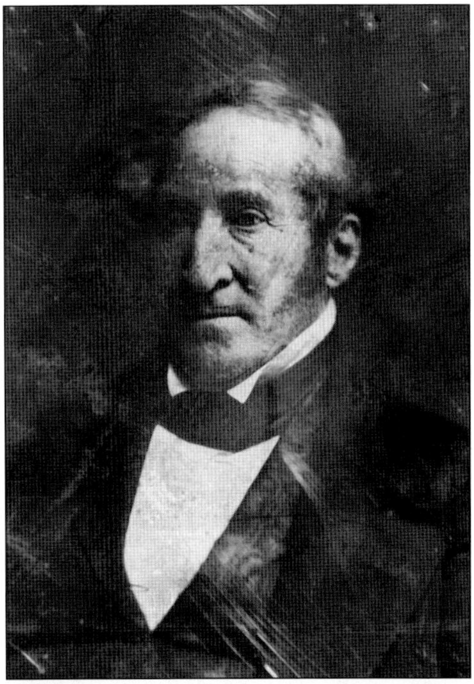

Thomas Hart Benton was a teenager when his family moved from North Carolina to Leiper's Fork in about 1799. He became a lawyer, a teacher, and a state representative while still in his twenties. After a fist fight with his friend Andrew Jackson, Benton moved to Missouri and became one of the most powerful men in the US Senate, where he championed "manifest destiny," the Homestead Act, and the limitation of slavery. (LOC.)

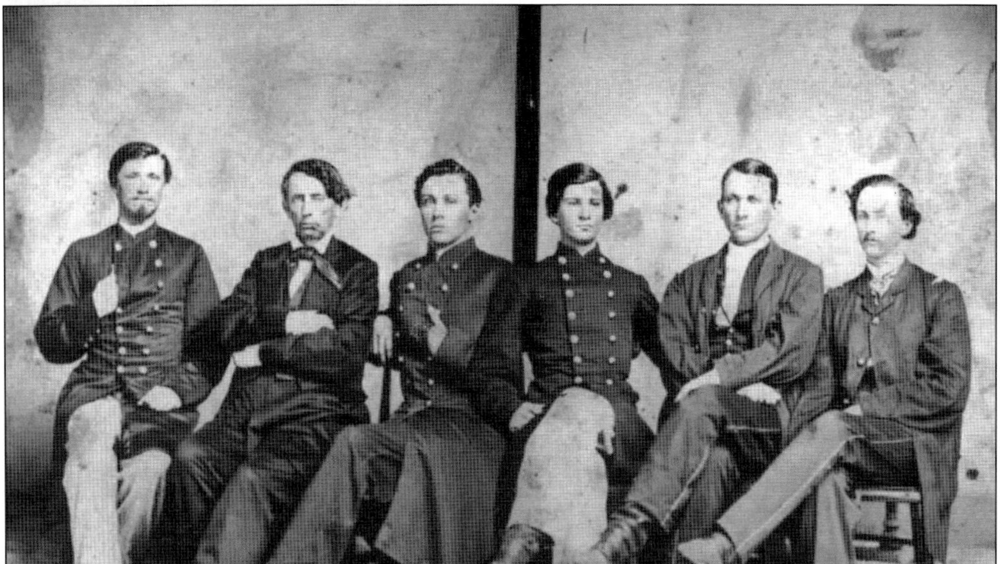

Brig. Gen. James Brownlow (left) is seated beside his father, Gov. William G. Brownlow, and the rest of the governor's cabinet in this 1866 photograph. At the time, James was adjutant general of the state, and he and his wife Belle were residents of Franklin. The Brownlows worked hard to heal the state's post–Civil War wounds, and when James, a Union veteran, died, his pallbearers included Confederate veterans.

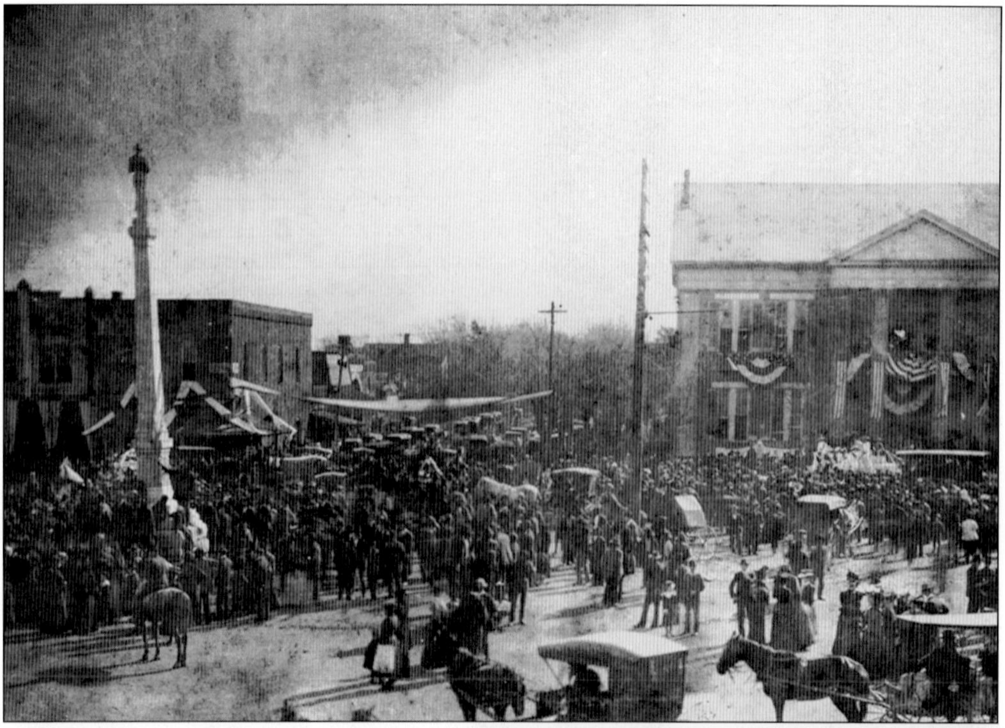

On November 30, 1899, on the 35th anniversary of the Battle of Franklin, the United Daughters of the Confederacy erected the Confederate Monument on Public Square. Rising over 37 feet, and surmounted by a six-foot tall soldier at parade rest, it stands at the center of the traffic circle in the figurative heart of Franklin life. After more than a century, the Confederate monument in the town square still gives testimony to the brave men who fought and died for the South, while its presence is a reminder of the healing and rebuilding done by all who have followed in their footsteps. During installation, a piece was broken from the brim of the statue's hat, earning him the nickname, "Chip." (Both, TSL.)

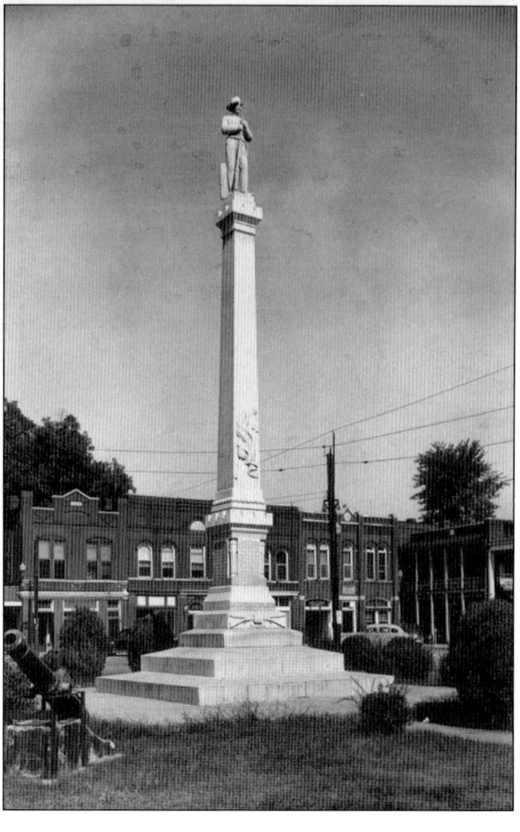

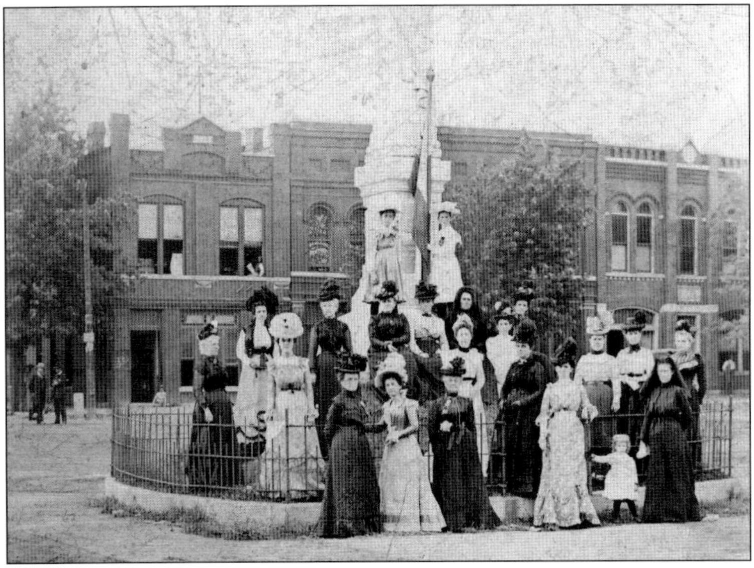

Shortly after the dedication of the monument in the square, The United Daughters of the Confederacy gathered for this portrait. It was they who conceived the idea for the statue, raised the money, and commissioned the sculpture. As evidenced by their mourning clothes, some of these women were Civil War widows. (BNTC.)

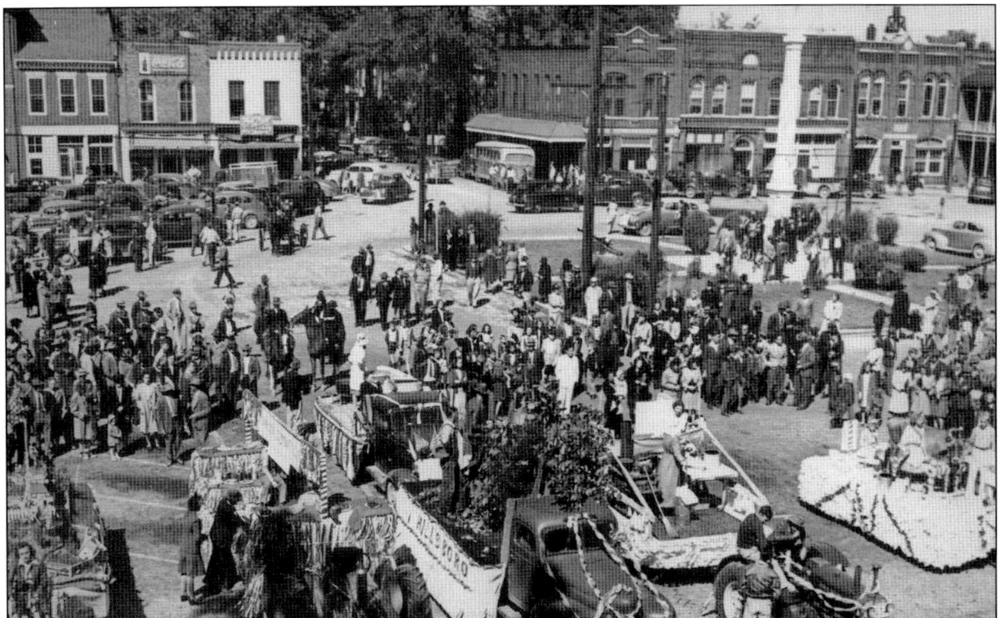

Citizens from all over Williamson County gather at the Franklin square for the annual county parade in this 1946 photograph. The celebration is in full swing, with each community contributing a float as the country emerges from the shadow of World War II. The Hillsboro float can be seen front and center on the flatbed truck, and at far right is a float featuring a girl milking a live Guernsey cow. (TSL.)

The Grand Lodge of United Brothers of Friendship and Sisters of the Mysterious Ten meet at Shorter Chapel in this photograph from 1926. The UBF and SMT were men's and women's African-American organizations founded in Louisville in 1861. One of the Franklin leaders was John Reddick, son of former slaves Bolen and Mariah Reddick. (TSL.)

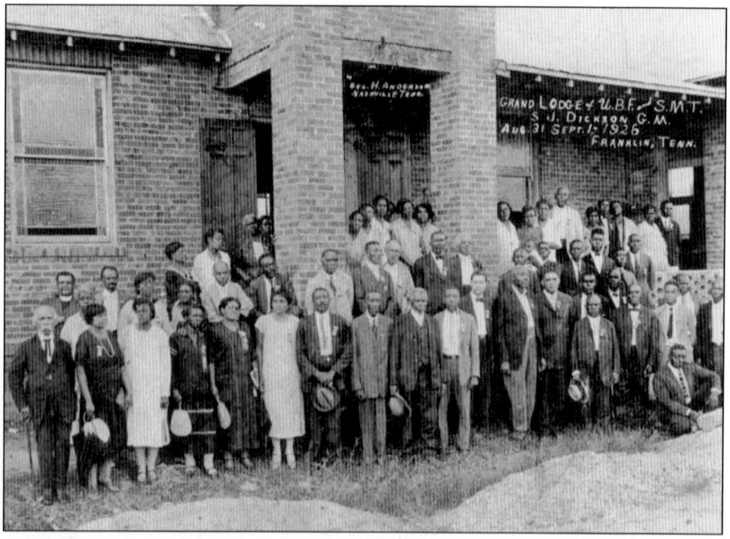

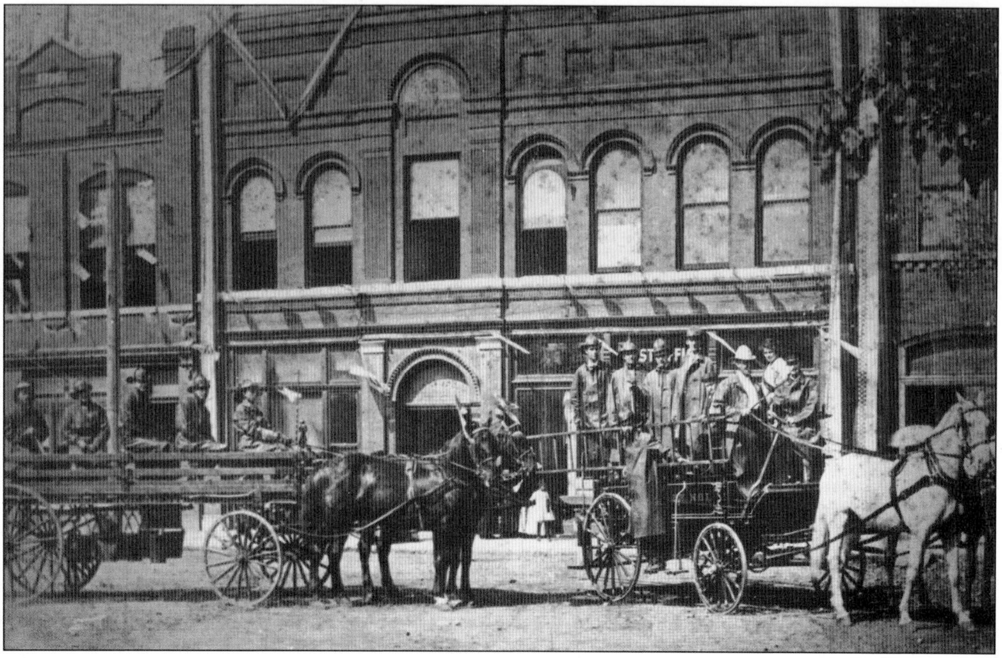

Throughout most of its history Franklin had a volunteer fire department, like the one pictured here in the early 1900s. As late as 1980, there was a single fire hall, which shared the building with the city hall and police department. Today, the department is housed in half a dozen fire halls and responds to over 6,000 calls per year.

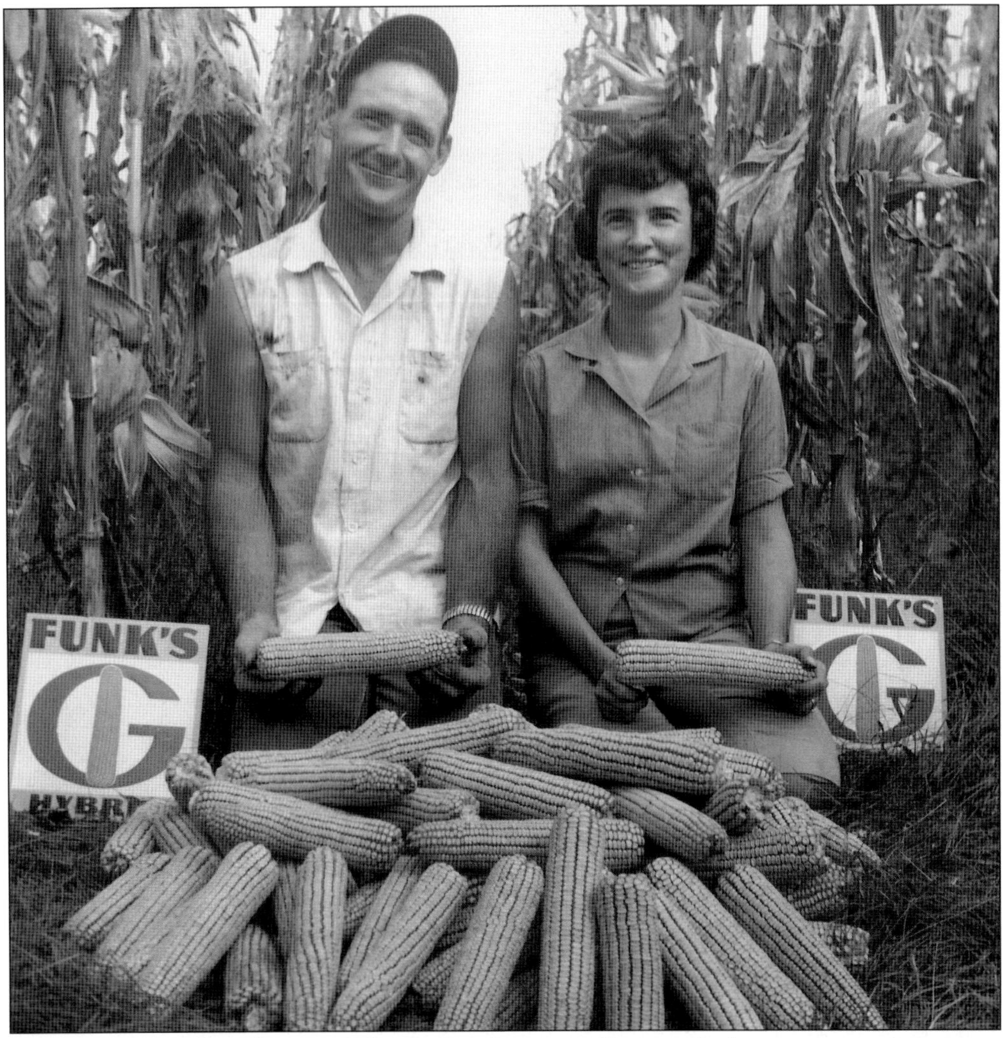

Clyde Dorris Lynch and Louise Gillespie Lynch, pictured here with their corn crop, were civic-minded farmers. Clyde was a Navy veteran and served as president of the Williamson County Farmers Co-op. All of that was in addition to becoming a county commissioner—a post he held for almost four decades. For much of that time he was the budget committee chairman, and was known to his friends as "Gatekeeper of the Budget." He also served for 20 years on the board of Williamson County Medical Center, and helped select the site for the hospital. Louise was director of the Williamson County Archives for many years. Starting as a volunteer and organizing files in the cramped basement of the post office, she relied on donated supplies. She was responsible for organizing the displays, moving the archives into the previous library, and creating an inviting public resource for education and research. The old library building now bears her name as the Louise G. Lynch Archives and Museum.

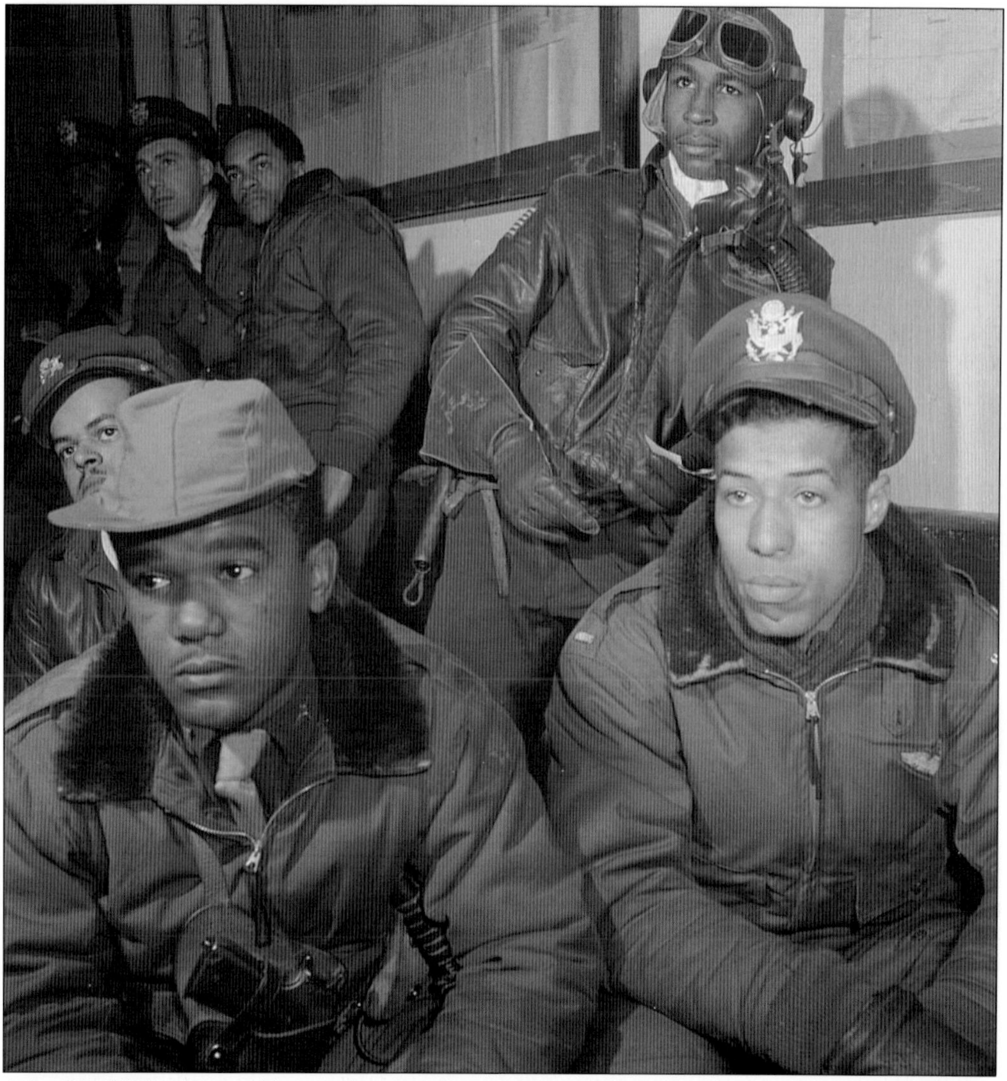

After World War II, Franklin was home to three of the famed Tuskegee Airmen. Robert J. Murdic Jr., pictured center as he leans against a wall during a briefing in Ramitelli, Italy, grew up in Franklin, as did Thomas G. Patton. Dr. Joseph C. White was originally from Chattanooga. The three of them were among 450 Tuskegee pilots to fly combat missions over Germany, providing fighter escorts for US heavy bombers. Also called "Redtails" because the tails of some of their airplanes were painted red, the Tuskegee Airmen included the 332nd Fighter Group and 477th Bombardment Group. They were America's first African American military pilots, and their great success was a major step in integrating the nation's armed forces, which had been segregated until that time.

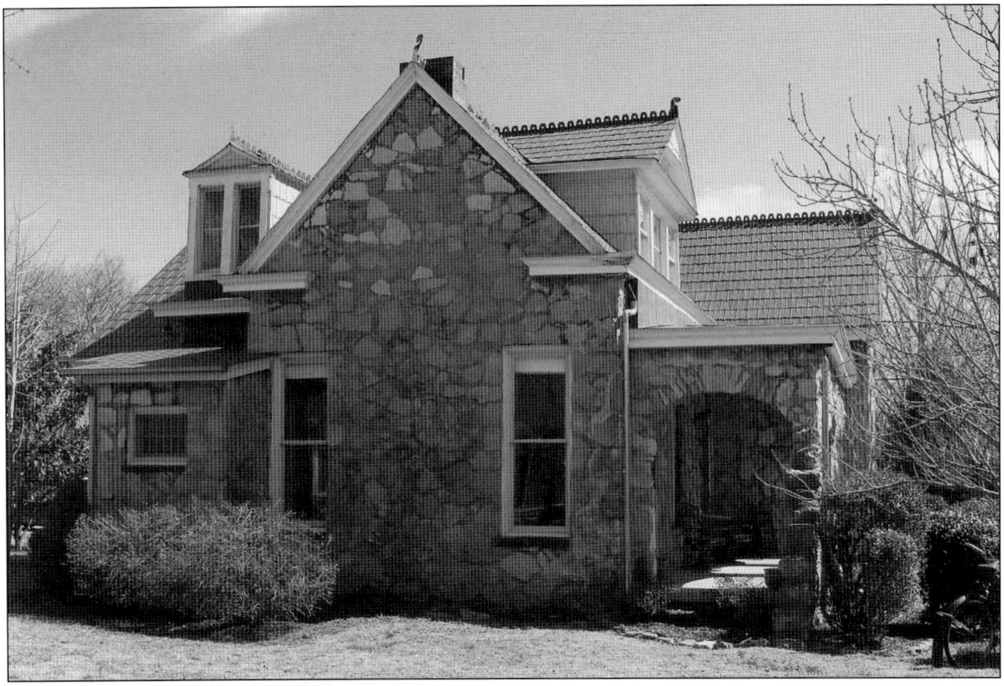

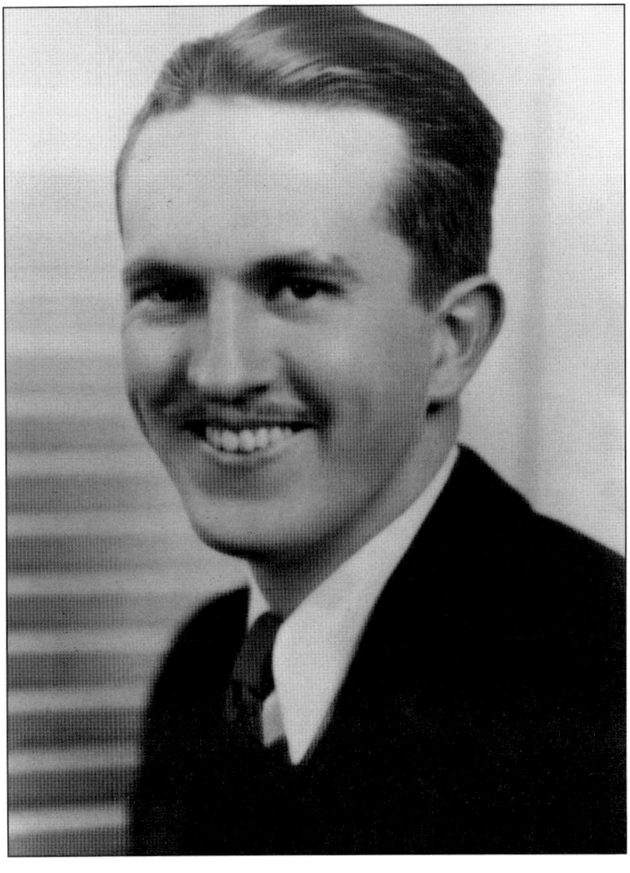

Dr. Dan German bought the above private home in 1938, and, with his son-in-law, Dr. Tandy Rice (left), turned it into a hospital. Dr. Harry Guffee and German's brother Richard, a dentist, also had offices in the hospital. There were four patient rooms and a ward, and a wing was added later. Though there were separate waiting and operating rooms for white and African American patients, the hospital's commitment to serving people of all colors was progressive and compassionate for the era. The hospital served as the county's health care center for 20 years, finally closing when the Williamson County Hospital opened. The building has been preserved as a monument to Franklin's early, caring health professionals.

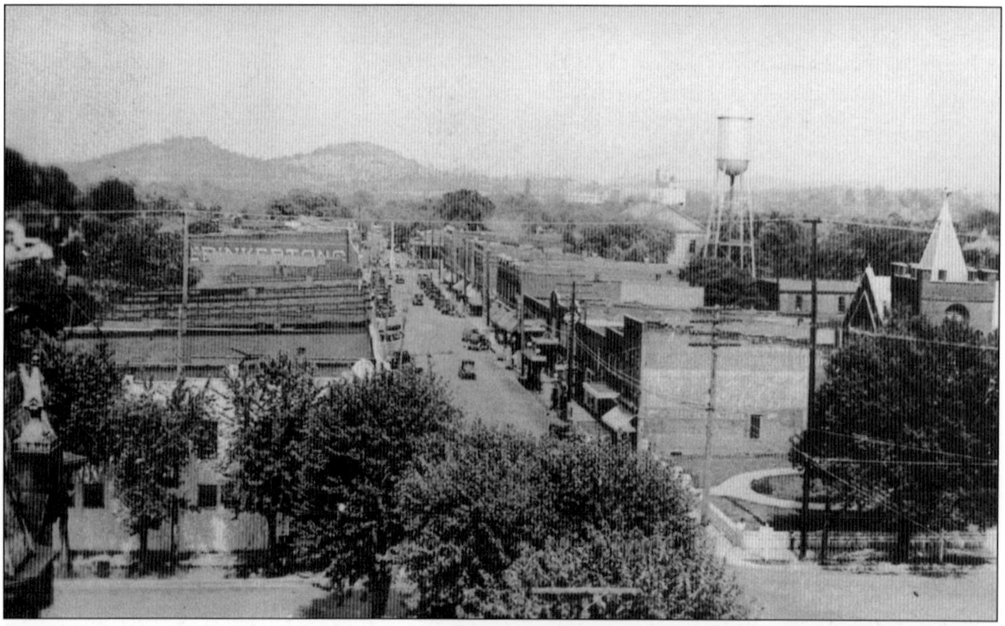

In this 1925 photograph looking north from the tower of St. Paul's Episcopal Church, the city's water tank rises over Main Street and its web of electric lines. On the right is the historic Presbyterian church, and in the distance are the grain elevators of the Lillie Mill. Cars line the street, and one pulls away from the gas pumps on the sidewalk. (TSL.)

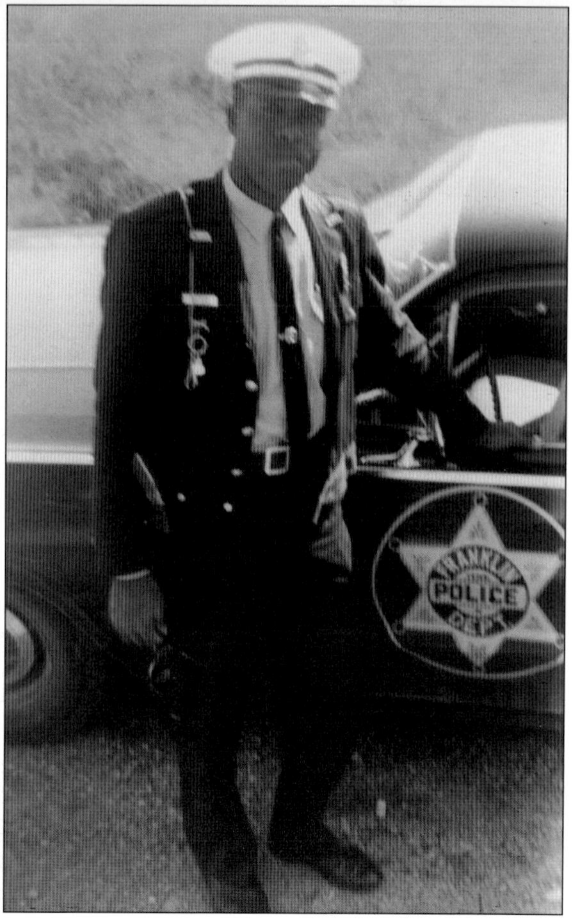

In the 1960s, Lee Douglas Waters, a graduate of Franklin Training School, became Franklin's first African American police officer. He was a husband and father, as well as a Mason, an Optimist, and a youth sports coach. Barbara Lane Derricks, also an African American, was the first permanent female officer. After becoming an officer in the 1980s, she quickly rose to detective sergeant and served the department for 16 years.

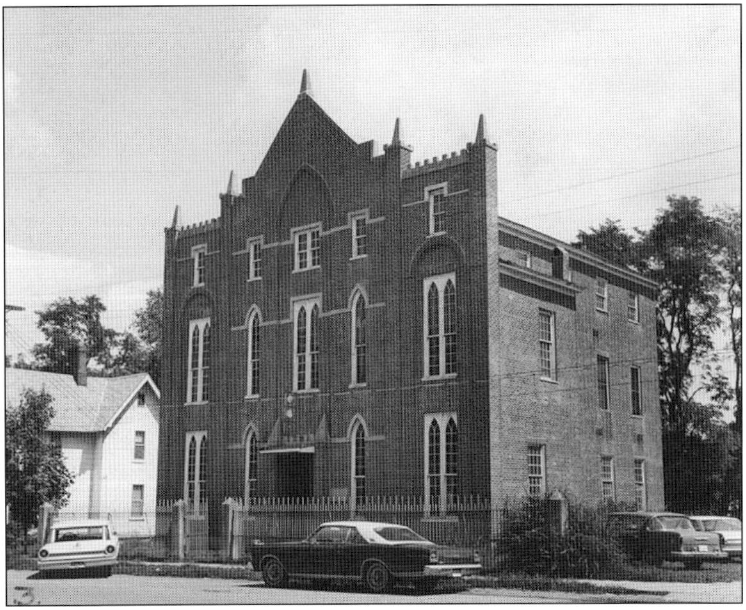

The Hiram Masonic Lodge was founded in 1809, and the Masonic hall was built in 1823. It was the first public building in Franklin, and the first three-story building in Tennessee. It served as a hospital for wounded Civil War soldiers, as a public meetinghouse, and as a temporary home for several churches. Today, it is the oldest Masonic hall in continuous use in the state. (TSL.)

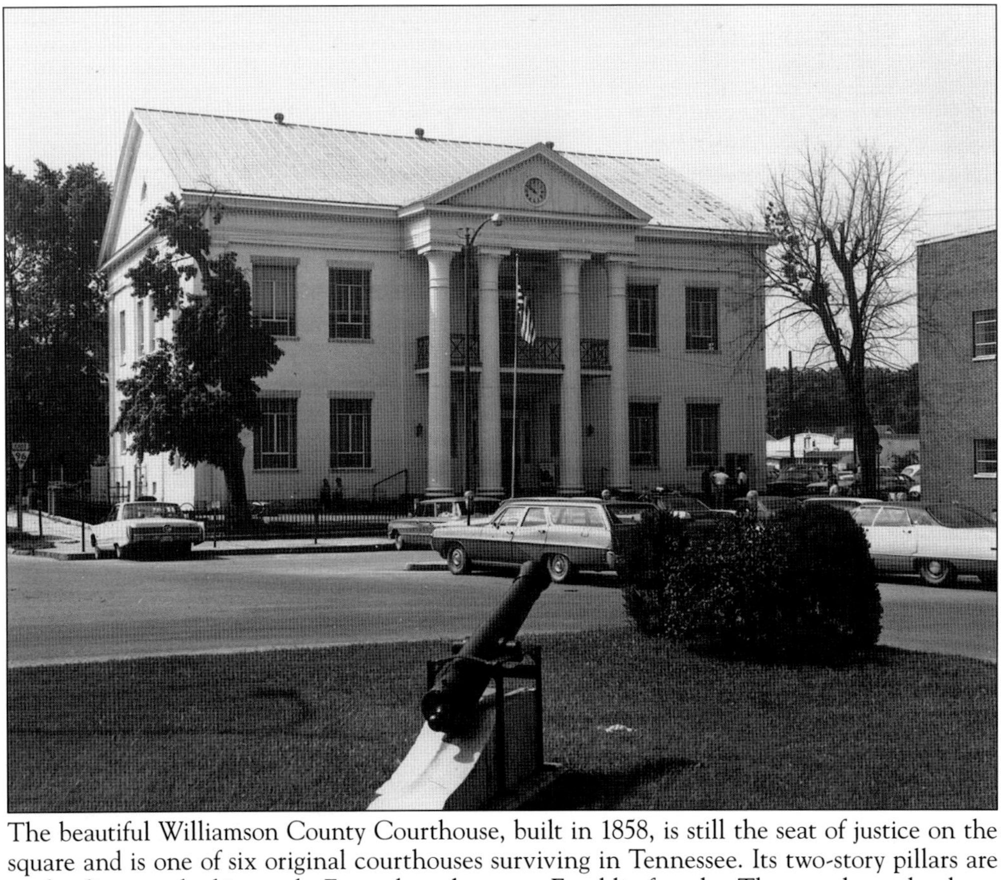

The beautiful Williamson County Courthouse, built in 1858, is still the seat of justice on the square and is one of six original courthouses surviving in Tennessee. Its two-story pillars are made of iron smelted in nearby Fernvale and cast at a Franklin foundry. The courthouse has been remodeled several times, and an annex was added in 1976. (TSL.)

The carriage and parts in this 1924 photograph suggest that a livery was using this vacant lot for storage, but the space would soon become the home of a stylish new post office. To the left is the Franklin School, with the tower of the Cumberland Presbyterian Church peeking over its roof, and on the right is St. Paul's Episcopal Church. A campaign banner stretches over Main Street near the church. (WCA.)

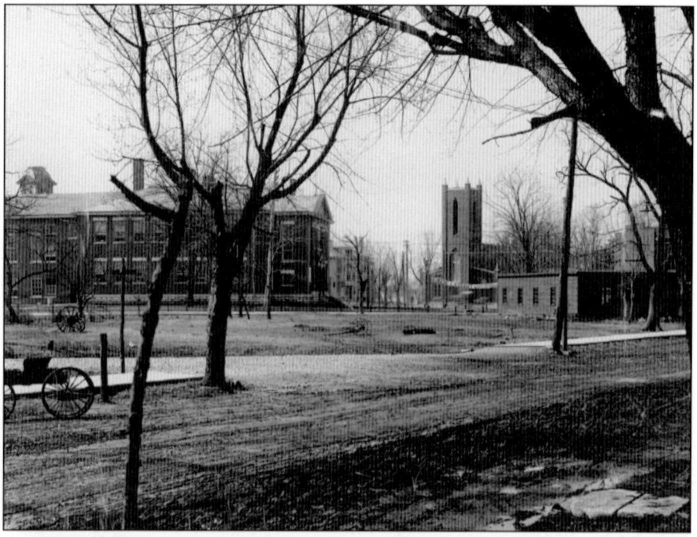

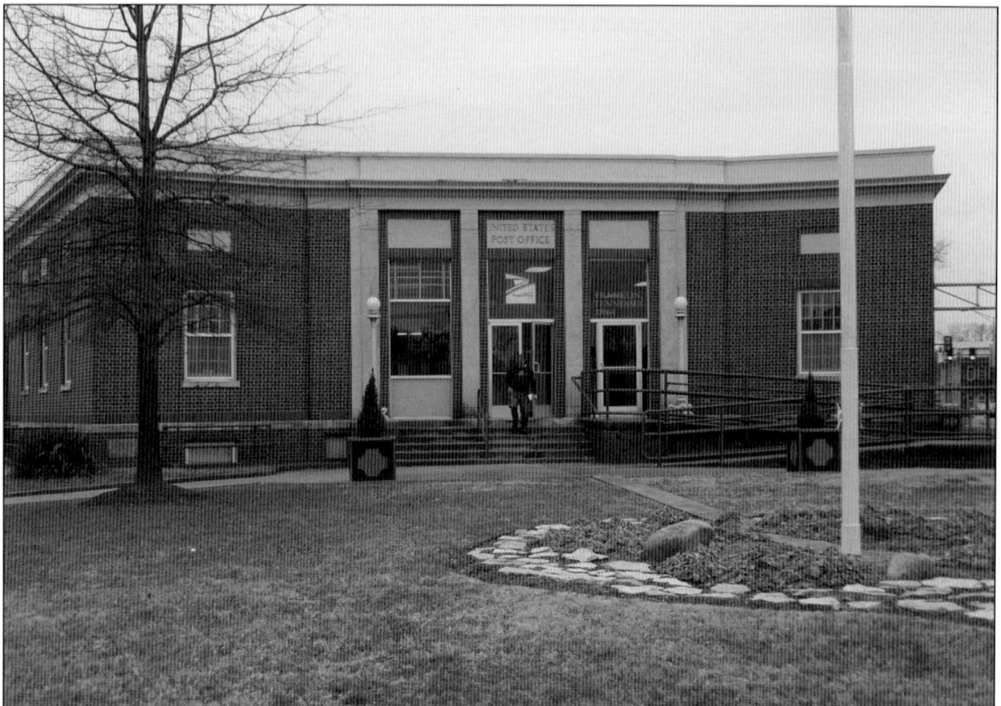

Franklin's post office at Five Points was built in 1925. Its angled shape and clean lines gave it a truly unique and futuristic design for the time. In 1990, when the US Postal Service planned to close the branch, citizens fought for its protection through the National Trust for Historic Preservation. An agreement was reached that preserved the old building, while the post office also opened a new location. (TSL.)

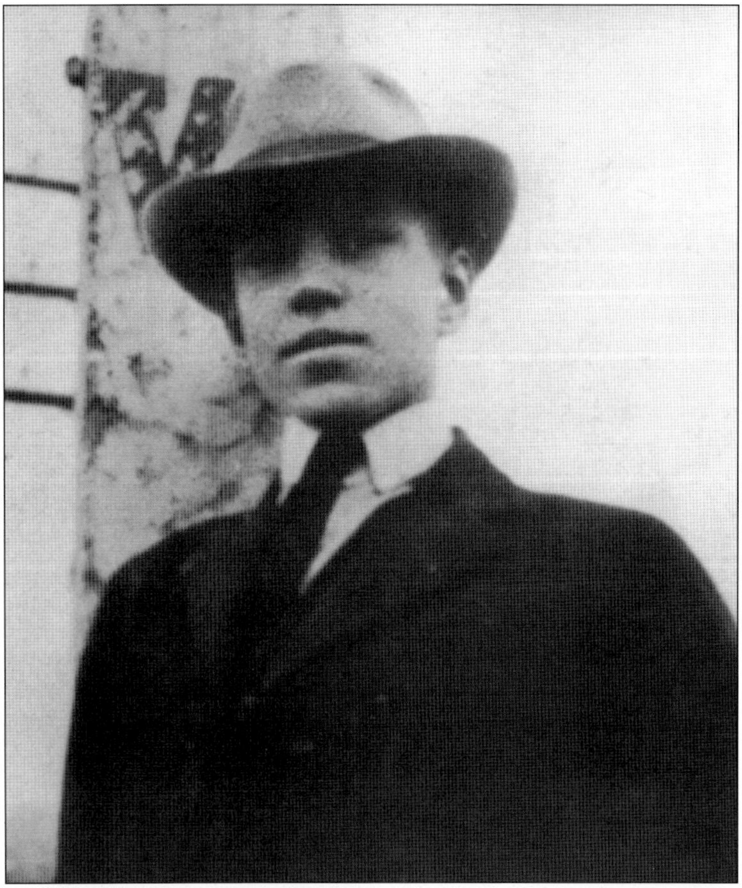

Sam M. Fleming, pictured here in 1922, started his banking career in New York, returned to his hometown Franklin, served in the Navy Reserve in World War II, and then rose to become chairman of Third National Bank. He was a director of the Federal Reserve Bank of Atlanta, and was an uncommon philanthropist. He chaired the board of Vanderbilt University, and served other schools and numerous charities and organizations, including the Boy Scouts. (TSL.)

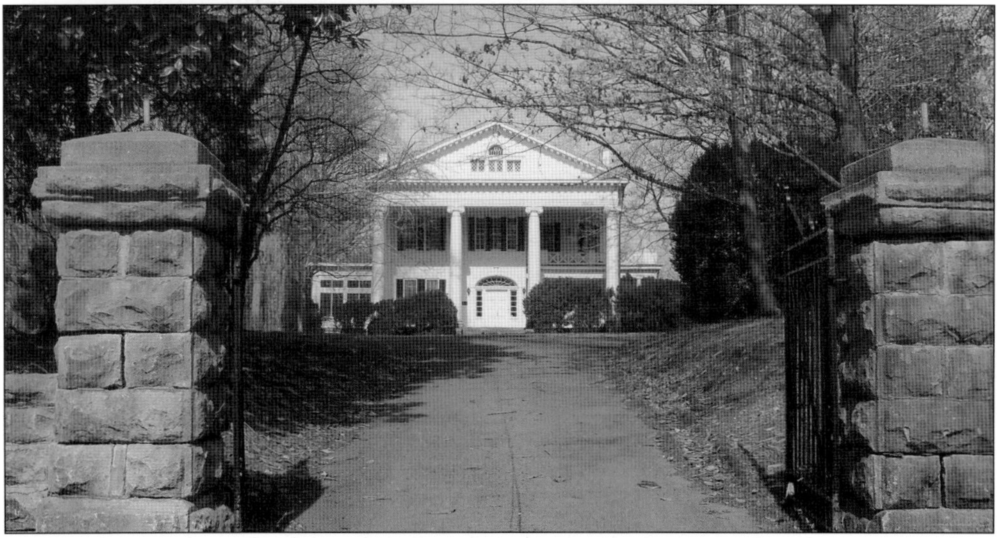

Built in the Neoclassical style in 1902, Riverview sits on 20-plus acres where horses graze along the north bank of the Harpeth River. It is one of several Franklin homes of exquisite design and construction that are listed in the National Register of Historic Places. Franklin has eight National Historic Districts, and one Local Historic District within a Historic Preservation Overlay.

Seven

Franklin's Spiritual Life

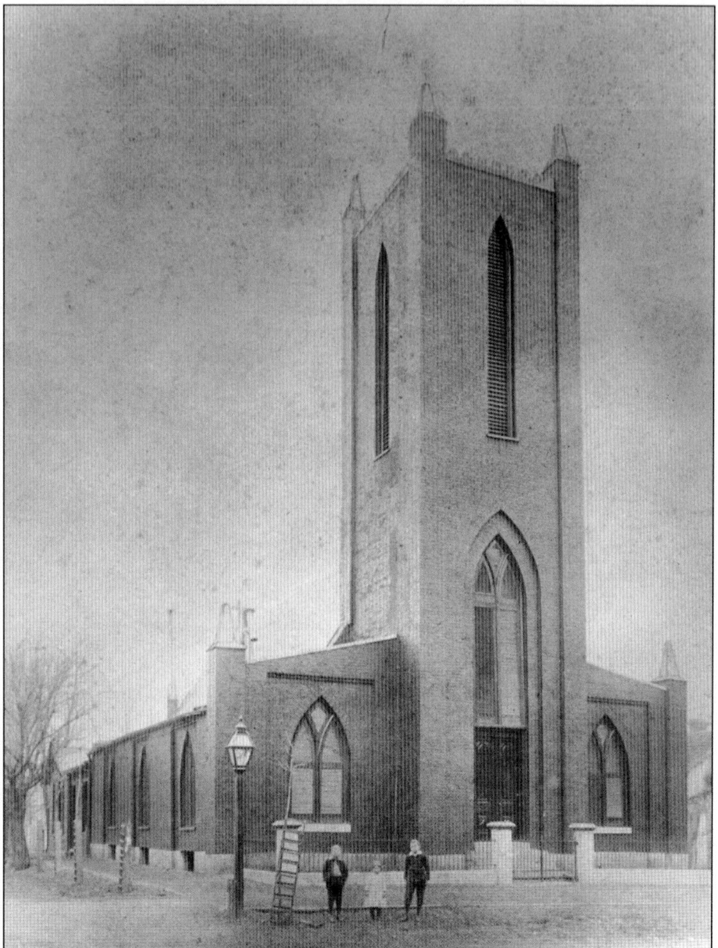

By 1834, the Episcopal congregation founded by Bishop Otey had built St. Paul's Episcopal Church, shown in this photograph taken around 1900. It originally had a second story "slave gallery," but the building was heavily damaged by Civil War troops. When it was restored, the second floor was removed. Today, St. Paul's doors are never locked, and it continues to serve an active congregation. (Courtesy of St. Paul's Episcopal.)

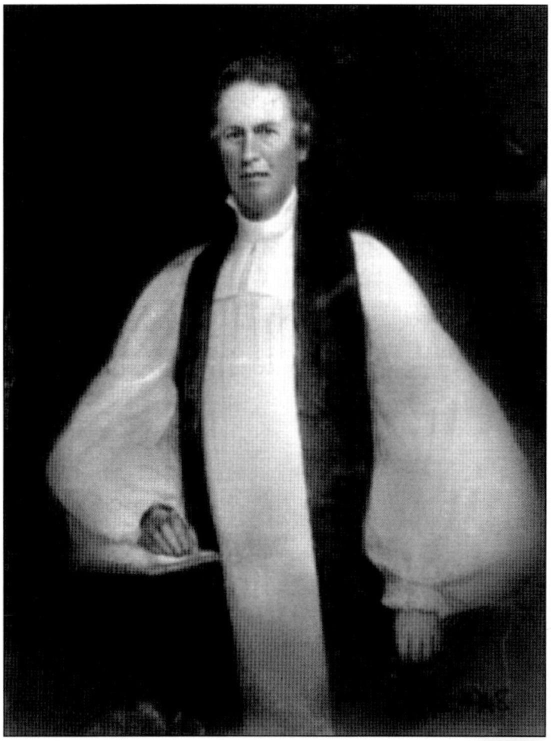

In 1827, the newly ordained James Hervey Otey organized the first Episcopal church in Tennessee, holding services at the Masonic hall in Franklin. Otey was a native of Virginia educated in North Carolina. He organized other Tennessee churches before founding the Episcopal Diocese of Tennessee (headquartered in Nashville), becoming its first bishop, and going on to plant churches from Pennsylvania to the Indian Territory. (TSL.)

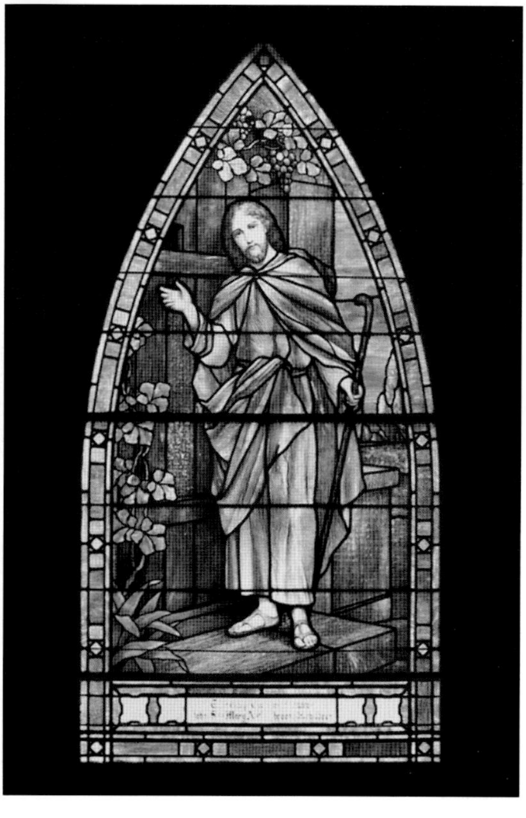

St. Paul's Episcopal is the home of eight opalescent windows created by Louis Comfort Tiffany. The artistry is striking, and the windows seem to come to life on close inspection. Because the glass is three-dimensional, the folds of the garments seem to billow toward the viewer. Tiffany used a special type of glass called Favrile glass, and carried the formula for it to his grave. It has never been duplicated. (Courtesy of St. Paul's Episcopal.)

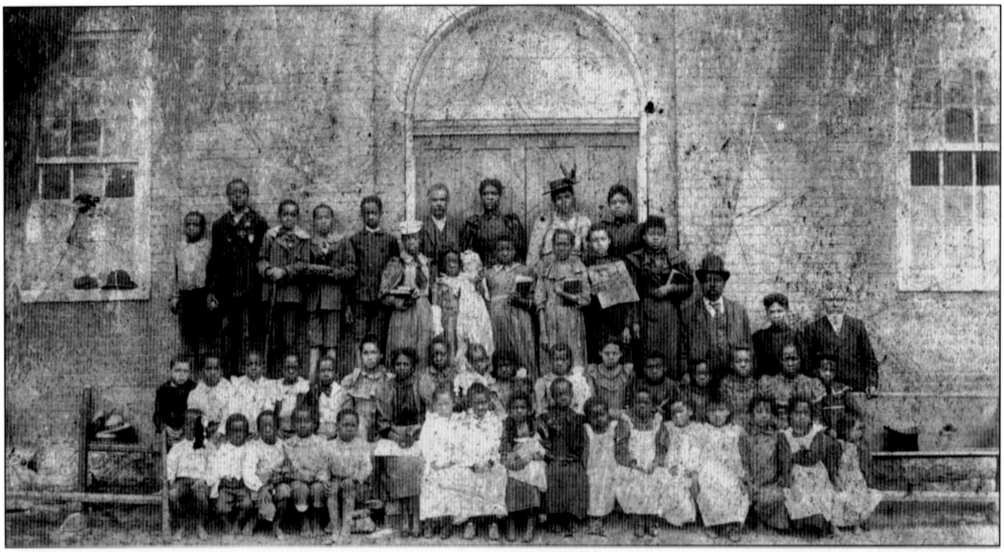

The congregation poses on the steps of Shorter Chapel African Methodist Episcopal Church in this 1900 photograph. Like all of the local African American churches, it was vital to the spiritual, social, and civic lives of the community following emancipation. Shorter Chapel was founded in 1868, and the church bought this building on Second Avenue from the Methodists in 1873.

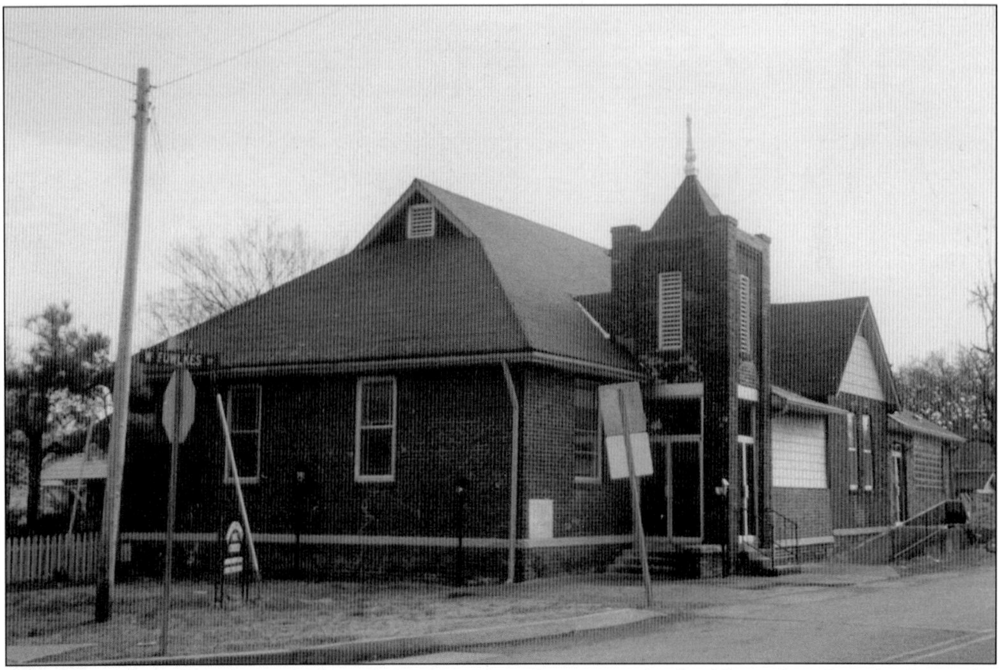

For about 50 years, Shorter Chapel A.M.E. Church met in the building they bought from the Methodists. Then, in 1925—to be closer to its African American members—the church was dismantled and the slave-made bricks were hand-carried to Natchez and Folkes Streets, where they were reassembled as this inviting Victorian-style building. The church still meets there today. (WCA.)

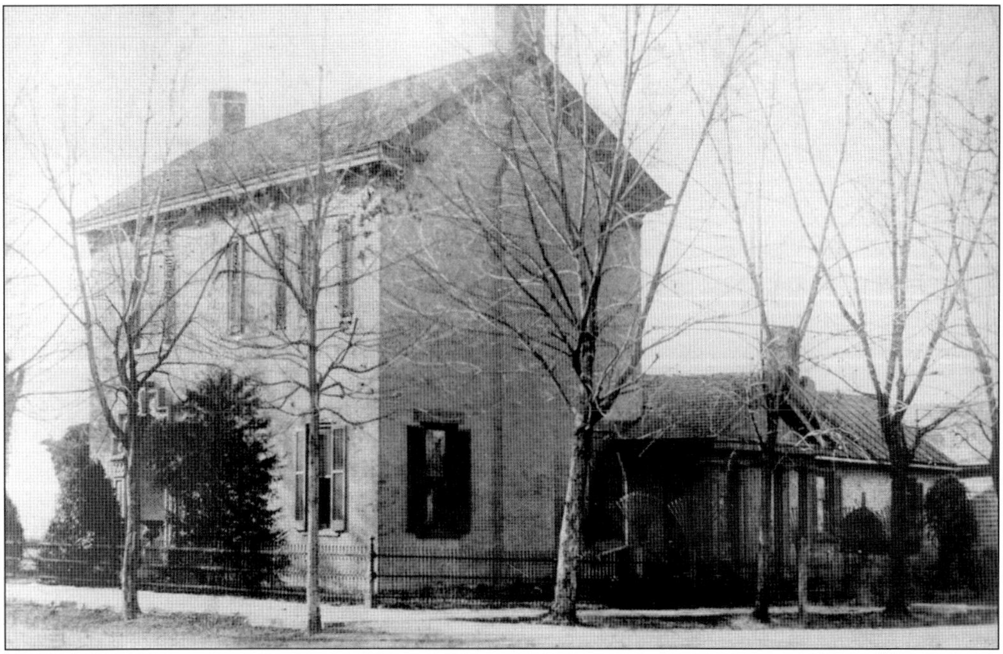

The home of the Joe L. Parkes family stood across the street from St. Paul's Episcopal Church. When the Civil War started, Federal troops occupied Franklin, including the church, so, to keep the church's silver service and other valuables safe, they were taken out and hidden in a box that was lowered into the cistern of the Parkes house.

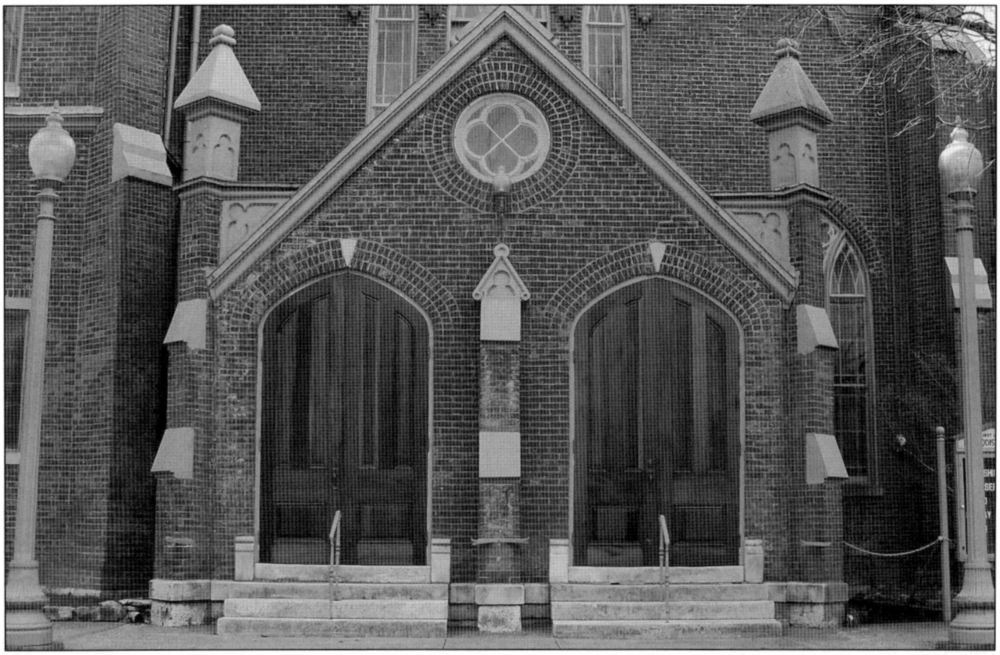

When Abram Maury laid out the city in 1799, he donated a site for the town's Methodist church and the original two-story brick building was constructed using slave labor. Today, the First United Methodist Church meets in the historic sanctuary, which was built in 1871. The building's steeple was lost to a tornado, but has been replaced and still uses the original bell.

Presbyterians have been worshipping in downtown Franklin since Rev. Gideon Blackburn organized the first church in 1811. They built at this Five Points location in 1845, which, like many buildings in Franklin, served as a hospital during the Civil War. In 1888, the building was replaced with a beautiful brick structure that was destroyed by fire in 1905. It was rebuilt and is still in use today. (WCA.)

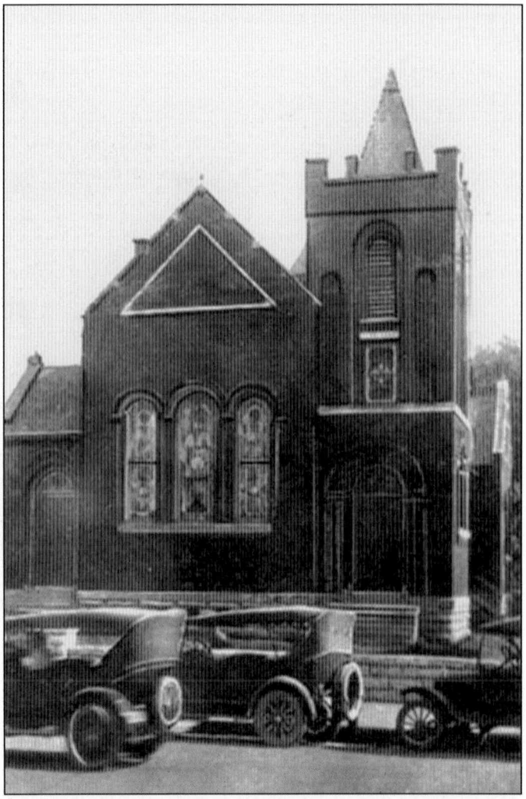

The Franklin Cumberland Presbyterian congregation was founded in 1871 and worshipped in various places until this brick building was designed by H.C. Thompson, the architect of Nashville's Ryman Auditorium. It was dedicated in 1877, making it the fourth oldest church in town. Its steeple was lost in a tornado but was replaced, and the church still serves the community on the corner of Main Street and Seventh Avenue.

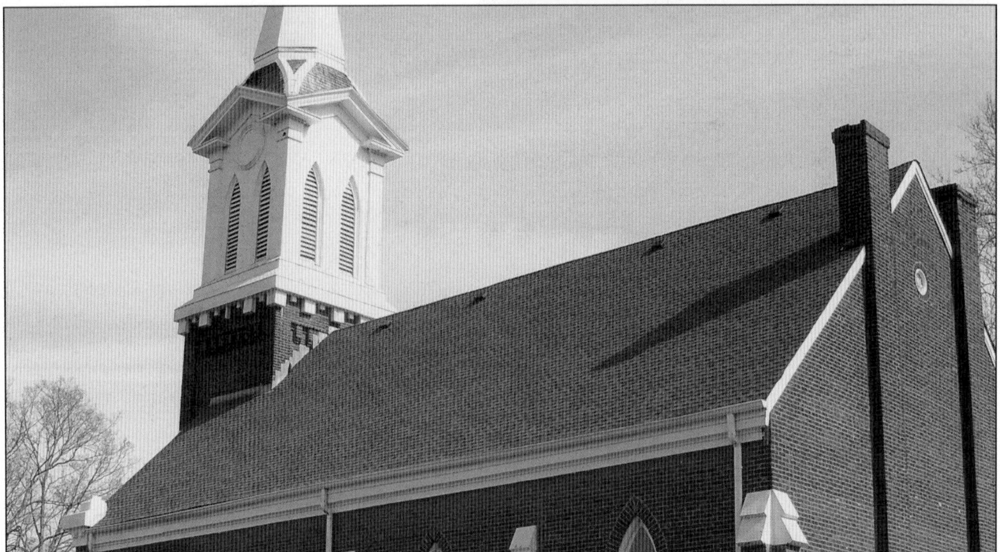

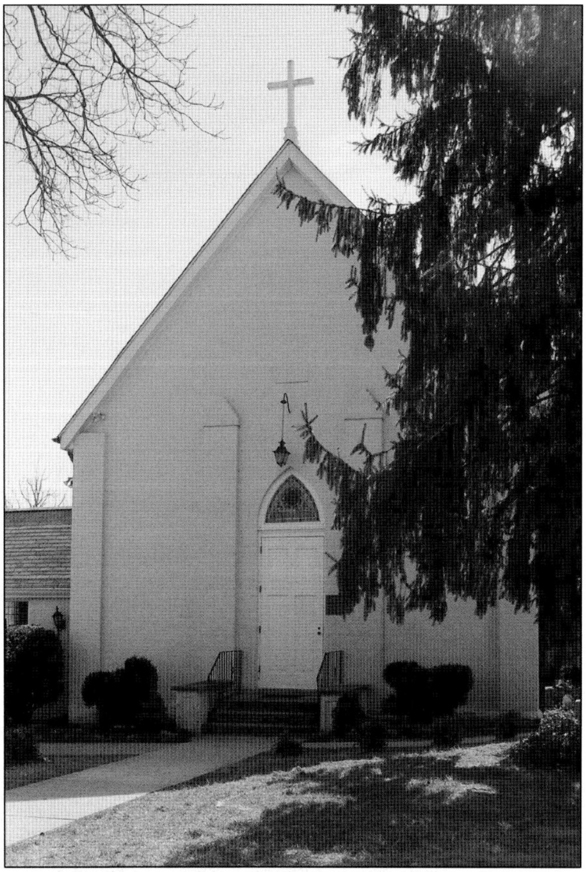

Many of the railroad workers who came to Franklin were Irish, and many of them decided to stay. This gave the city a substantial Catholic population. However, they had no church until well after the Civil War. In 1871, they dug the clay, fired the bricks, and built St. Phillip's on Second Avenue. Today, with several newer, connected buildings, the church stands at the same location.

A group of 17 people organized the Fourth Avenue Church of Christ in 1833, making it one of the oldest congregations of the American Restoration movement. In 1852, they erected their first brick house of worship (pictured), which stood until it was destroyed by a tornado in 1927. The new building stood for another 50 years before it was replaced by the current structure. Each of these buildings stood at the same location.

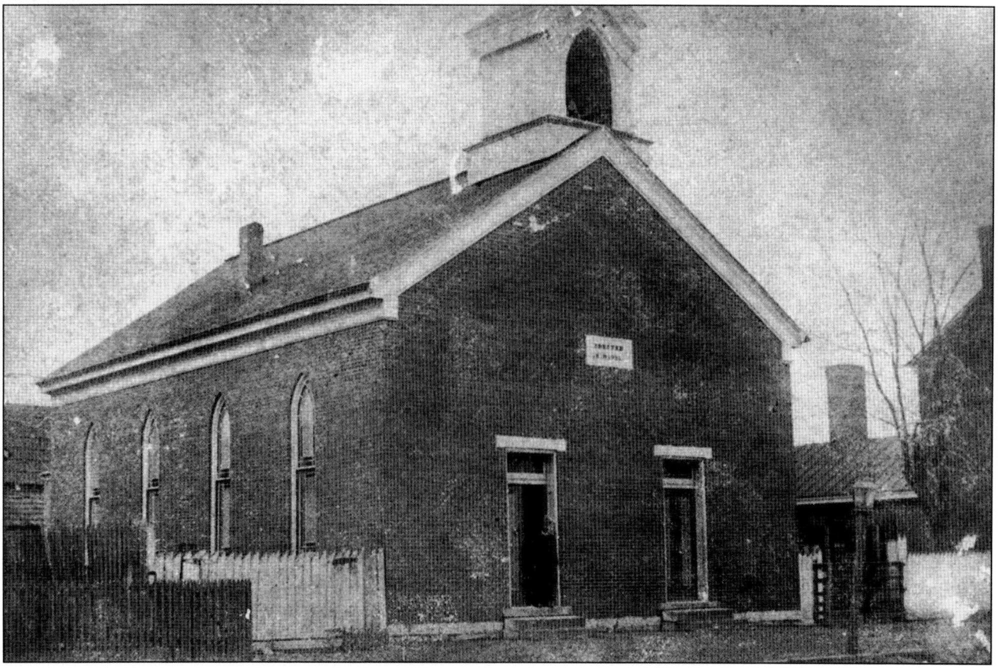

Eight

The Spirit of Franklin

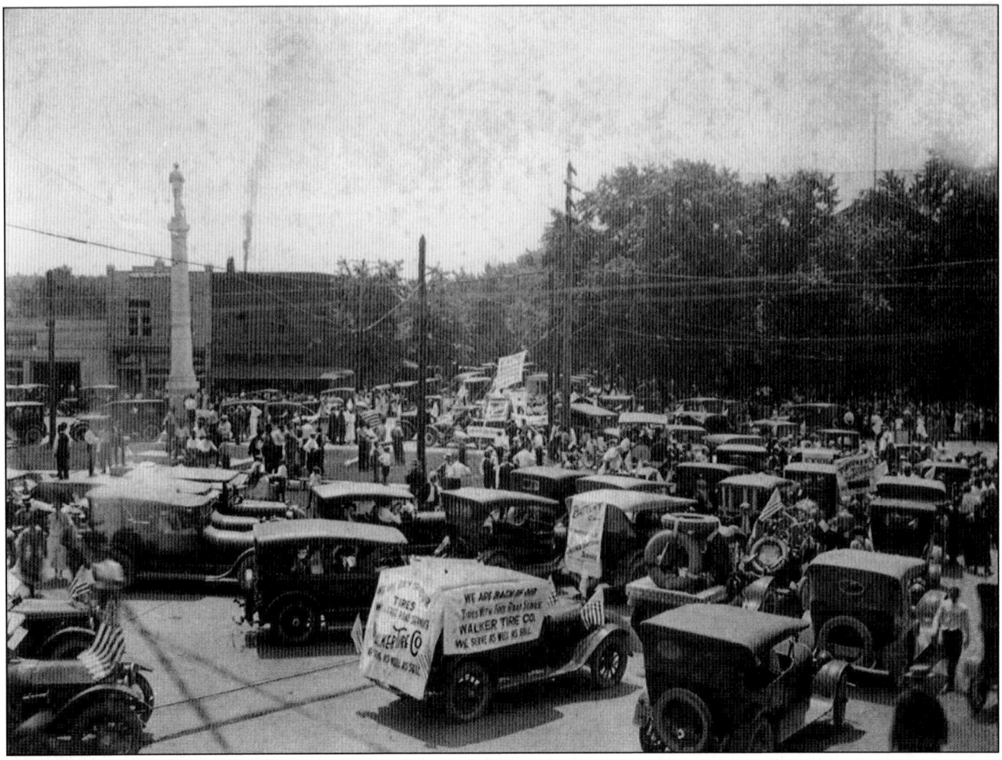

For many years, Franklin businesspeople would decorate their vehicles and travel the county in a Booster Parade. Participating businesses advertised their goods and services with signs, and local dignitaries and business leaders addressed large crowds in each town along the route. All of this was aimed at inviting people to do their shopping in Franklin. Everybody was welcome to join in, and some families went along for the ride.

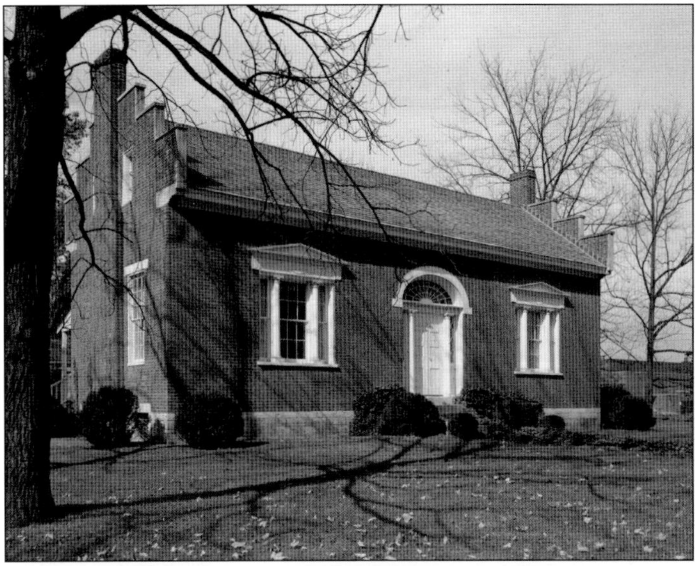

In 1951, a developer was planning to demolish the Carter House, one of the city's historic treasures, and replace it with a service station. Two years later, the house was opened to the public, and, in 1961, it was listed in the National Register of Historic Places. In 1994, the house was fully restored to look as it did at the time of the battle, November 30, 1864. (BOFT.)

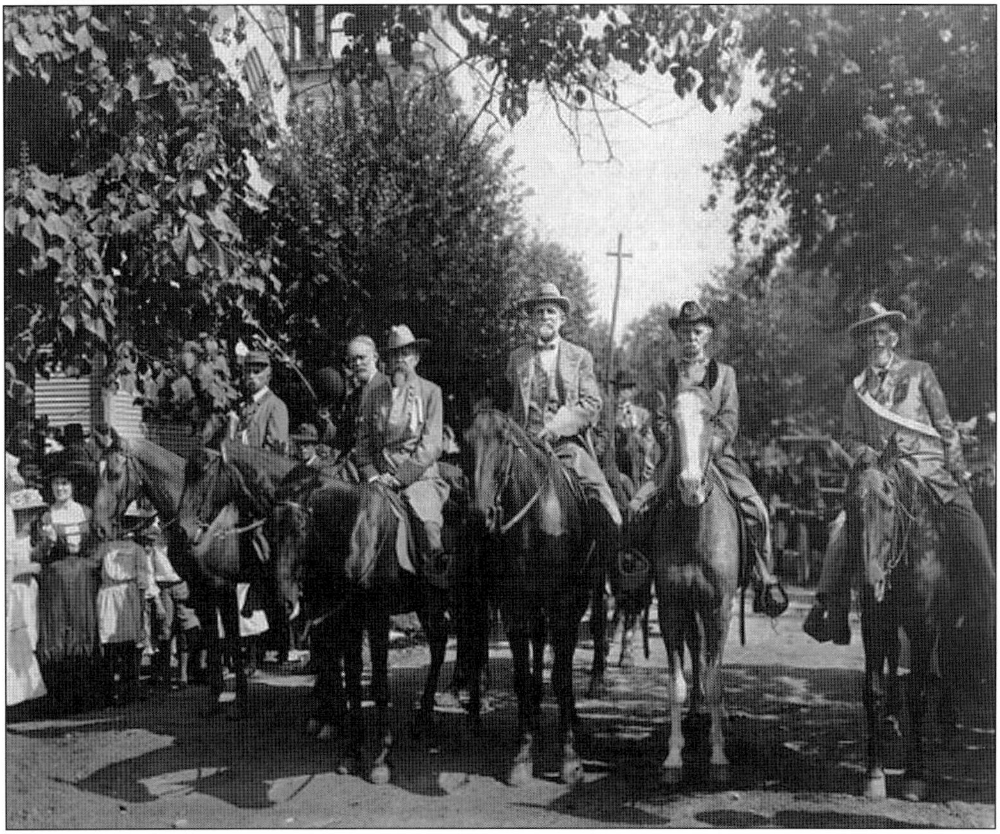

One of the remarkable contributions Franklin made to the legacy of the Civil War was the way she welcomed veterans, including hosting several reunions. At the pictured reunion, held at Carnton Plantation in October 1910, Brig. Gen. George W. Gordon is seen with his staff. One of the youngest generals in the battle of Franklin, Gordon was wounded and captured. After the war he became an attorney, Indian agent, and US congressman. (BNTC.)

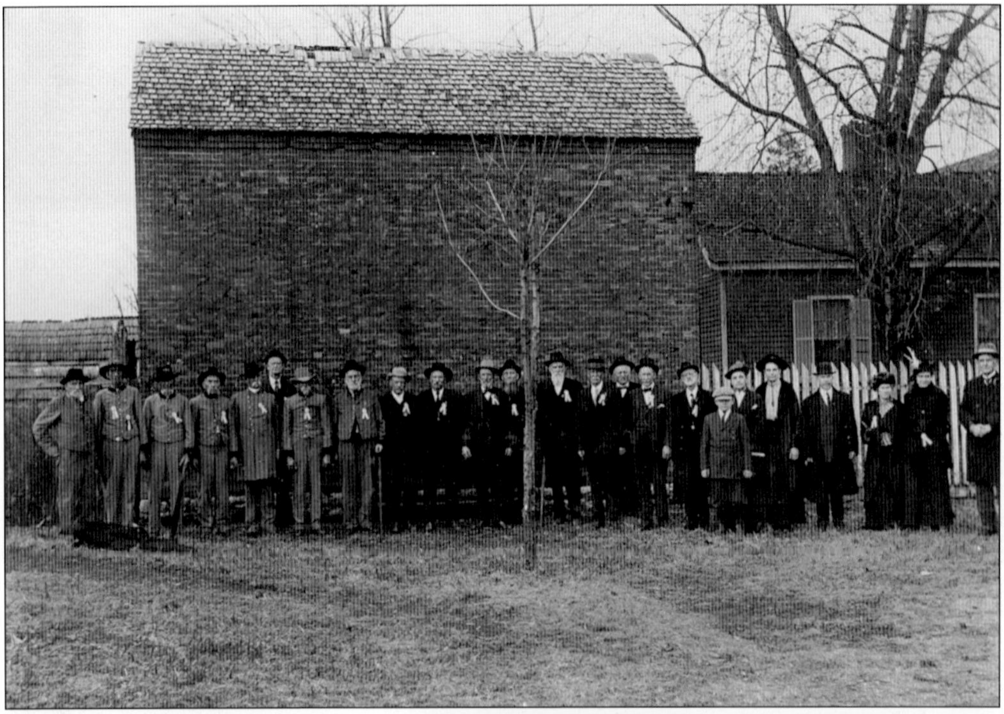

The spirit of Franklin showed brightly at "The Blue and Gray Reunion" in 1914. Veterans of both armies, most of them survivors of the Battle of Franklin, gathered while wearing souvenir buttons bearing a picture of two soldiers in blue and gray shaking hands. Pictured here beside the bullet-scarred smokehouse on the Carter farm, they opened the door to a new era of honoring the past and embracing the future. (BOFT.)

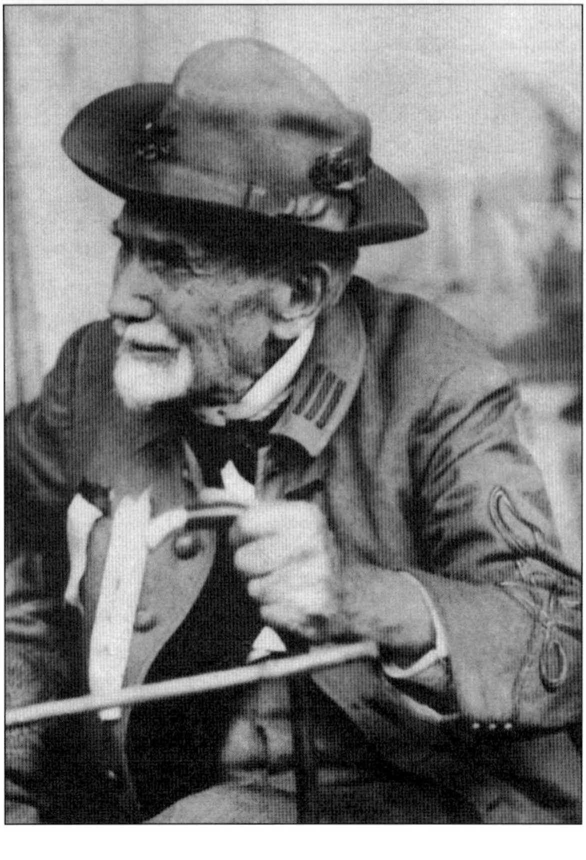

Hardin Perkins Cochrane was a teenager when he enlisted in the Confederate army, and later resigned his position as a drill sergeant to join the 2nd Alabama Cavalry. After the Civil War he completed his medical training in New York, where he became head of the Colored Home Hospital. He married his cousin, Leighla Perkins, a descendant of Franklin's founder, Abram Maury, and, together they owned one of Franklin's first automobiles.

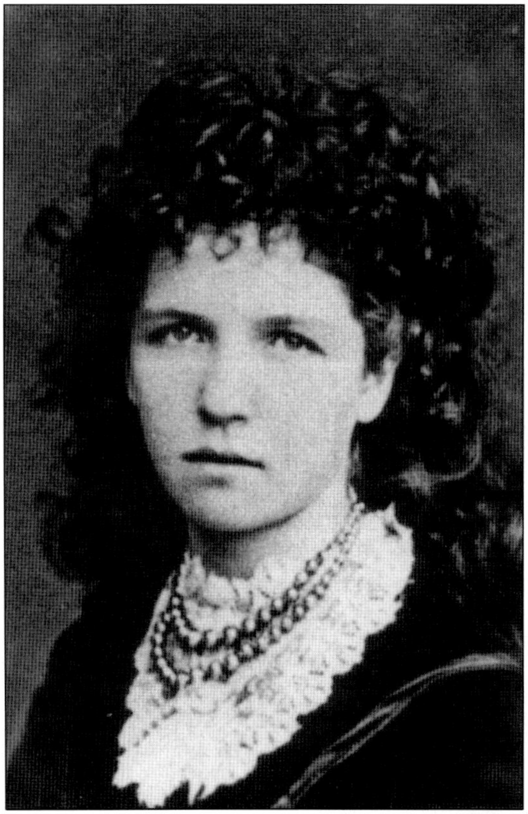

There is an apparent sadness in the eyes of Matilda Lotz in the picture to the left of her as a youngster. The daughter of Albert Johann and Margaret Lotz, she suffered the trauma of the Battle of Franklin at the age of six. But Matilda would not let that define her life. She loved farm animals, and enjoyed painting the wonders of the natural world around her. She became a self-sufficient, fiercely independent woman, wearing pants rather than the long dresses other women wore in the late 1800s, and even traveling abroad without a chaperone. After studying in France and traveling the world, Matilda became an internationally recognized artist, with her portraits of people, horses, wild animals, and pets being in high demand. The below portrait of her looking self-assured with her palette was painted in Paris. (Both, Lotz House.)

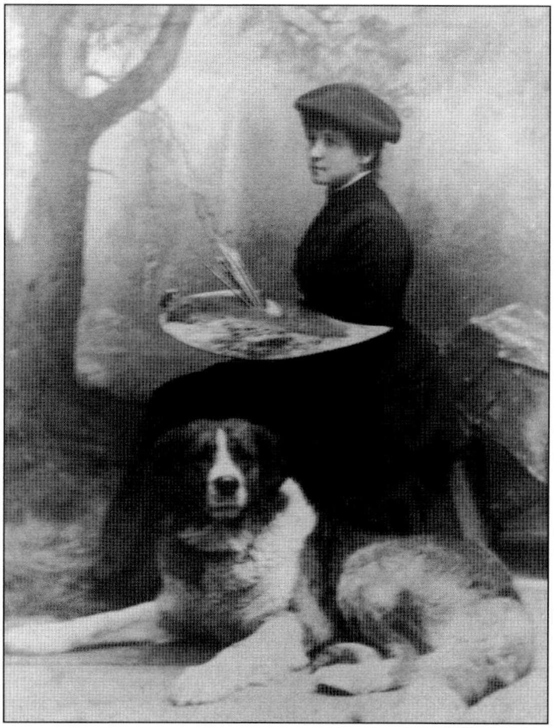

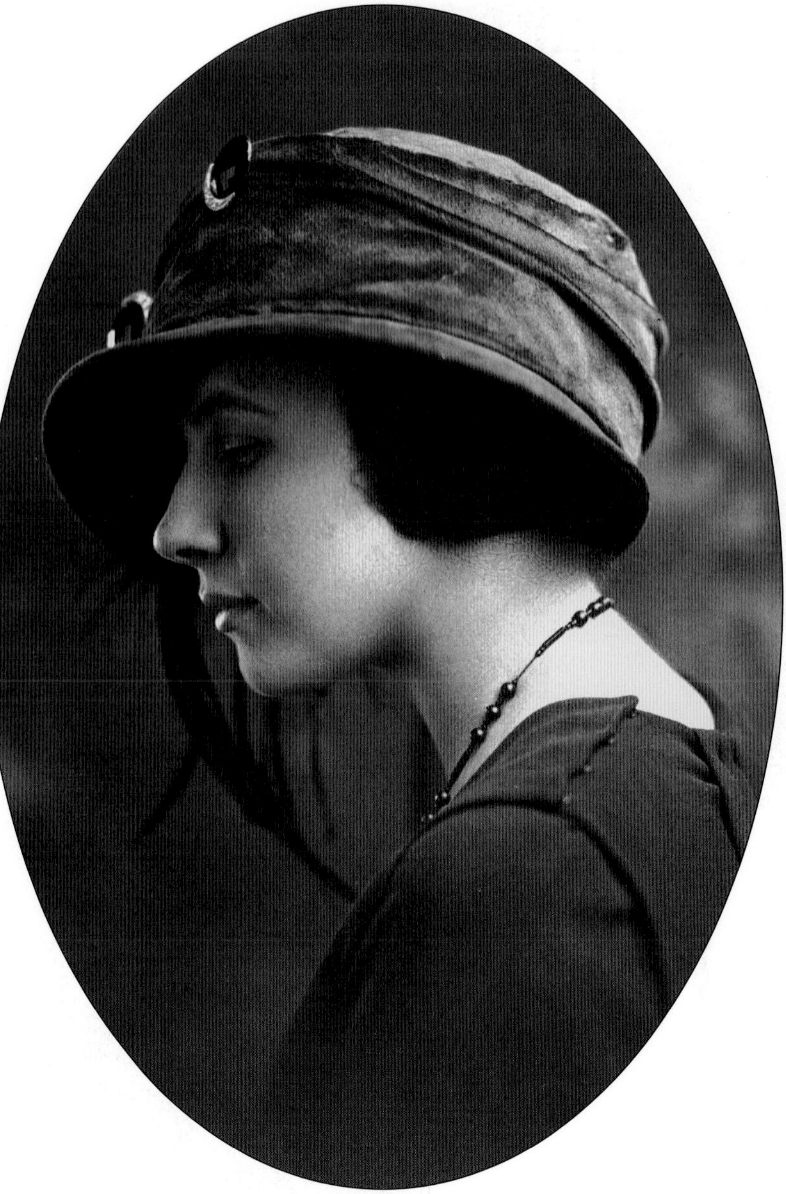

Dr. Rosalie Carter, pictured in 1925, was the beautiful great-granddaughter of Fountain Branch Carter. Though she was descended from an iconic Confederate family and lived her entire life in a cottage beside the Carter House, she was an educated, stylish, and thoroughly modern woman. Like her father, Moscow Branch Carter Jr., Rosalie was a Franklin dentist, and held state and national offices in dental organizations, including a term as president of the Association of American Women Dentists. Rosalie wrote booklets preserving the countless stories she heard from the Civil War veterans who returned for reunions in Franklin, and one of her books details the brief life of her heroic great-uncle, Todd Carter. Her passion for keeping history alive in the midst of contemporary progress is evidenced by her membership in Daughters of the American Revolution and her presidency of the National Federation of Business and Professional Women's Clubs. Dr. Carter's life reflects Franklin's exuberant spirit for life, learning, growth, tradition, philanthropy, and family.

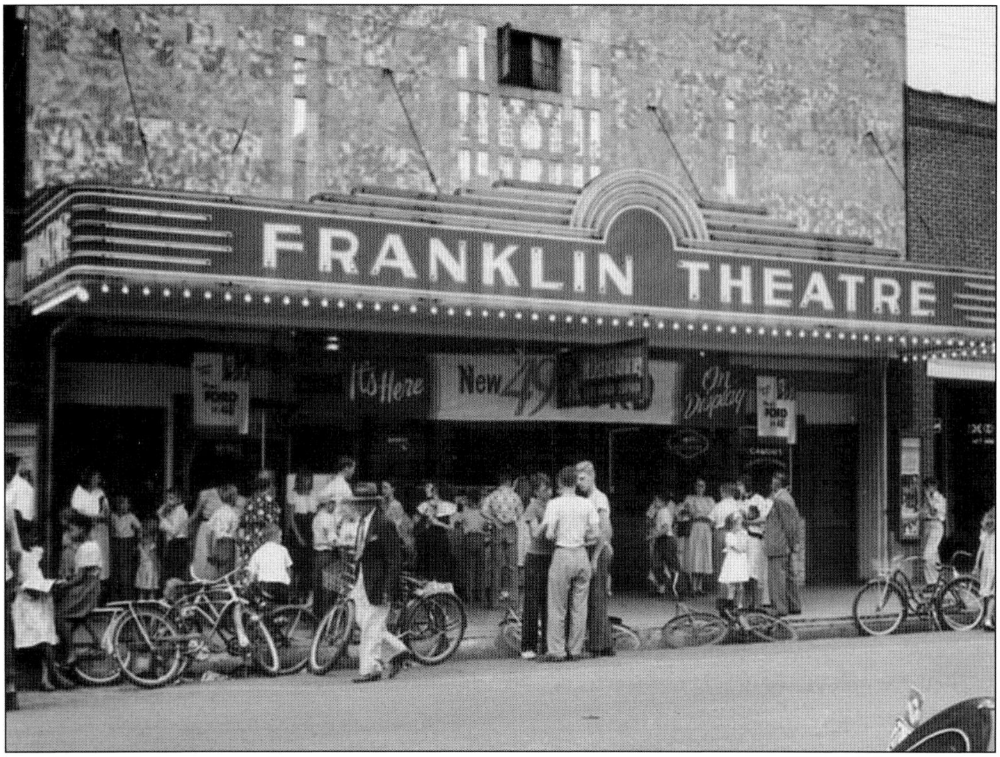

The Franklin Theater opened on Main Street in 1937, and was at the heart of Franklin entertainment for 70 years, showing movies for generations of families. Every year, school children from all around the county could come to town for the Blue Ribbon Parade, a reward for children who had their vaccinations and dental checkups. They would dress up, parade down Main Street, and enjoy a free movie. The theater eventually closed due to declining ticket sales, but after years of neglect, it was purchased by the Franklin and Williamson County Heritage Foundation and restored to its former glory. The grand reopening was captured on dozens of cell phones, and today the theater is busy with a calendar of movies, live music, and special events. (Above, TSL; below, courtesy of Debbie Smartt, Smartt Images.)

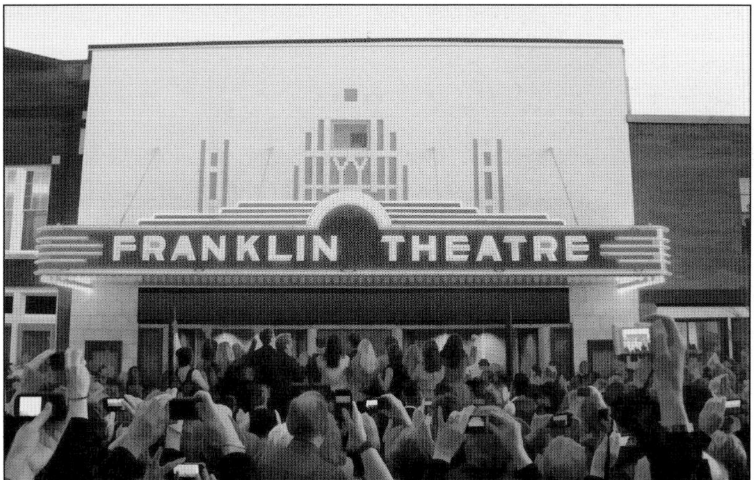

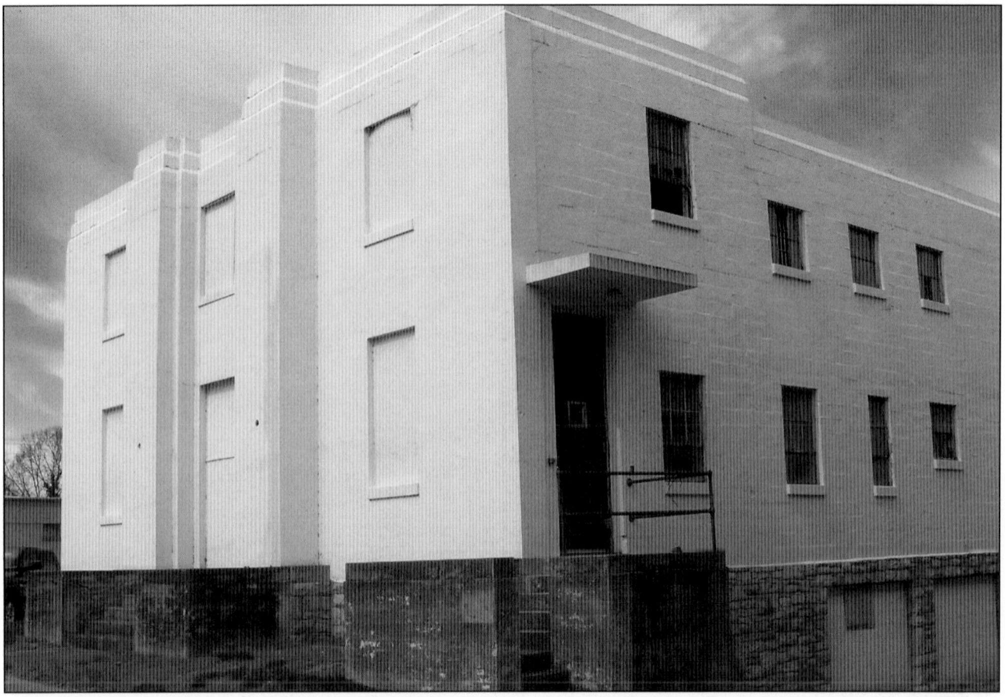

Franklin's Old, Old Jail, with its Art Deco facade, was built in 1940. It served city and county law enforcement for three decades before becoming offices and storage space until 2008. It then became vacant and fell into disrepair. When its restoration is complete, it will be Franklin's first permanent center for historic preservation.

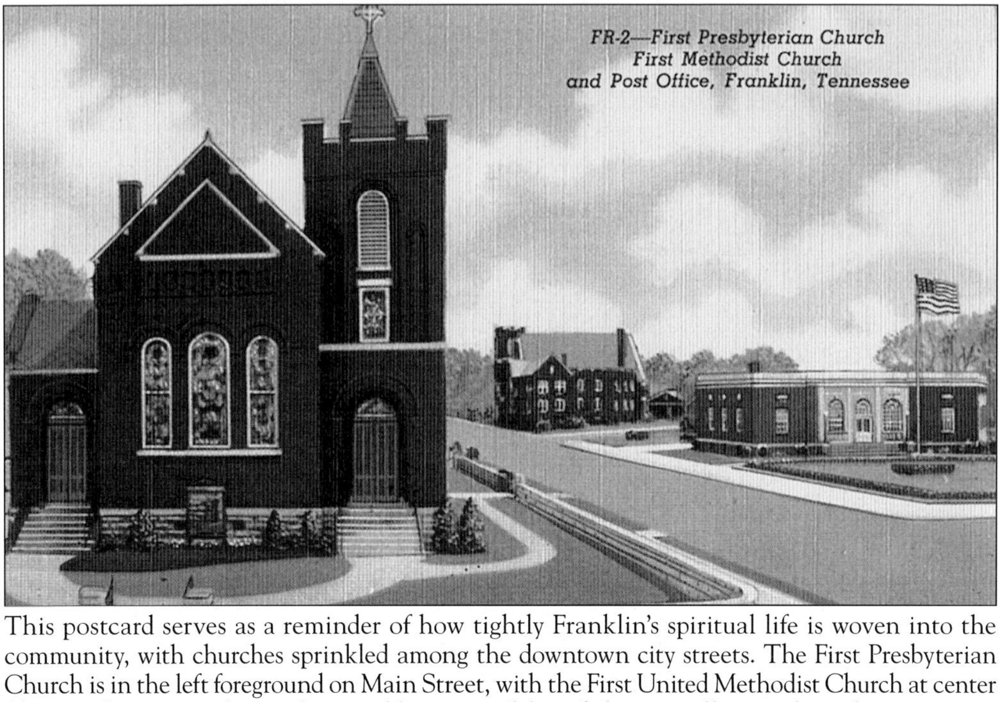

This postcard serves as a reminder of how tightly Franklin's spiritual life is woven into the community, with churches sprinkled among the downtown city streets. The First Presbyterian Church is in the left foreground on Main Street, with the First United Methodist Church at center (shown after its steeple was destroyed by a tornado), and the post office on the right

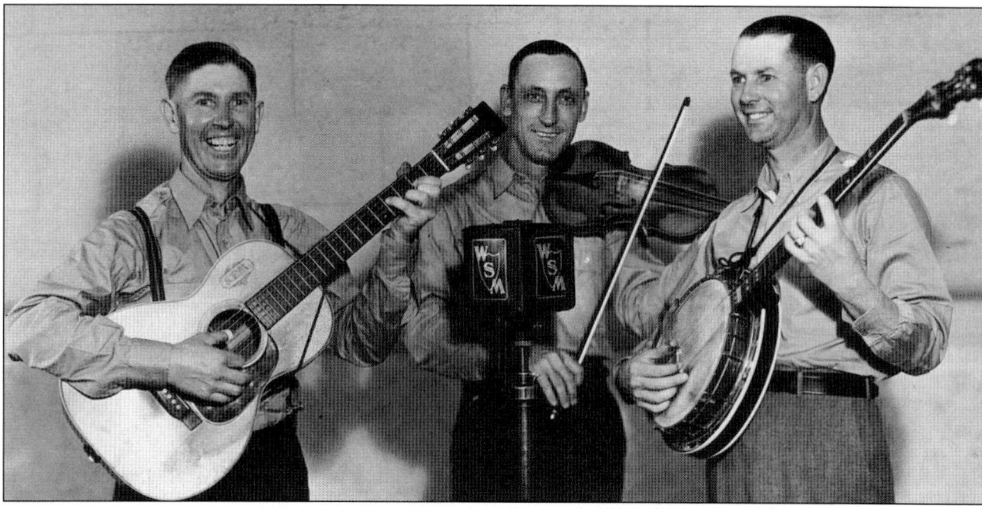

Franklin natives Sam and Kirk McGee joined the Grand Ole Opry in 1926. Learning blues slide guitar techniques from the African American players around Franklin, the brothers developed a unique style. They played in Uncle Dave Macon's Fruit Jar Drinkers, formed a band called the Dixieliners, and toured with Bill Monroe. The McGees appeared on the Opry as long as they lived, and were included in the last Opry show at the Ryman Auditorium.

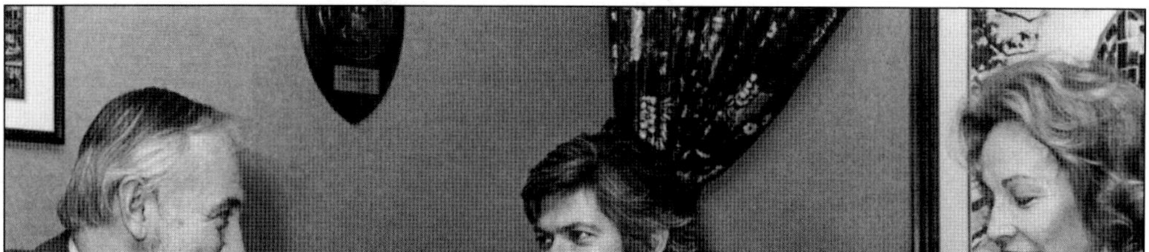

Tandy Rice Jr. (center), the president of the Country Music Association, meets with record executive Bruce Lundvall (left) and CMA executive director Jo Walker-Meador in this 1981 photograph. Tandy, whose father was a leading Franklin doctor, headed the Top Billing International talent and marketing agency. Rice has been a member of many corporate and charitable boards, and is in the Franklin High School Hall of Fame as a 1956 state track champion. (Courtesy of CMA.)

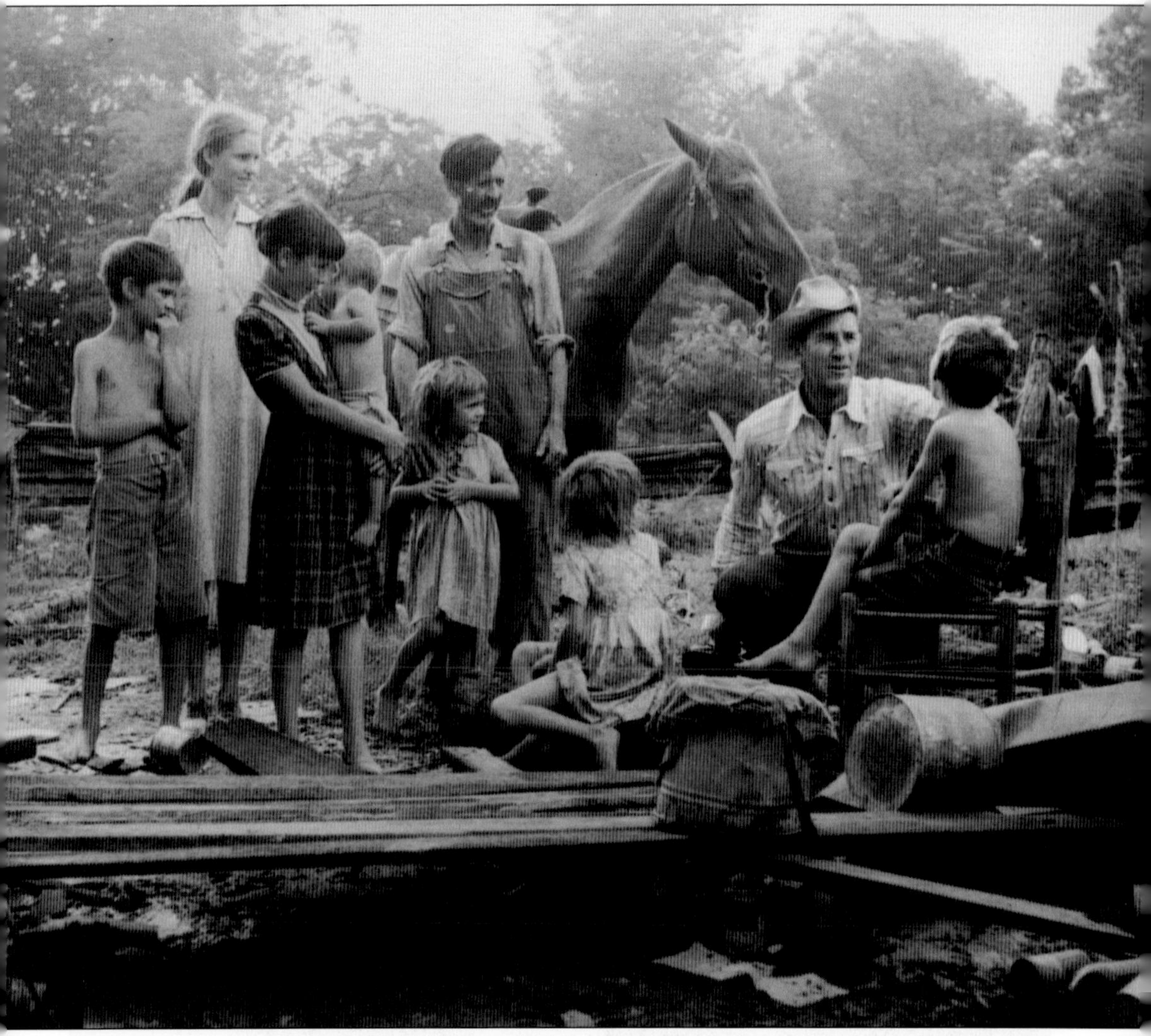

One of the best examples of Franklin's colorful and civic-minded people is Dr. Harry Jasper Guffee. He was born in 1913, educated in Franklin, captained the football team at Vanderbilt University while playing both offense and defense, and returned home to practice medicine at the Dan German Hospital. During World War II, he became a US Army medic assigned to a special unit serving the front lines. While advancing after the Normandy invasion, he became a prisoner of war, and was one of only 32 survivors of the 84th Division's 3,500 men. As a member of the Rotary, Guffee was a key organizer of the annual rodeo, and rode his horse to lead the rodeo parade for many years. A banjo player and avid horseman, he would trailer his horse into the hills, riding back in the hollows to make house calls on people who were otherwise unable to get medical care. In his career, he delivered well over 4,000 babies. Guffee is pictured here kneeling beside a member of the Bill Dorton family in the 1950s.

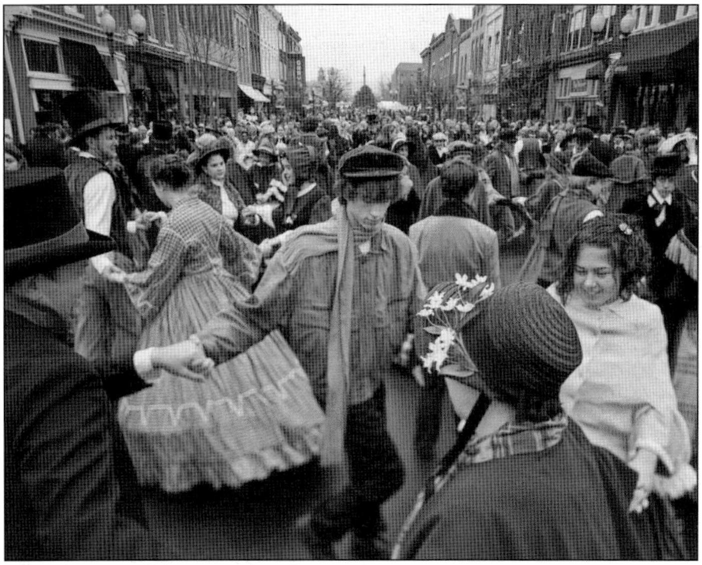

Dancers in costume look like they have stepped from the pages of *David Copperfield* and filled the streets of downtown Franklin in this photograph from the annual Dickens of a Christmas celebration. Franklin is one of the few cities where visitors can walk to so many stores, restaurants, and galleries—all within the 15-block Historic District—with free parking. (Grandin Hood, courtesy of Downtown Franklin Association.)

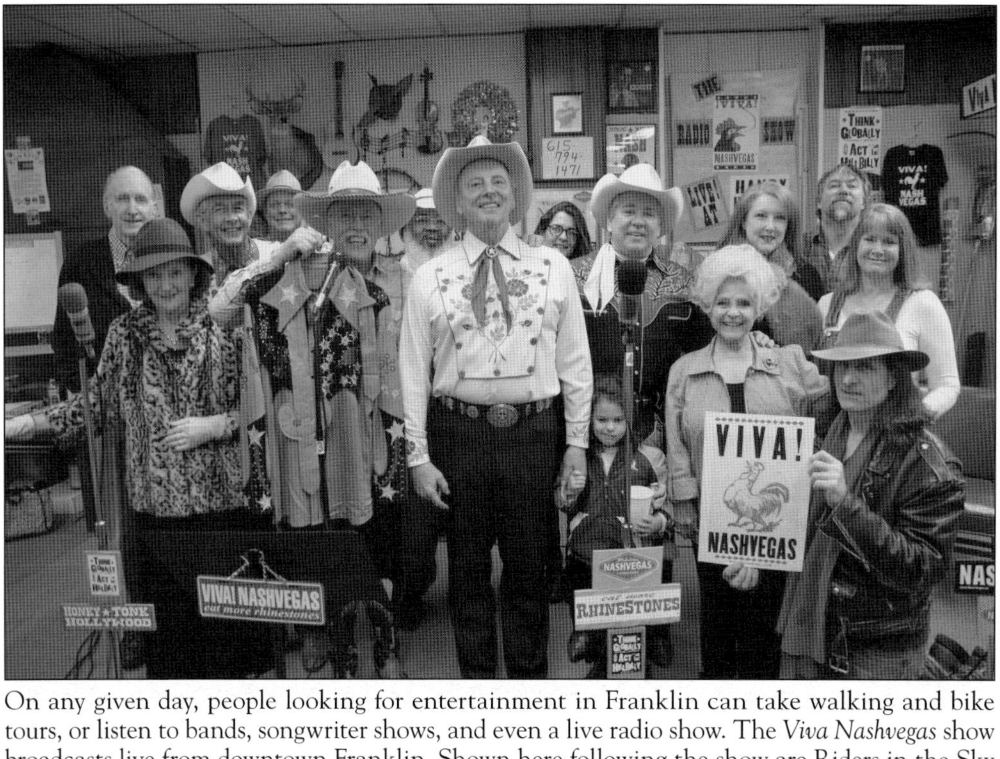

On any given day, people looking for entertainment in Franklin can take walking and bike tours, or listen to bands, songwriter shows, and even a live radio show. The *Viva Nashvegas* show broadcasts live from downtown Franklin. Shown here following the show are Riders in the Sky in white cowboy hats, Brenda Lee behind the Nashvegas sign, George Hamilton V (kneeling), and George Hamilton IV (back row left). (Courtesy of Interactive Media Service.)

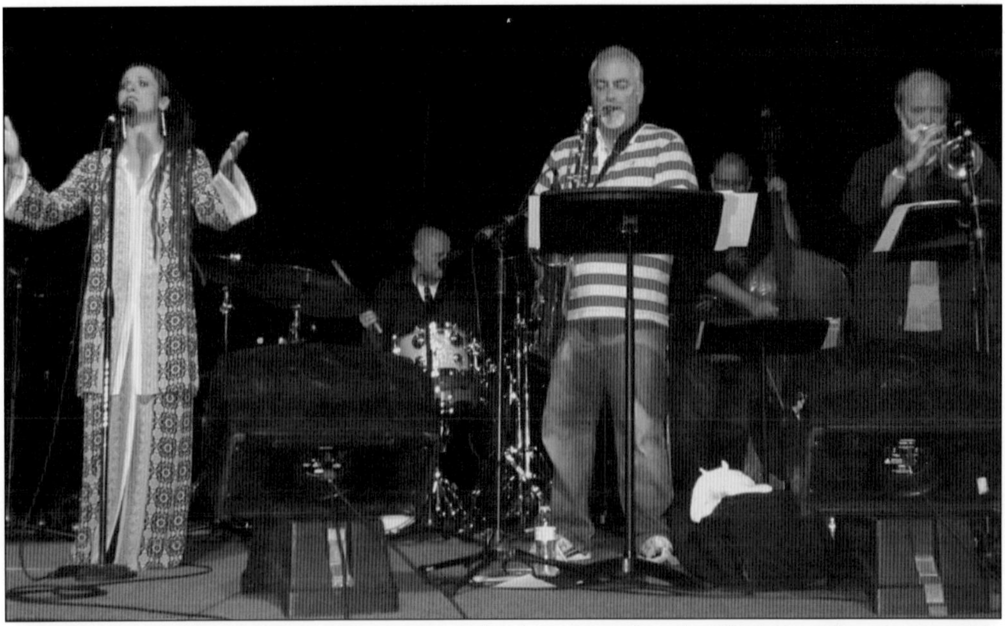

The Franklin Jazz Festival, seen here, has been held for three decades. With Brewfest, the monthly Art Crawl, Pumpkinfest, and other celebrations, there's always something going on in Franklin. Throughout its history, downtown Franklin has been known for its festivals and parades, and locals and tourists alike are still drawn in by the city's hospitality. (Courtesy of Scott Ducaj.)

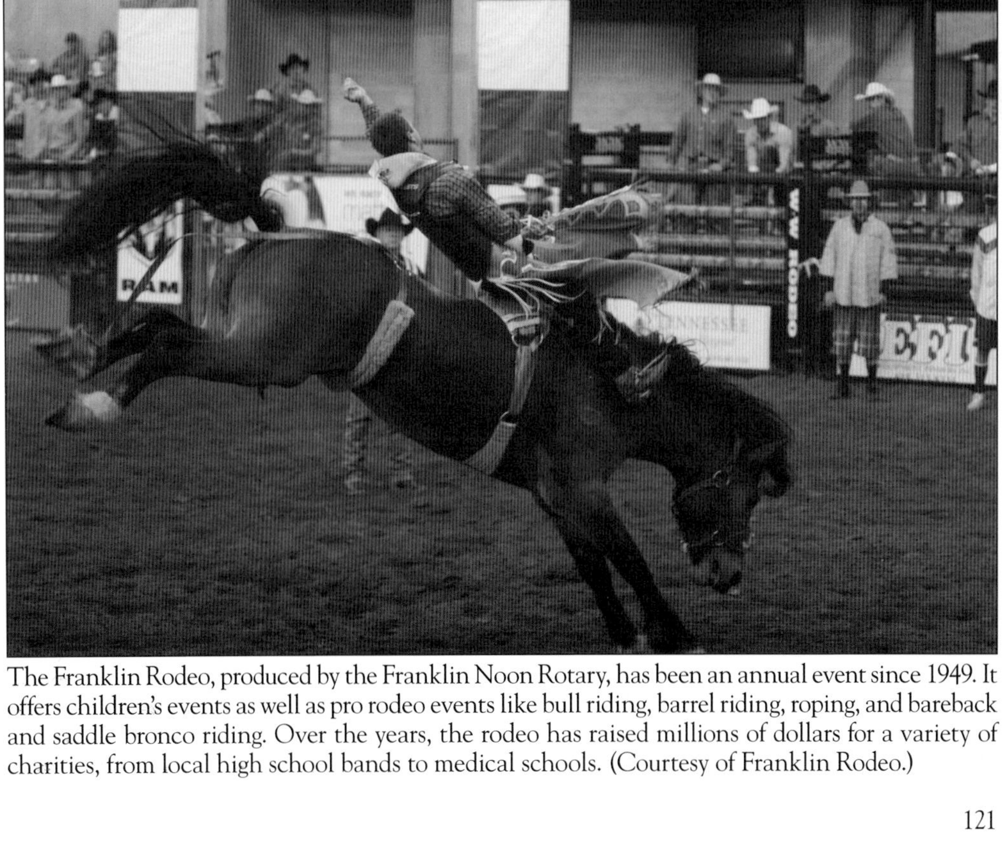

The Franklin Rodeo, produced by the Franklin Noon Rotary, has been an annual event since 1949. It offers children's events as well as pro rodeo events like bull riding, barrel riding, roping, and bareback and saddle bronco riding. Over the years, the rodeo has raised millions of dollars for a variety of charities, from local high school bands to medical schools. (Courtesy of Franklin Rodeo.)

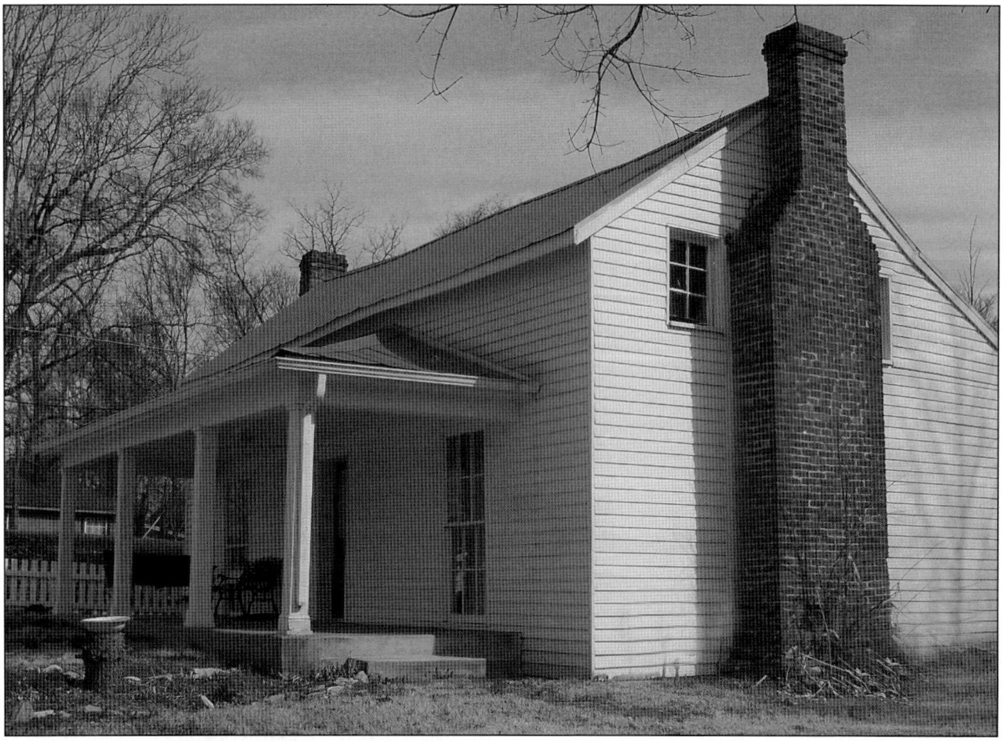

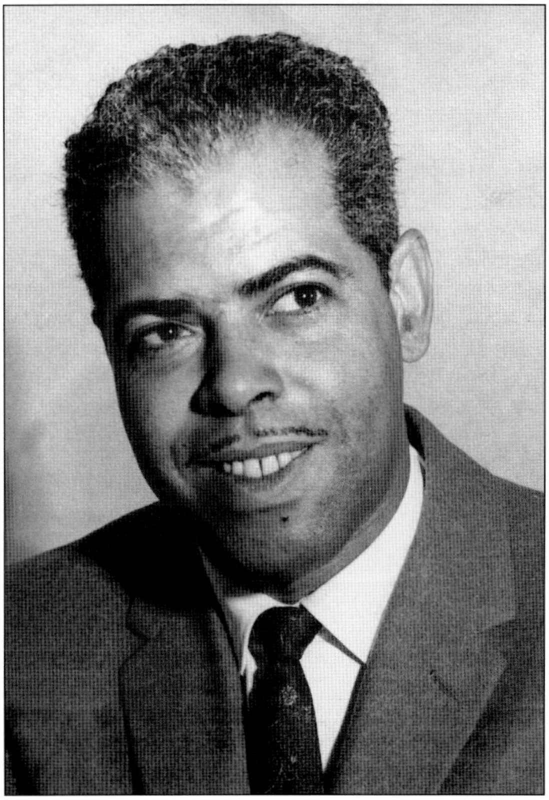

In 1880, ex-slave Harvey McLemore bought two acres from his former owner, Judge W.S. McLemore, and built this house. His descendants lived there for over 100 years, but the house fell into disrepair before it was saved by private citizens. In the city's spirit of restoration, the house was preserved as a museum by the African American Heritage Society, and hosts programs and events to preserve Franklin's African American history.

Fred Williams, grandson of pioneering merchant A.N.C. Williams, was a popular figure in Franklin and an early civil rights activist who advocated peaceful integration in the 1960s. At Franklin Training School he captained the football team and played in the band at halftime, still wearing his football uniform. He played trumpet in dance bands, operated a taxi company, and was a Boy Scout troop leader. (Courtesy of Cassandra Taylor.)

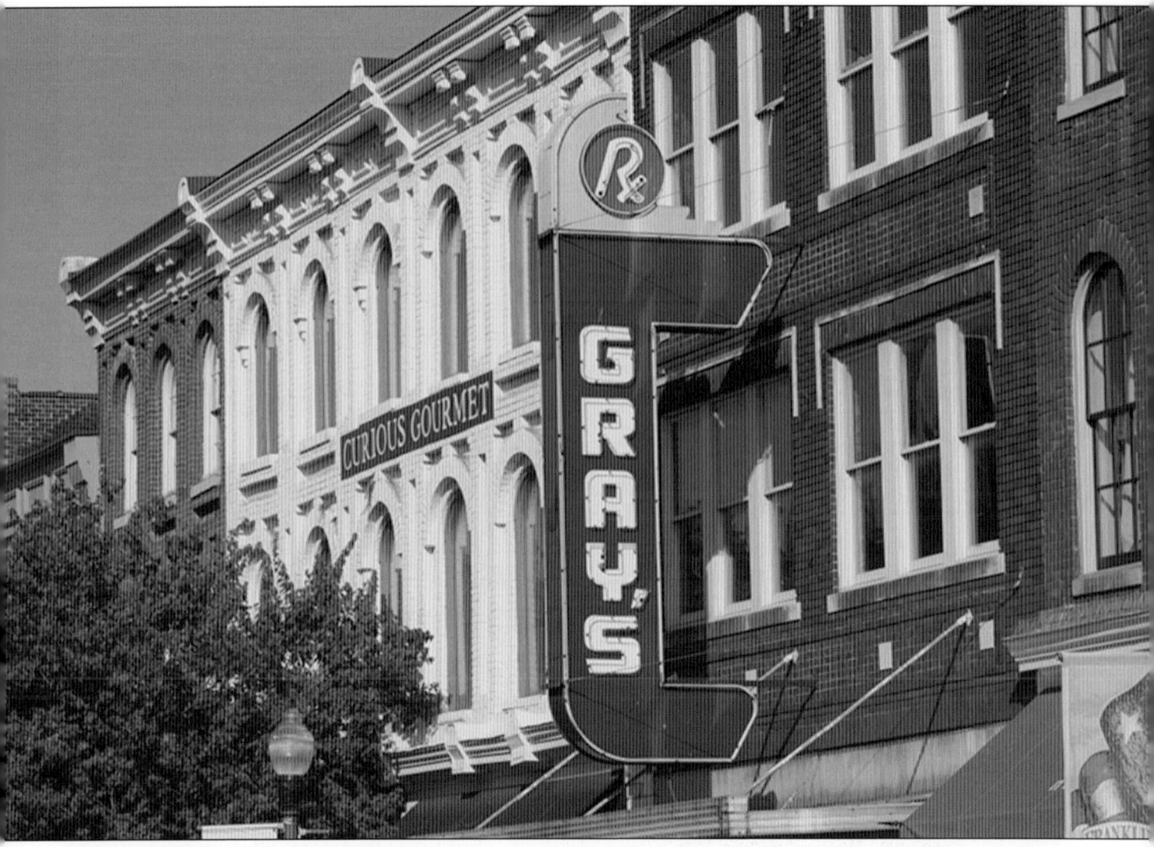

When the Moran Drug Company opened on Main Street in the late 1920s, it was a popular gathering place and pharmacy. Then, after more than 60 years as Gray's Drug, the store finally closed and sat vacant for almost a decade. Eventually, Joni and Michael Cole reopened the space as a restaurant with an upstairs music venue, which was once the bedroom of the first owner, John Moran. The original wood flooring was reused in other areas, including the upstairs bars, and the decor includes new fixtures along with antiques like medicine bottles, pharmacy products, and other treasures recovered during the building's restoration. During the restoration, the building even yielded prescriptions written during its first years. A crowd filled Main Street for the grand reopening, and today, Gray's iconic neon sign still greets visitors as a shining symbol of the restorative spirit of Franklin. (Courtesy of Debbie Smartt, Smartt Images.)

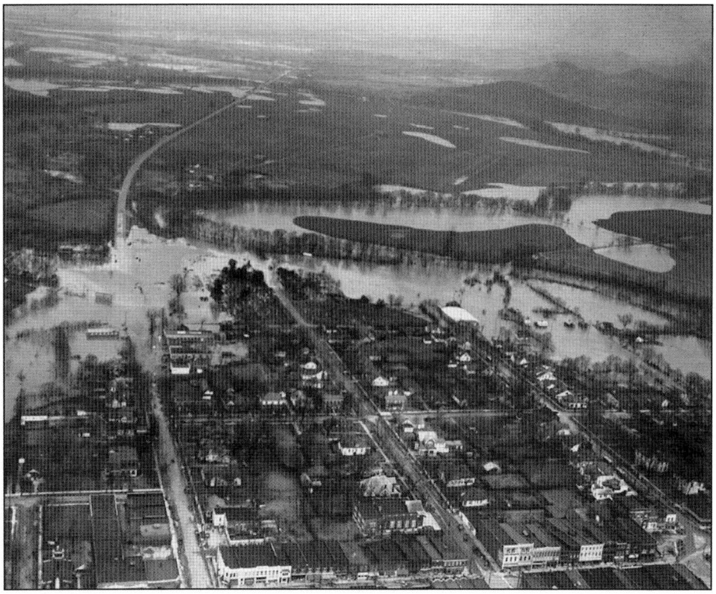

The flood of 1948 was a Middle Tennessee disaster, as the Harpeth River inundated streets, homes, and businesses. Main Street runs along the lower edge of this photograph, with St. Paul's Episcopal Church at the lower left and the public square at the lower right. Highway 431 curves northwest out of the city. In the wake of floods, tornadoes, and fires, the spirit of Franklin has always recovered, rebuilt, and endured. (TSL.)

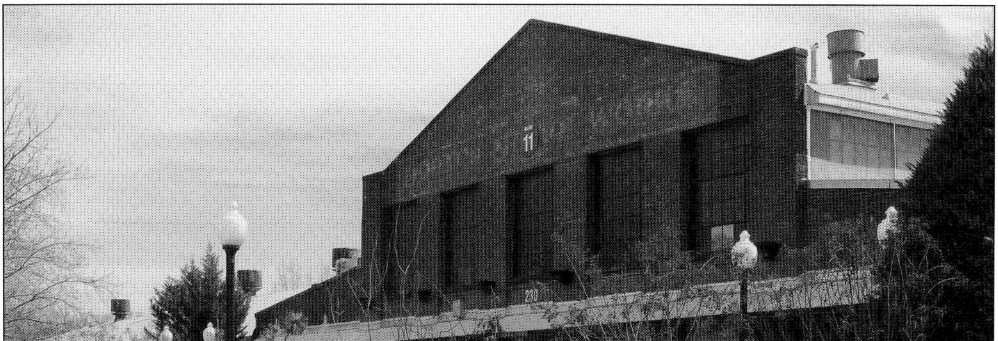

The abandoned factory on Franklin's north side sat empty until 1998, when the long-ignored complex was renovated into an iconic commercial and entertainment center called the Factory. Offering retail, restaurant, and office space, and hosting charity events, weddings, and concerts, it is thriving once more and reflects the vibrant spirit of Franklin.

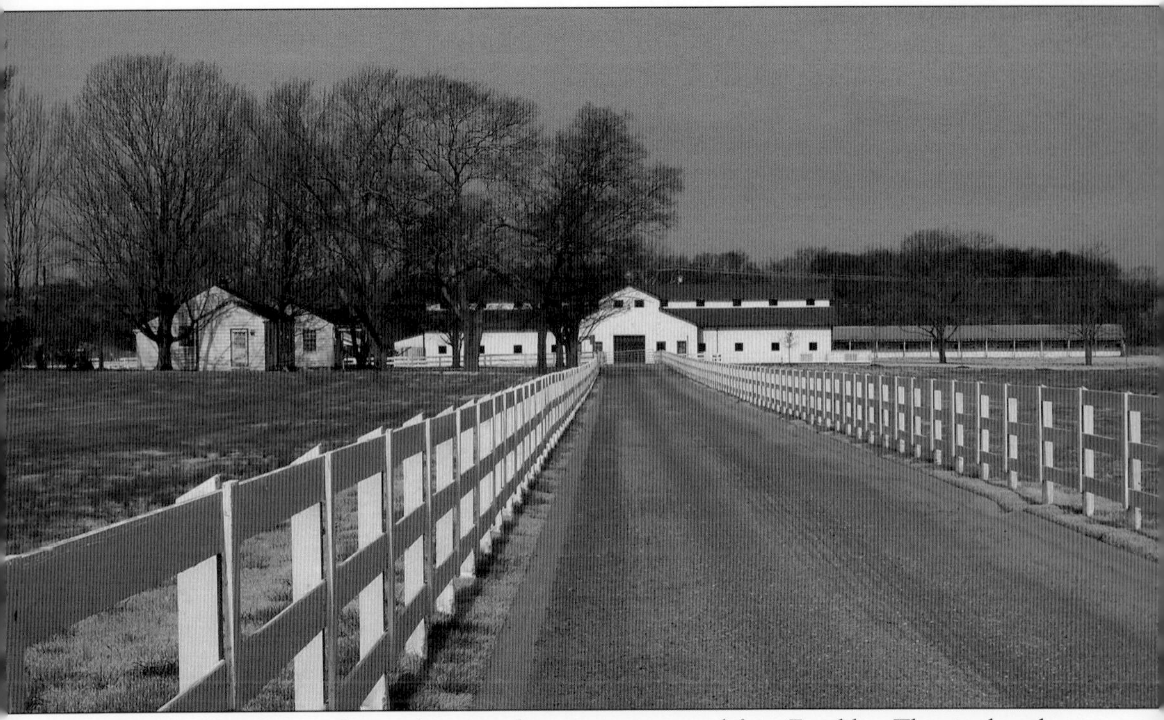

Harlinsdale Farm is one of many historic places enjoying new life in Franklin. The city bought the 200-acre farm across the Nashville Highway from the Factory to use as a public park that will preserve the Walking Horse history of the property. The long-term plan for the scenic park includes a dog park and fishing pond.

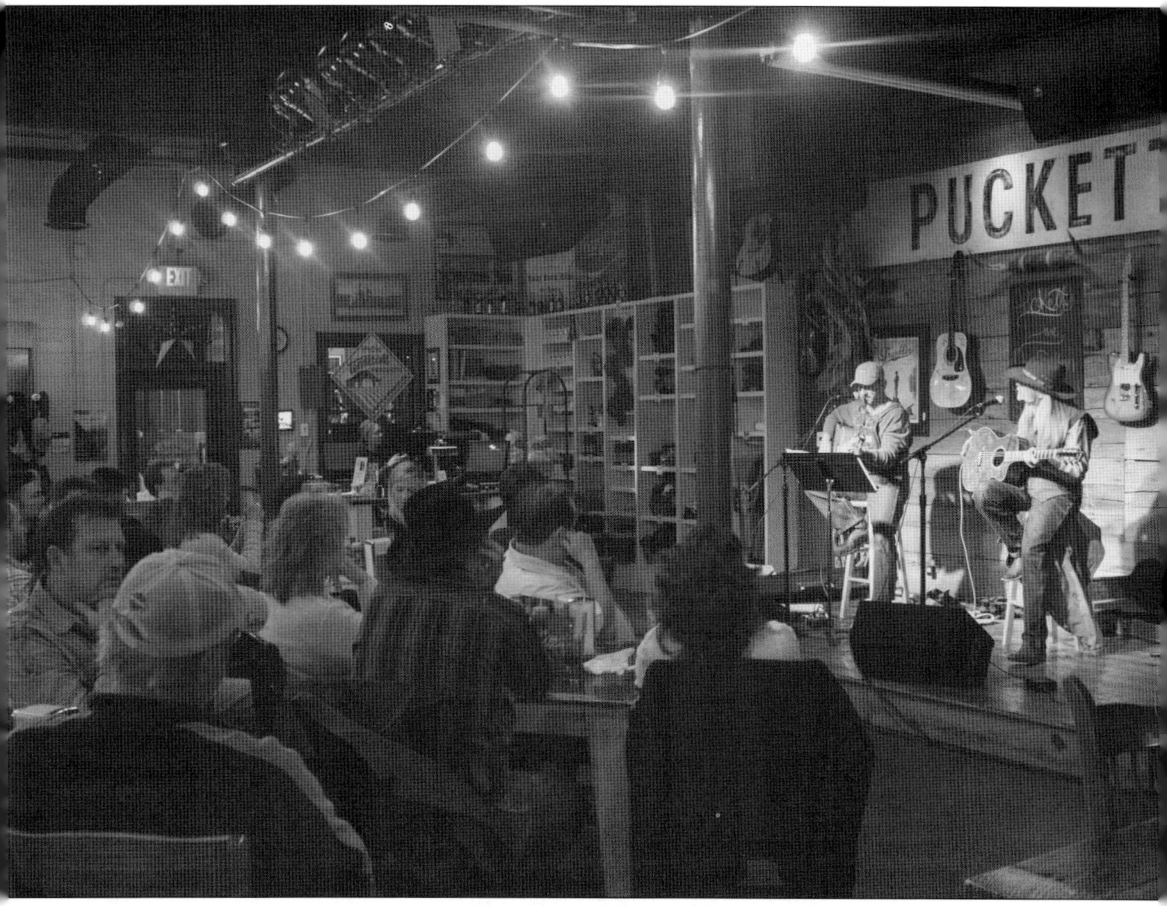

Puckett's Grocery in Leiper's Fork was already a local institution when it started serving a Southern-style meat-and-three dinner and offering live music in 2002. Then, Franklin's Andy Marshall opened Puckett's in Historic Downtown Franklin, with the same combination of southern-influenced food and live entertainment, and has continued to expand to other locations. (Courtesy of Debbie Smartt, Smartt Images.)

The Methodist Episcopal Church was built on Second Avenue in 1869. Even after a tornado took the roof and the building was converted from two stories to one, it was in use until 1945. When the church sold the building, it still held plenty of life. It became a grocery, and then an antique store. Well into its second century, it is now the home of a local theater group, the Pull-Tight Players.

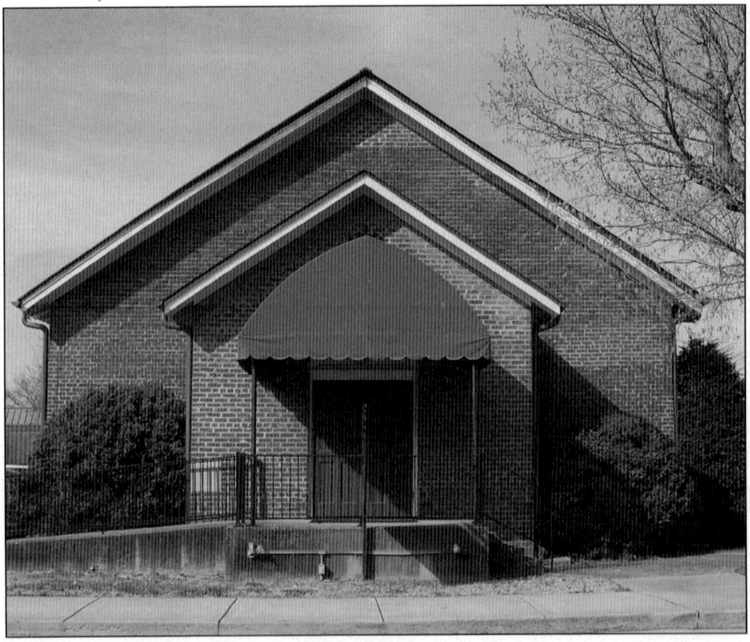

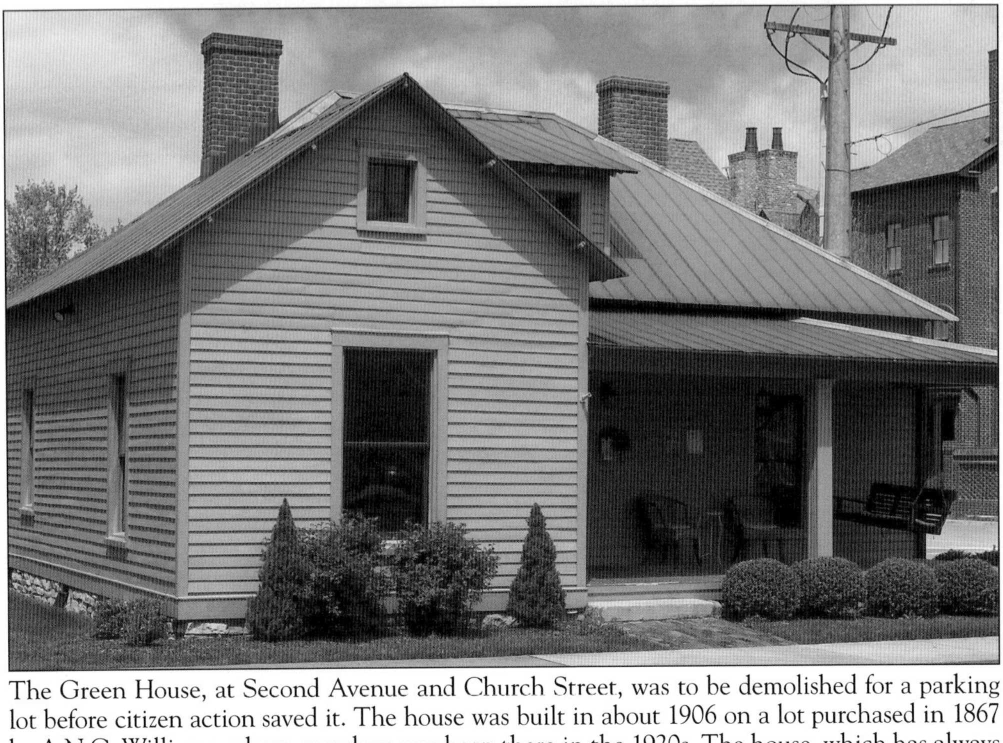

The Green House, at Second Avenue and Church Street, was to be demolished for a parking lot before citizen action saved it. The house was built in about 1906 on a lot purchased in 1867 by A.N.C. Williams, whose grandson was born there in the 1920s. The house, which has always been painted green, has now been fully restored as office space and is listed in the National Register of Historic Places.